The deregulation of financial markets in various nations in the 1980s brought about not only a qualitative change in their operation but also a greater integration among these markets. These changes enabled the free flow of financial resources across borders, and private and public institutions in each economy now have the ability to draw on the strengths of foreign markets to meet their individual needs. But many observers in Japan, Europe, North America, and elsewhere fear that the new freedom has contributed to a greater instability in individual markets and the transmission of these swings to other markets. The introduction and individual chapters in this book examine the ramifications of these trends.

Japan, Europe, and international financial markets

Japan, Europe, and international financial markets

Analytical and Empirical Perspectives

Edited by

RYUZO SATO
RICHARD M. LEVICH
RAMA V. RAMACHANDRAN

CAMBRIDGE
UNIVERSITY PRESS

Published by the Press Syndicate of the University of Cambridge
The Pitt Building, Trumpington Street, Cambridge CB2 1RP
40 West 20th Street, New York, NY 10011-4211, USA
10 Stamford Road, Oakleigh, Melbourne 3166, Australia

© Cambridge University Press 1994

First published 1994

Printed in the United States of America

A catalog record for this book is available from the British Library

ISBN 0--521-45228-7   hardback

Library of Congress Catatoging-in-Publication Data

Japan, Europe, and international financial markets: analytical and
    empirical perspectives / edited by Ryuzo Sato, Richard M. Levich,
    Rama V. Ramachandran.
        p.   cm.
    Includes index.
    ISBN 0-521-45228-7
    1. Japan--Foreign economic relations.   2. Japan--Foreign economic
relations--Europe.   3. Europe--Foreign economic relations--Japan.
4. International finance.   I. Satō, Ryūzō, 1931–.   II. Levich,
Richard M.   III. Ramachandran, Rama V.
HF1601.J3534   1993
332'.042--dc20   93-3810
                                                              CIP

Foreword

KENJI KAWAKATSU

The latter half of the 1980s was a turbulent period for international financial markets. Worldwide deregulation, globalization of industry, and innovations led to rapid expansion in spite of the persistence of Third World debt problems. By the decade's end, this rapid expansion stopped, and markets entered a period of adjustment.

The Center for Japan–U.S. Business and Economic Studies of New York University and the Sanwa Bank Limited jointly organized a series of three conferences on International Financial Markets to study these changes in New York, Tokyo, and Honolulu between 1988 and 1990. More than 50 leading scholars, officials from monetary and financial institutions, and economists from the private sector participated and actively exchanged views.

Today, as the market tries to meet the challenges that it faces with the formation of the European Union, the reconstruction of East Europe after the collapse of communism, and the restructuring of the post–World War trade system, we see that these discussions are very valuable in understanding the contemporaneous issues.

The Sanwa Bank, as a member of the international financial community, provided support for these conferences. I was pleased to attend these conferences and found the discussions extremely stimulating. The depth of discussion and diversity of participants' views are vividly conveyed in this volume of papers presented at the conferences. I am confident that it will be widely read by those who study the issues within the academic and financial communities.

We are also pleased to have established an endowment at the Leonard N. Stern School of Business of New York University to provide continuing support for research on international financial markets. One of the activities supported by the endowment is to give an annual award to write a monograph on international financial markets. I am looking forward to these scholarly studies.

In closing, we would like to express our particular gratitude to Dr. Richard R. West, former Dean of the Stern School of Business, for his support in furthering this project, and to Professor Ryuzo Sato, the C. V. Starr Professor of Economics and the Director of the Center, for his work in organizing the conference and editing the book.

Editors' preface

It is often argued that the liberalization policies of the 1980s led to dramatic changes in international financial markets. The rise to international prominence of Japanese commercial and trust banks was one of the interesting characteristics of this change. Many explanations were given for their success, including access to considerable savings within the Japanese economy and to monetary policies followed by the Bank of Japan.

With a research grant from Sanwa Bank Ltd., the Center for Japan–U.S. Business and Economic Studies organized a group of scholars to analyze the role of Japan in the changing world market. Their ongoing research was presented at three conferences: the first in New York in 1987, the second in Tokyo in 1989, and the third in Honolulu in 1990. This format allowed the participants to interact with each other and to benefit from suggestions about their individual research projects.

This book contains the papers that were developed as part of the project. After an overview at the very beginning, the book is in four parts. In his introduction, Richard Levich provides a succinct summary of each paper and then explains its relation to the overall research program. The first section contains three papers by James Tobin, Richard Cooper, and Paul Krugman that provide an overview of international trade and finance interrelations. The second section presents three papers on capital flows and the exchange rate mechanism. Jayendu Patel, Richard Zeckhauser, and Darryll Hendricks discuss the evidence pertaining to factors influencing cross-border investments. Masahiro Kawai discusses the demand for foreign securities in Japan. Robert Cumby and John Huizinga discuss the role of imperfect competition in determining relative prices of trade goods as the exchange rate varies.

The third section is on new financial products and the Japanese firm. Annie Koh and Richard Levich discuss the evidence from synthetic Euro-currency interest rate futures. Menachem Brenner, Marti Subrahmanyam, and Jun Uno analyze the volatility of Japanese stock indices, while

Akiyoshi Horiuchi discusses agency problems affecting firms and capital markets. In the last section, Ryuzo Sato, Rama Ramachandran, and Bohyong Kang discuss risk-adjusted deposit insurance in Japan, while Shelagh Heffernan examines competition in retail banking of Britain and Japan.

We are grateful to the Sanwa Bank and, particularly to Chairman Kenji Kawakatsu not only for the financial grant that enabled these studies but also for the active interest they showed throughout the project. Both at Tokyo and Honolulu, they were the most gracious hosts.

But more importantly, the Sanwa Bank has given the Center an endowment to continue the study of international financial markets. Each year, on a competitive basis, the Center will award a grant to write a monograph. Additional conferences similar to those that led to this volume are also part of the activities funded by the endowment.

Organization of a research program and conferences of this magnitude are not possible without the support of many individuals. We wish to thank all those at New York University and Sanwa Bank who helped us in this endeavor. Last but not least, we thank Mr. Scott Parris of Cambridge University Press for his interest and assistance in the preparation and publication of this book.

March 1993   R. S.
                                              R. M. L.
                                              R. V. R.

Contents

ix

Introduction and overview

RICHARD M. LEVICH

The importance of national financial markets and the international linkages among them have increased dramatically in the last quarter century. Although the American economy, American financial markets, and the dollar still play important roles, the era of U.S. dominance on the world economic stage has passed. Real economies and financial markets in other parts of the world have developed both in size and sophistication. The savings and investment decisions made by individuals and firms in Japan, Germany, and elsewhere, along with real business decisions regarding the development of new products, new technologies, and their pricing have all had an impact on neighboring countries. The linkages among national financial markets, as well as those truly international markets like foreign-exchange and Eurocurrency markets, form a network for the transmission of economic disturbances as important as the trade linkages that bind the welfare of countries together.

A few examples of the stresses put on international financial markets and their importance to world economic welfare will be useful. At the macroeconomic level, consider first the magnitude of current account imbalances during the 1980s. For the United States, the current account deficit averaged nearly $130 billion per year (nearly 4% of GNP) over the 1984–88 period and rose further during 1989 and 1990. By the accounting axioms, the U.S. current account deficit required a capital account surplus, or capital inflow from the rest of the world. An international financial system largely free of capital flow restrictions was a necessary (but not sufficient) condition to enable the United States to run a current account deficit of the size of the 1980s.

In this book, the determinants of international investment flows are addressed by Patel, Zeckhauser, and Hendricks (PZH) and by Masahiro Kawai. PZH eschew a financial theoretic model and instead adopt a more behavioral approach, relating current investment flows to past security performance and other variables. They test their model on investment flows into American open-end mutual funds. The model performs well,

1

explaining 70% of the cross-sectional variation in flows over the sample period. PZH apply a similar model to flows from U.K., Japan, Germany, and Canada into U.S. securities. Again the data support their model, although the explanatory power is not as great as in the case of mutual funds.

Kawai also explores the demand for foreign securities, specifically the determinants of the Japanese stock demand for foreign securities in the 1980s. Kawai uses a more traditional financial modeling approach to determine that Japanese demand for foreign securities has been a function of the interest differential (adjusted for exchange rate expectations), exchange risk, and income. He also concludes that particular institutional factors (such as the one-time stock adjustment to exchange rate and capital market deregulation, and payout formulas affecting Japanese insurance companies) played an important role in the steady accumulation of foreign securities by Japanese investors throughout the 1980s.

Related to the trends on current account, the international investment position of the United States has shifted from being the world's largest creditor nation with a net investment position of $380 billion in 1980 to being the world's largest debtor nation with a net liability position of over $400 billion in 1990.[1] While many economists would advise caution in interpreting the absolute figures (because, among other reasons, real investments are measured at book values and the U.S. official gold stock is measured at $42/ounce), the relative shift of roughly $1 trillion in the U.S. investment position is probably a good estimate.[2] Again, an open international financial system and an appetite for foreign investments (both real and monetary) were necessary conditions to enable this substantial shift of ownership. Foreign ownership of U.S. federal debt reached nearly $400 billion in 1989, more than 13% of the total.[3] Foreign purchases of U.S. businesses – Pillsbury by Grand Metropolitan (U.K.), CBS Records by Sony, Firestone by Bridgestone, to name only a few – and the rise of *de nova* manufacturing businesses – Japanese car manufacturers such as Honda in Tennessee and Mazda in Michigan being conspicuous examples – are more visible reminders of the mobility of international investment capital. The switch toward real investments is also suggested in the paper by Kawai.

The major foreign-exchange rates, whether expressed in real or nominal magnitudes, also experienced substantial fluctuations in the 1980s. The

---

[1] Figures are from the *Survey of Current Business*, Jun. 1991, p. 26. These are revised figures prepared by the Bureau of Economic Analysis, U.S. Department of Commerce.
[2] See, for example, Eisner (1989) and Bame (1985).
[3] *Federal Reserve Bulletin*, January 1991, p. A30.

U.S. dollar real effective exchange rate appreciated by nearly 50% over the 1980–85 period, a remarkably large and swift rise when measured in real terms as an average against a group of currencies. However remarkable this rise, in the next $2\frac{1}{2}$ years the U.S. dollar depreciated just as sharply to its levels of 1980. These price swings show the nature of the disturbances faced by business leaders and portfolio managers in the present international economy.

In his overview, Richard Cooper analyzes some of the key principles of exchange rate theory, focusing closely on the role played by the Law Of One Price (LOOP). Cooper argues that LOOP is flagrantly violated by close (or even casual) observation and that these deviations may persist for several years or longer. Economists, Cooper argues, have rationalized these deviations by special factors (all amounting to imperfect competition), but models of exchange rate determination have failed to accommodate deviations from LOOP.

The paper by Cumby and Huizinga picks up Cooper's theme to analyze whether exchange rate changes have led to relative prices changes that could be consistent with a model of imperfect competition in manufacturing industries. Cumby and Huizinga adapt a model of Dornbusch (1987) to assess how relative prices (in the export market relative to the home market) might be affected by exchange rate changes and the pricing behavior of firms. They test their model on a cross section of 16 U.S. manufacturing industries covering the 1980–1985 U.S. dollar cycle. The results suggest that there is considerable variation across industries in the exchange rate elasticity of relative export and import prices. Further, these differences in price relative to cost are generally associated with differences in exchange rate elasticity, as in the Dornbusch model.

Accompanying the rise of foreign-exchange fluctuations have been proposals to reduce the degree of exchange rate volatility. Perhaps the most ambitious of these is the plan for European Monetary Union (EMU), which embeds a common currency within an evolving single political area, the European Community (EC). Paul Krugman reexamines the case for EMU. Krugman argues that the theoretical criteria for a common currency area remain those articulated nearly three decades ago by McKinnon (1963) and Mundell (1961). Empirically, Krugman feels that these criteria do not hold up any better today in Europe than in the past, and so there is little solid evidence to forecast either significant net benefits or costs to EMU. Nevertheless, Krugman argues that if, as a symbol of political unity, the EC is committed to EMU, then the changeover should be made sooner rather than later. Waiting for further convergence exposes the EC to a variety of shocks disrupting the European Monetary System and putting EMU beyond reach.

Besides the developments in the macroeconomy, individual financial markets are undergoing their own dramatic changes. Related to the price movements in the foreign-exchange markets, daily trading activity in these markets has soared from roughly $25 billion in 1977 to nearly $500 billion in 1989.[4] Assuming 250 trading days per year, annual trading volume in 1989 could be estimated at $125 trillion, perhaps 6 times as large as world GNP and 40 times as large as world exports.[5] With an order flow this size, it is easy to comprehend the depth and speed of the foreign-exchange markets.

Other financial markets also witnessed dramatic developments over this period. The nature of innovations that have occurred and some of the reasons for these changes have been examined elsewhere.[6] The Euromarkets, in particular the Eurocurrency market for offshore banking deposits and the Eurobond market for international bond issues, rose from virtually nonexistent markets in the early 1960s to become the major international venues for their respective financial functions. As largely unregulated and innovative markets, these Euromarkets have survived and prospered to become the markets of choice, even though – as Miller (1992) reminds us – some of the regulatory incentives for the markets are no longer in place.

The paper by Koh and Levich presents a specific illustration of the innovation process within the context of the Eurocurrency markets. Koh and Levich demonstrate how readily available contracts can be combined to create a new synthetic instrument. In this case the authors show that a Eurodollar interest rate futures contract combined with foreign currency futures contracts can be used to create a Eurocurrency (e.g., Euroyen) interest rate futures contract. The authors show that such a contract produces significant results for hedging Eurocurrency interest rate risks. The Eurodollar interest rate futures is thus a "vehicle contract" – a contract that might be used to create a synthetic hedge for interest rate risk in any currency.

Other markets that have existed for years, such as stock exchanges or futures exchanges, have seen their competitive positions and essential business activities altered by the development of new financial products (in particular, futures and options) and new financial trading strategies (for example, index arbitrage and program trading). These products and trading techniques originated in the United States, but they were quickly

---

[4] See "Survey of Foreign Exchange Market Activity," Bank for International Settlements, Monetary and Banking Department, Feb. 1990.

[5] GNP figures from *World Development Report*, World Bank, 1991, p. 182. World export figures from *International Financial Statistics*, International Monetary Fund, 1991.

[6] See Levich (1988) and Miller (1992) for a review of innovations in international financial markets.

copied and applied in exchanges around the world. It might seem that as redundant securities – i.e., securities that could be replicated using combinations of other existing financial instruments – futures and options could not have a deleterious effect on welfare (this is basically Merton Miller's position). But the market crash of Black Monday, October 19, 1987, made policymakers less certain. Debate over the impact of financial innovation on price behavior and risk to the trading system has ensued.

The paper by Brenner, Subrahmanyam, and Uno (BSU) offers some evidence on the impact of futures trading on cash market volatility in the case of the Japanese stock market. The causes of changing cash market volatility are numerous: greater macroeconomic uncertainty, financial market deregulation, tighter international financial market linkages, and new (automated) trading technologies, in addition to the rise of derivative securities. BSU examine the course of volatility both before and after the advent of futures trading on Japanese securities. The authors find that after an interim rise in cash market volatility (associated with futures trading in Singapore) cash market volatility has indeed fallen. And curiously, futures market volatility is less than in the cash market. The authors conclude that there is no evidence that the introduction of futures trading has exacerbated cash market volatility in the Japanese market.[7]

Another phenomenon to hit the stock market in the 1980s was the wave of corporate takeovers in the United States, many of them viewed as "hostile." Cross-border takeovers also flourished in Europe in the 1980s, in part as a lead-up to the 1992 single market initiative.[8] However, Japan has not been the scene of any hostile takeover activity. On the contrary, Akiyoshi Horiuchi describes a variety of Japanese business practices (in particular the main bank relationship, long-term labor contracting, and mutual business stockholding, *zai-tech*) that actually remove much of the threat of takeover from Japanese corporate managers. Despite capital market liberalization and enhanced market linkages, Horiuchi argues that these practices form a distinctly different attitude among Japanese business managers than in their American counterparts that strengthens their discretionary powers.[9] Only now at the beginning of the 1990s does Horiuchi sense any changes in Japan that might alter these mechanisms.

As a final illustration of the turbulence affecting international financial markets, consider the banking sector. As regulatory changes, innovation, and technological changes have led to a change in the competitive position

---

[7] The reader should note that the paper by BSU was written in 1990 using data for the period Jan. 1984–Nov. 1989. The dramatic slide in the Tokyo stock market occurred after this paper was written.

[8] See Walter and Smith (1989) for an analysis of European mergers and acquisitions.

[9] See Franks and Mayer (1990) for a comparison of U.K., German, and French corporate financial practices.

of various financial centers and financial products, so too have these changes affected the banking industry. In 1964, for example, U.S. banks occupied 9 slots in the top 20 international banks ranked by deposits. By 1991, only one U.S. bank (Citibank) ranked (by assets) in the top 20, however there were 10 Japanese banks in this category.[10] While illustrative of the developments that affect the policymaking environment, these rankings only reflect the fundamental changes and economic disturbances affecting the banking industry. As a worldwide trend, policymakers have been driven to liberalize a variety of banking practices, both involving wholesale and retail banking activities.

Regarding wholesale activities, the Bank for International Settlements has undertaken a new commitment to harmonize bank regulatory practices and, in particular, capital adequacy guidelines. The need for global rules again stems from the openness of international financial markets and the mobility of capital. Regarding the retail sector, increased openness has also lead to pressures for change. In her paper, Shelagh Heffernan argues that liberalization has resulted in substantially more competitive behavior in Britain than in Japan. Heffernan stresses that measures of competitive behavior should include both price and nonprice considerations. On the price side, Heffernan observes that British depositors receive higher spreads (over markets rates), while British borrowers pay lower spreads in comparison with Japanese counterparts. Moreover, British banks introduced considerably more retail product innovation in the 1980s than did the Japanese. Heffernan suggests that dismantling of the banking cartel systems in Britain appears to have been sufficient to induce competition, whereas this has not been the case in Japan.

Another development over the last decade with global proportions has been the surge in lending to developing countries and the massive defaults and write-offs that have been the result. Both the scale of lending and the scale of defaults have been such as to cause policymakers to rethink the entire process of sovereign lending – from the alternatives for structuring sovereign loan contracts, to the decision of countries to default or pay, and to the role of international organizations in recommending macroeconomic adjustment policies and monitoring macroeconomic performance.

A final shock to hit the banking sector over the last decade has been the demise of the two deposit insurance funds in the United States, the Federal Deposit Insurance Corporation (FDIC) and the Federal Savings and Loan Insurance Corporation (FSLIC). The massive losses absorbed by these agencies have raised serious questions regarding the design of

[10] Figures for 1964 are from Roger Orsingher, *Banks of the World*, London: Macmillan, 1967, p. 271. The 1991 data were reported in the *American Banker*, Jul. 1991.

deposit insurance programs. The most common proposals are for flat-rate schemes with severe regulatory guidelines (as the FDIC has administered) and flexible-rate schemes where the cost of deposit insurance is linked to the riskiness of the banks loan portfolio. In their paper in this volume, Ryuzo Sato and Rama Ramachandran use an option pricing approach to estimate the actuarially fair price of deposit insurance for major banks in Japan and the United States. Their key finding is that the range of premiums in both countries appears to be quite large. The results suggest that flat-rate insurance could entail serious distortions and that variable-rate insurance could cause banks to dramatically alter their lending activities. In either case, their results suggest that policymakers face a serious challenge to designing a suitable safety net for bank depositors.[11]

As this brief overview attempts to show, the environment of international financial markets has changed in fundamental ways over the last quarter century. To address this broad topic our book is organized into four sections. Part I contains three papers that address policy aspects of foreign-exchange rates. This section begins with a keynote address by James Tobin offering his views on the fundamental relationships and fallacies in the analysis of international macroeconomics. The papers referenced earlier by Richard Cooper and Paul Krugman complete Part I. The remaining three sections of the book are structured broadly around topics in international macroeconomics, financial markets, and banking. Papers were commissioned to address research and policy concerns in each of the areas. The authors were asked to prepare original research papers highlighting the various facets of international financial markets. The authors comprise a variety of perspectives: American, Japanese, and those of other countries; macroeconomics, finance, banking, and other disciplines. These papers only scratch the surface of a broad and important range of topics. We hope that you find these contributions stimulating.

References

Bame, Jack (1985), "A Note on the United States as a Net Debtor Nation," *Survey of Current Business*, Jun.

Dornbusch, Rudiger (1987), "Exchange Rates and Prices," *American Economic Review*, 77 (Jan.), 93–106.

Eisner, Robert (1989), "Budget Deficits: Rhetoric and Reality," *Journal of Economic Perspectives*, 3, no. 2 (spring), 73–93.

---

[11] The reader should note that the paper by Sato and Ramachandran was written in 1990, prior to the slide in Japanese stock prices that has indirectly affected the capitalization of Japanese banks.

Franks, Julian, and Colin Mayer (1990), "Capital Markets and Corporate Control: A Study of France, Germany and the UK," *Economic Policy*, 5, no. 1 (Apr.), 191–231.

Levich, Richard M. (1988), "Financial Innovations in International Financial Markets," *in* M. Feldstein (ed.), *The United States and the World Economy*, Chicago: University of Chicago Press.

McKinnon, Ronald I. (1963), "Optimum Currency Areas," *American Economic Review*, 53, no. 4 (Sep.), 717–25.

Miller, Merton (1992), "Financial Innovation: Achievements and Prospects," *Journal of Applied Corporate Finance*, 4, no. 4 (winter) 4–11.

Mundell, Robert A. (1961), "A Theory of Optimum Currency Areas," *American Economic Review*, 51, no. 4 (Sep.), 657–65.

Walter, Ingo, and Roy C. Smith (1989), *Investment Banking in Europe*, Oxford: Basil Blackwell.

PART I

Policy aspects of exchange rates

CHAPTER 1

Policies and exchange rates: a simple analytical framework

JAMES TOBIN

How do exchange rates, trade balances, and international capital movements react to national fiscal and monetary policies and to other events of macroeconomic significance? Divers answers to such questions may be heard in financial circles, political arenas, and academic conferences. All these propositions depend on models, implicit or explicit. Whether or not they would avow it, even practical traders in foreign-exchange markets have models in their heads, models probably borrowed unconsciously from economists. They interpret and act upon macroeconomic news in the light of their models or, more important, the models they think other traders depend on.

I propose here to set forth a simple open-economy macroeconomic framework, reflecting a model in the heads of many economists, though not all to be sure. It is certainly not a quantitative forecasting model. Economists are pretty poor at forecasting exchange rates, and evidently markets are not very good either. Here I am interested in a model that yields qualitative comparative static or dynamic results for policies and other exogenous shocks. It is also, I confess, what I teach undergraduate students. I have learned that what professors really believe, stripped of secondary complications and reservations, is what they teach.

Sometimes sharp students, more likely undergraduate than graduate, want to know what economists know that other people, including their roommates, do not. First of all, I tell them, are identities. From non-economists in public debate, and sometimes alas even from economists, we hear or read plenty of arguments that are fallacious because they ignore identities. Likewise identities are frequently misused to imply causation. By themselves they do not, for example, tell us that government deficits generate trade deficits or that import surpluses finance themselves by inducing capital inflows or that business investments generate business profits. Those statements may be true, but you can't prove them by equations that are true by definition. Identities are only the beginning of wisdom.

11

I think open-economy macromodel builders can feel some intellectual satisfaction about the events of the past 20 years, especially the last 10. Fiscal and monetary policies under the floating-rate regime have worked out pretty much the way the textbooks said they would. Just as the IS/LM model, for all the hard knocks it has received from pure theorists, remains a good working approximation, so its international extension, Mundell-Fleming, has been a good guide. Thanks to that model, economists were prepared for the regime change in 1971–73. Qualitatively, that is. The quantitative extent of the open-economy effects of policies has exceeded our *ex ante* imaginations. But so, of course, have the experiments obligingly run by governments, particularly by the Reagan administration.

A Mundell-Fleming model

Let's begin with three important identities. First, the output-expenditure identity for a single economy,

$$C + I + G - CAD = Y \tag{1.1}$$

which implies the identity of the sources and uses of national saving,

$$S^p - D^g = I - CAD \tag{1.1'}$$

where C is consumption, G government purchases, I net private domestic investment, CAD the current account deficit (if negative, a surplus), Y net national product, S^p private saving equal to $Y - TX - C$, TX taxes net of transfers, D^g government deficit (if negative, a surplus) equal to $G - TX$.

Second, the current account deficit equals the capital inflow,

$$CAD = F \tag{1.2}$$

Third, across countries both current accounts and capital flows sum to zero,

$$\sum CAD = 0 = \sum F \tag{1.3}$$

Now I present a one-country model, motivated to apply to contemporary United States, running a current account deficit with "Japan" and borrowing in dollars to finance it.

The exchange rate is market-determined. The nominal value of the foreign currency, "yen," in terms of dollars is e. The real exchange rate E is ep^*/p, where p^* is the price of foreign goods in yen and p is the price of local goods in dollars.

The volume of U.S. exports in constant dollars depends on foreign economic conditions, in particular positively on foreign income Y^* and positively on the real exchange rate. Thus export volume is given by

$X(\overset{+}{E}, \overset{+}{Y}{}^*)$. Signs over the variables in functions indicate directions of effects. Real depreciation of the dollar makes U.S. goods more competitive and also has positive income effects, in that the command of given yen income over U.S. goods is increased.

The volume of imports of foreign goods in yen is $p^*IM(\overset{=}{E}, \overset{+}{Y})$. Depreciation of the dollars makes foreign goods relatively less attractive and also has negative income effects on home demand for foreign goods. Converted into dollars, imports are $ep^* \cdot IM(E, Y)$. Thus dollar depreciation, while reducing import volume, might increase its dollar value.

The current account deficit CAD is the difference between imports and exports, both in dollars. The current account deficit includes also the net outpayments of investment income – interest, dividends, rents, etc. In the model, capital transactions take place in dollar assets bearing an interest rate r and priced, inversely to r, at $q(r)$. Let VF be the volume of such assets held by the Japanese, as valued at a standard interest rate $\bar{r}$ at which $q = 1$. Let ΔVF be the change in those holdings during the period; $q\Delta VF$ is the capital inflow at current asset prices. The net outpayments of investment income are $rqVF$. Thus the equality of the U.S. current account deficit to the capital inflow is the following:

$$CAD = ep^* \cdot IM(E, Y) - pX(E, Y^*) + rq(r)VF = q(r)\Delta VF \qquad (1.4)$$

The inflow $q\Delta VF$ increases the stock of external debt. Of course the aggregate value of the stock might also change because of changes in r, i.e., by $q'(r)VF\Delta r$.

From the viewpoint of the foreign holders of U.S. debt VF, its value in yen is what matters. That value is qVF/e. Appreciation of the dollar is a possible source of capital gains.

Suppose that Japanese wealth owners hold VF at the beginning of this time period and wish to hold at the end of the period an aggregate of dollar assets of value p^*J in yen. They will buy ΔVF at price q such that $qVF/e + q\Delta VF/e = p^*J$. Thus

$$q\Delta VF = ep^*J - qVF \qquad (1.5)$$

The desired real-yen amount J depends on their previous accumulations of yen and dollar assets and also on contemporary market outcomes at home and abroad. I model the latter dependences as $J(\overset{+}{s}, r\overset{=}{*}, \overset{+}{Y}{}^*)$. Here r^* and Y^* are local Japanese interest rate and income, while s is the expected yield to Japanese investors of dollar assets: $s = r -$ expected $\Delta e/e$.

Perfect substitutability between Japanese and American assets is *not* assumed. Note also that the nominal exchange rate appears here. The real rate that concerns Japanese investors is the difference between the yen yield of holding dollar assets and the *Japanese* inflation rate. The U.S.

inflation rate is irrelevant to them except as a possible indicator of likely changes in the nominal exchange rate. They do not necessarily believe in purchasing power parity, and they should not if this model is correct.

In summary, the balance of payments equation in dollars is

$$CAD = ep^* \cdot IM(E, Y) - pX(E, Y^*) + rqVF$$
$$= ep^* \cdot J(s, r^*, Y^*) - qVF \tag{1.6a}$$

In real dollars, this is

$$CAD/p = E \cdot IM(E, Y) - X(E, Y^*) + rqVF/p$$
$$= E \cdot J(s, r^*, Y^*) - qVF/p \tag{1.6b}$$

I shall not in this brief presentation consider price movements in the two countries. In the upper panel of Fig. 1.1, CAD is measured on the horizontal axis, and the nominal exchange rate e (or interchangeably for present purposes the real exchange rate E) is measured vertically. The curve XX shows their relationship as determined by trade in goods, imports and exports, for given values of the other relevant variables. As drawn, XX assumes that depreciation of the dollar, increase in e, lowers the trade deficit. The slope would be positive if the import and export elasticities with respect to E were too low in absolute value to overcome the "J curve" effect of the higher dollar costs of imports. XX shifts right for increases in U.S. income Y and for increases in investment outflows, for example from increases in r.

Net capital inflows, $q\Delta VF$ as in Eq. (1.5), are depicted by JJ. It is upward sloping in Fig. 1.1 on two assumptions, both having to do with behavior of Japanese investors. First is a portfolio balance effect, implicit in the role of the exchange rate in Eq. (1.5): the higher is e, the lower is $1/e$, and the lower is the value in yen of Japanese holdings of dollar assets. This negative wealth effect increases the Japanese appetite for dollar assets, given interest rates in the two markets and exchange rate expectations. Second is a regressive expectations effect. The higher is e, the lower is expected $\Delta e/e$, and the higher is expected $\Delta(1/e)/(1/e)$, the better dollar assets look to Japanese investors. Extrapolative expectations are a different story. The higher is this period's e, the higher the expected $\Delta e/e$. This speculative response could reverse the slope of the JJ curve. In what follows I assume the standard shapes of XX and JJ as illustrated; the results depend on those assumptions.

A particular JJ curve assumes a given interest rate r in the U.S. A rise in the U.S. rate, holding the Japanese rate r^* constant, shifts JJ to the right, increases CAD and appreciates the dollar. JJ will also be shifted right, CAD increased, and e lowered by an autonomous increase in Japanese

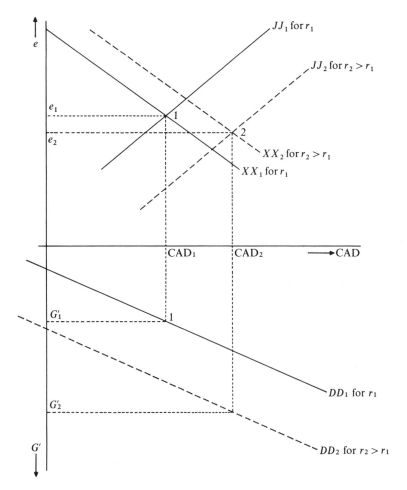

Fig. 1.1. Determination of current account deficit and capital inflow by fiscal policy (see text for explanation).

preference for dollar assets, whether by private investors or by the central bank.

The next step is to relate the U.S. CAD to the "IS" balance of aggregate demand and output in the U.S. The relevant equation is

$$D(r, Y) + [G - bT(Y)] - \text{CAD} = Y \tag{1.7}$$

where G is federal purchases of goods and services, $T(Y)$ is taxes net of transfers, b is the private marginal propensity to spend with respect to net taxes, and thus $G - bT(Y)$ is the aggregate demand effect of the budget deficit. Let us call this measure of fiscal policy G' for short. $D(\bar{r}, Y)$ is the remainder of private demand for goods and services.

Here I assume, as I believe is realistic for the U.S. nowadays, that Y is chosen by the Federal Reserve. Monetary policy, here represented by r, is geared to achieve the Fed's desired path of Y. Given the Fed's target Y, Eq. (1.6) relates the three variables G', CAD, and r. This relation is illustrated by loci DD in the lower panel of Fig. 1.1, where CAD is again the horizontal axis and G' is measured vertically downward. As is illustrated, these two variables are positively related to each other for a given interest rate. If G' is increased, CAD must increase to keep aggregate demand constant at Y at the same interest rate. A higher interest rate allows a higher G' for the same CAD, DD_2 instead of DD_1.

A (short-run) equilibrium is illustrated by points 1 in the two panels of the figure, where DD_1, XX_1, and JJ_1 all correspond to the same U.S. interest rate r_1. Fiscal policy is G_1'. Another equilibrium, at point 2, corresponds to fiscal policy G_2'. The second policy is less austere than the first; therefore the CAD is larger, the interest rate is higher, and the dollar is appreciated. Although the higher interest rate shifts XX in the same rightward direction as JJ, because of the higher interest payments on outstanding foreign-held debt, the assumption in the figure is that the XX shift is relatively small. That is a safe assumption if the initial stock of debt is small; there would be no shift in XX if it were zero.

In this model, bad news about future fiscal policy should cause the dollar to rise, e to fall, on the grounds that the Fed will raise interest rates to stay on its desired path for output Y. One of the missing ingredients in this short-run model, however, is "Japanese" investors' views of the exchange rate e that will eventually be required in a sustainable current account equilibrium. If that should rise, expected $\Delta e/e$ will rise too, s will be lower for given r, JJ will move left and up; the current value of the yen e will rise and CAD will fall. A rise in the Japanese interest rate r^* would have similar effects.

Dispelling some myths about the dollar

Let's put our simple model to work on some common misconceptions.

1. Eliminating the federal budget deficit will automatically eliminate the deficit in the U.S. external current account.

Imagine a political miracle. The President and Congress agree to a package of tax increases and spending cuts that balance the budget in fiscal year 1994, or even in fiscal year 1995. Will our $100 billion CAD

vanish simultaneously? Much rhetoric on the twin deficits seems to answer my question Yes. Common sense says No.

The dollar might strengthen in the exchange markets on news of a tough compromise budget package. That response might be rationalized on very general grounds of "confidence" in American political leadership, strengthened by evidence that the President and Congress can jointly accomplish a mission they undertook for themselves. Yet it would be difficult to rationalize on macroeconomic grounds. The myth reflects a misunderstanding of the mechanics connecting fiscal deficits and external deficits. In fact, the way that fiscal austerity could eventually balance our trade is precisely by *depreciating* the dollar.

How would this come about? Via Federal Reserve policy. If the Fed tries to stay on the modest growth track along which its policy has steered the economy since mid-1984, then the Fed will ease money and credit and lower interest rates to counter the fiscal contraction in aggregate demand. As our model says, this will depreciate the dollar. Monetary policy is exchange rate policy.

Whatever happens to fiscal and monetary policies and to interest rates and exchange rates, correction of the trade deficit is not automatic. The nation has to earn an improvement in its net exports in competition with foreign producers. As we have seen over the last 8 years, the trade deficit responds quite slowly to changes in exchange rates, terms of trade, and other determining variables. Quick fiscal contraction, giving the Fed the opportunity to ease interest rates, would still leave us with a big and stubborn trade deficit. In terms of the figure, imagine XX to be nearly vertical in the short run. Although the JJ curve would be shifting left and raising E, CAD would respond very little in the short run. The decline in r might give some slight relief in outpayments of interest and profits.

2. Recession is the inevitable consequence and deserved punishment of America's profligacy, and its essential natural cure.

A decline in GNP would reduce our demands for imports. Assuming the marginal propensity to import is 0.25 or 0.2, it would take a $400 to $500 billion loss of GNP (8 to 10%) to wipe out a $100 billion trade deficit. That's not recession but depression. The moral is that, even with recession, we need some help from prices relative to those of our competitors, help provided by exchange depreciation.

Don't worry. A $100 billion fiscal package would reduce GNP by much less, $150 to $200 billion, and that only if the Fed refused to counteract it. Recession is not the inevitable result of fiscal tightening, especially if we phase in fiscal tightening gradually. But the Fed must pursue a low-interest-rate policy and allow the dollar to depreciate.

We could have a recession without any drastic fiscal correction. All it takes is for the Fed to heed the warnings that higher U.S. interest rates are needed to keep the dollar from falling.

Whether we Americans deserve recession for our macroeconomic sins, as our Asian and European critics say, is a question of ethics and justice, not of economic analysis. Those critics are not alone in believing this nation is undersaving. The victims of our binges of consumption and arms buildup are our own children and grandchildren. They will be helped if we save more of our prosperity incomes and accumulate capital assets for them, instead of debts. But increased thrift will not help them if it goes to waste in recession, unemployment, and idle capacity.

3. The United States can balance its external current account without an adverse shift in its real exchange rate.

A decline in the real value of the dollar in external trade – in the quantity of foreign goods obtainable by a given amount of our labor and other resources – is a decline in American real wages and other real incomes. It is bad news, for sure, but accepting it is essential if we are to avoid indefinite accumulation of ever more onerous foreign debt.

It would be wonderful to restore competitiveness and trade balance by a burst of American productivity, a favorite refuge of politicians. Alas, no one knows how to bring that about; certainly it can't be done in a hurry. Our foreign rivals may be better able to speed up cost savings and quality gains than we are.

There are two ways of bringing about a decline in our real exchange rate, i.e., a reduction in the costs and prices of U.S. goods relative to those of foreigners. One is depreciation in the nominal exchange rate, assuming it is not offset by increases in dollar wages and other costs. As argued above, the U.S. is in a good position to bring this off. The other is to have a domestic deflation, of prices, wages, and other costs in excess of the deflations of our competitors. We are not in a good position to win at this game. The Germans and Japanese already have near-zero inflation and are prepared to operate their economies with even more slack if need be.

A few years ago our government was quite justifiably chastising Japan and Germany and other European countries for the sluggishness of their macroeconomic performances since the second oil shock. They should stimulate their economies by fiscal and monetary policies. The resulting increases in their imports would help to correct the trade imbalances. Recently their growth rates have picked up, while the United States economy, having reached full employment, has turned sluggish. Anyway, faster foreign growth is not likely to be a major contribution to the solution.

German and Japanese marginal propensities to import are not high enough to eliminate their surpluses.

Somehow there have to be relative price adjustments. The next time someone tells you devaluations do not work, are simplistic solutions, etc., etc., ask what the alternative solution is. Dollar appreciation?

4. The United States has to have high interest rates to induce foreigners to lend us the funds to finance our budget deficit and our excess imports.

We are being warned incessantly that we depend on foreigners – mainly Japanese banks, insurance companies, and pension funds – to buy U.S. Treasury bonds and other dollar assets. Their purchases both finance our budget deficit and provide us the foreign currencies we need to import Toyotas and Sonys. Should they decide not to buy dollar securities, the consequences, we are told, would be calamitous. That is why Washington must get its act together and follow policies of which these foreigners approve.

In terms of our model, the "calamity" we must avoid is a leftward shift of JJ. This will not by itself raise U.S. interest rates, which are under the Fed's control. Likewise, by assuring the liquidity of domestic financial intermediaries and markets the Fed can get the federal deficit domestically financed at prevailing interest rates. The natural result of a leftward shift in JJ is a higher e, a depreciation of the dollar. This would actually reduce CAD, per se a desirable outcome. However, if the U.S. economy is already at full employment, then in the absence of a fiscal correction there is no room in the economy for more exports or for substitution of domestic production for imports. Thus to prevent inflation, the Fed might have to react to a leftward shift of JJ by tightening credit and raising interest rates.

Obviously this obstacle would not be present if domestic aggregate demand were weakening, whether from fiscal contraction or private thrift. In those circumstances, a fall in the dollar could correct the disequilibrium by taking the exchange rate to a more realistic level, from which the dollar could be expected to rise. It is a bad idea for the G-7 central banks to peg the dollar at a rate where the risk is all on one side, that it will go down. What we do not need is an exchange value of the dollar too high for timely and significant improvement in the trade position, too high for anyone even to entertain the possibility of appreciation. What we do not need, especially, is a U.S. commitment to defend an overvalued dollar with high interest rates, independently of domestic economic circumstances.

We frequently hear warnings of a "free-fall" of the dollar. I guess this means that exchange rate expectations become extrapolative instead of regressive. This can happen in any financial market. No one can tell when it might happen or what might trigger it or how far a price could move before more sober expectations took over. Our central bank cannot keep interest rates uneconomically high forever just to ensure against this contingency.

International capital flows vs. intercurrency flows

My simple framework has numerous shortcomings, and I want to discuss some of them in this section and in the next and concluding sections.

Interregional trade occurs between geographical regions and their resident populations. It is international trade when the regions are those of national political jurisdictions. Balance-of-payments accounts refer to trade and capital transactions across national boundaries. We commonly regard those transactions as the ones that determine demands for and supplies of various national currencies and their exchange rates. That is, we identify transactions across boundaries with transactions across currencies.

The correspondence is imperfect. For one thing offshore currency markets—Eurodollars, for example – move exchange rates without being recorded in nationally based payments statistics, and without disturbing the accounting identities of current account deficits and capital account surpluses. Less obvious and more important is that some international capital flows may not really change relative demands for currencies or alter their rates of exchange.

Consider, for example, Japanese direct investments in the United States, in particular the acquisition of facilities for producing internationally traded goods like automobiles. In the first instance Japanese investors use dollars they bought from Japanese exporters to buy or build a factory, instead of purchasing U.S. Treasury bonds or other nominal dollar assets. This substitution of American equity for bonds may be only transitory. Japanese investors' demand for nominal dollar assets should not decline by the full amount of their direct investments in the U.S. The reason is that an automobile factory in Ohio may well be a closer substitute for factories, properties, and equities in Japan than it is for future dollars *qua* dollars.

The international car market can be supplied from Tennessee or from Tokyo. The long-run real returns from owning a plant in Tennessee are not very dependent on the dollar/yen exchange rate and not very vulnerable to the factors that might generate losses to Japanese holders of American bonds. U.S. inflation, for example, would raise the dollar earnings from operating the plant at the same time as it depreciated the dollar against the yen. Direct investment of this kind in the U.S. is portfolio reallocation vis-à-vis Japanese plants, real properties, and equities more than vis-à-vis dollars per se. When the investments overseas are in real assets productive of nontraded goods, like office space in Rockefeller Center, they are not so obviously substitutes for similar real assets in Japan. But neither are they particular substitutes for U.S. bonds or other U.S. nominal assets.

My model above, for these reasons, overstates the dependence of capital flows, specifically Japan to U.S., on nominal interest differentials and exchange rate expectations. For direct investments and equities, differences in net real marginal productivities are of prime importance. One should say, of course, *expected* differences. While these are not wholly independent of current differences in nominal interest rates and of expected movements of exchange rates, they mainly reflect longer-run estimates of the profit-abilities of producing particular goods and services in different nations and jurisdictions.

Thanks to Reaganomics, the U.S. has been following loose-fiscal–tight-money policies for nearly a decade. Combined with a low rate of private saving, these policies created a nominal interest differential that attracted financial inflows, the more so because, partly in response to U.S. pressure, Japan had just relaxed restrictions on holdings of foreign assets by Japanese financial institutions. The policies kept the cost of capital high in the U.S., higher than in previous cyclical recoveries and higher than in other major economies. As domestic investment was crowded out, the marginal efficiency of capital was lifted, creating an opportunity for foreigners who could tap cheaper foreign sources of finance. In this light, the surge in Japanese direct investment in U.S. business is not surprising. What is perhaps surprising is that U.S. firms and Japanese lenders do not make more deals.

Stock adjustments vs. sustainable flows

Observed flows of capital can reflect either or both of two conceptually distinct phenomena: reallocations of portfolio stock and allocations of new wealth in established patterns. Stock reallocations occur in response to changes in current and expected asset yields and in perceived risks. These are one-shot effects. Because of transactions costs and other frictions, they do not take place instantaneously in response to news. They take time, but as they are completed and portfolios are reshaped they die out. In the absence of further changes of yields and risks, i.e., without new news, these flows between markets and across frontiers and currencies become zero. Accretions to wealth, on the other hand, are a continuing source of capital flows.

For example, suppose U.S. assets are about 10% of fully adjusted Japanese portfolios. In stable circumstances we should expect 10% of the regular annual additions to these protfolios to flow to U.S. markets. Japan's wealth is estimated to be 6 times its GNP. Steady-state growth for both wealth and GNP is in nominal terms 9% per year. Thus the steady flows into U.S. assets would be $.10 \times .09 \times 6 \times$ GNP, about \$16 billion. In the recent decade, of course, Japanese holdings of U.S. assets have grown sharply in relation both to Japan's wealth and to U.S. wealth. I infer that a stock adjustment has been occurring, and still is. Obviously it must taper off sooner or later. But when? It's impossible to say. But catching up to target portfolio allocations is not the only force tending to slow down these capital flows. The increasing interpenetrations of loan markets, equity markets, and goods markets narrow the differentials between the two countries in both nominal interest rates and real costs of capital.

A second-approximation model

The Mundell-Fleming style model presented above does not disaggregate the asset menus offered investors in the two countries. It does not model the two countries symmetrically. Neither does it distinguish between stock reallocations and steady flows. Here I can only sketch briefly some amendments to remedy these shortcomings.

Assets in both countries are available to wealth owners and portfolio managers in both countries. (Some assets may be held in negative amounts.) The notation is tedious, because the identity of the asset, its country of origin, and the residence of its holders must all be described. Amounts of American assets are designated by a_i, amounts of Nipponese assets by n_j. Holdings by Americans are denoted by superscript A, those by Japanese by superscript N. Thus $a_i = a_i^A + a_i^N$ and $n_j = n_j^A + n_j^N$. The units of assets are par values for nominally dominated securities and commodity units for equities or real properties. The economies' steady-state growth trend rates are g_a and g_n.

The prices of assets are q_{ai} and q_{nj}, in dollars or yen per asset unit. These prices are related, normally inversely, to rates of return r_{ai} and r_{nj}. In each country there is one asset, base money, whose price is identically 1 in local currency and whose nominal return is zero or some other constant. As before, the exchange rate is e dollars per yen.

The values of desired asset holdings in currency of the country of issue are for Americans A_i^A and N_j^A, for Japanese A_i^N and N_j^N. In the currency of the holder they are A_i^A and eN_j^A, $(1/e)A_i^N$ and N_j^N. These latter are functions of the vectors of rates of return (r_{ai}, r_{nj}), of prices and expected inflation rates, of NNP in the investors' home country, and of expected change in the exchange rate.

Here are the flow demands for the various assets, all expressed in dollars:

$$fa_i^A(t) = g_a A_i^A(t-1) + \alpha_i(A_i^A(t) - q_{ai}(t)a_i^A(t-1))$$
$$fa_i^N(t) = g_n e(t)[(1/e(t))A_i^N(t-1)] + \beta_i e(t)([(1/e(t))A_i^N(t)]$$
$$- (q_{ai}(t)/e(t))a_i^N(t-1))$$
$$fn_j^A(t) = g_a[e(t)N_j^A(t-1)] + \alpha_j([e(t)N_j^A(t-1)]$$
$$- e(t)q_{nj}(t)n_j^A(t-1))$$
$$fn_j^N(t) = g_n e(t)N_j^N(t-1) + \beta_j e(t)(N_j^N - q_{nj}(t)n_j^N(t-1)) \qquad (1.8)$$

In each case, the first term is the flow required to make the holding grow at the rate of the economy's growth. The second term is the stock adjustment. The α's and β's are the speeds of adjustment, which are multiplied by the excess of desired holdings over the value of previous holdings at the prices of the current period.

The flow demands for each asset – $f_{ai}^A + f_{ai}^N$ and $(f_{nj}^A + f_{nj}^N)/e$ in local currencies – are to be equated to the new supplies. For equities and direct investments in business capital, these are the increments in capital stocks, evaluated at current replacement costs or commodity prices. For government obligations, these are the changes in outstanding supplies resulting from central bank and Treasury transactions with the public. These equal in total the government deficit. New asset supplies need not be exogenous; domestic capital investments and government deficits are in part policy decisions and in part functions of other variables.

Total wealth stocks and total private saving in both economies are implicit in the above equations. They are just the sums of stocks and flows for the wealth owners of the country. In steady states, with stock adjustments zero, asset supplies and holdings and total wealth would be growing at rates g_a and g_n.

There are two more supply-demand equations than there are endogenous asset prices (or corresponding rates of return) to be determined. That is because the local prices of currencies and their nominal returns are fixed. And there is one more equation, the payments balance equation. It is natural to think of the equality of net capital flow to current account balance as determining the exchange rate, just as in the simple framework exhibited above. Here is the equation, expressed as the net capital inflow to the United States in dollars on the left-hand side and on the right-hand side the American CAD. This CAD has two parts, the trade deficit and the deficit in investment incomes.

$$\sum_i f_{ai}{}^N - \sum_j f_{nj}{}^A = X^N(ep^N/p^A, Y^A) - eX^A/(p^A/ep^N, Y^N)$$

$$+ \sum_i r_{ai}q_{ai}a_i{}^N - e\sum_j r_{nj}q_{nj}n_j{}^A \qquad (1.9)$$

What variables do the two extra equations determine? In some contexts these would be the two Y's, or the two price levels. If aggregate supply equations, "AS curves," were added for each economy, all four of these variables could be determined. However, in the spirit of the simple model above, price levels would be taken as predetermined in the short run and the two Y's would be those chosen by the monetary authorities. The two free variables would be local interest rates r indicative of monetary policies, or, alternatively, values of the monetary base in each country.

Crucial parameters in a portfolio model of this kind are the partial derivatives of desired asset stocks with respect to rates of return, the r's. It is intuitively natural to expect the own partials, the responses to changes in the asset's own rate, to be positive, at least non-negative. Furthermore, a "gross substitutes" assumption is convenient and plausible, though not mandated by rationality. This says that cross partials, responses of a given asset demand to other rates of return, are non-positive and that the sum of all of them is not greater in absolute value than the own partial. High absolute values of cross partials indicate high substitutability between assets, low values the reverse. Common vulnerabilities to certain risks make for high substitutability. Assets whose returns, including capital gains or losses, do not share the same risks, or move in opposite directions in response to the same shocks, will be poor substitutes. I gave an example above, when I argued that equities and real properties in the two countries could be good portfolio substitutes for each other but poor substitutes for nominal assets in either currency.

Figure 1.2 is a schematic illustration of the accounting underlying Eqs. (1.8) and (1.9). In the matrix, the columns represent sectors of the two economies, America on the left and Japan on the right. Only four sectors of each economy are distinguished here. The rows represent assets, American at the top, Japanese at the bottom. Seven asset categories are shown for each country. A plus sign $+$ in a cell indicates that the sector holds positive quantities of the asset, a minus sign $-$ that the sector is a debtor in this category of asset. The entries in a column, for both local and foreign assets, describe the sector's portfolio; they sum to the sector's net worth. The entries in a row show how the positive and negative holdings of a given asset are distributed among sectors in the two countries. The row sums, in the final column, are zero for all the assets that are

Fig. 1.2. Illustrative two-country sectoral portfolio matrix.

	American portfolios				Japanese portfolios				Total
	Hhs	Bus	Bks	Gov	Hhs	Bus	Bks	Gov	
American assets									
$ Base money	+	+	+	−					0
$ Deposits	+	+	−			+	+	+	0
$ Treas. debt	+	+	+	−	+		+	+	0
$ Hh debt	−	+	+						0
$ Bus. debt	+	−	+		+		+		0
Equity	+	−	−		+	+			0
Real property	+	+			+	+			+
A-owned A-assets	+	−	−	−					+
N-owned A-assets					+	+	+	+	+
Japanese assets									
YEN base money					+	+	+	−	0
YEN deposits		+	+	+	+	+	−		0
YEN treas. debt	+		+	+	+	+	+	−	0
YEN Hh debt					−	+	+		0
YEN bus. debt	+		+		+	−	+		0
Equity	+	+			+	−	−		0
Real property	+	+			+	+			+
A-owned N-assets	+	+	+	+					+
N-owned N-assets					+	−	−	−	+
Net worth	+	0	0	−	+	0	0	−	+

obligations of one or more of the sectors. They are positive only for real property, capital, in the two economies. The sum of the values of the two capital stocks is equal to the sum of the sector net worths. Of course, one country – in present circumstances, Japan – may have a net worth greater than its own capital stock by the amount of its net claims on the other country.

Figure 1.2 is a schematic balance sheet, in which the entries are stocks. An analogous schema would describe the flows in any period, as in the "second approximation model" above. The illustration is for a two-country world, but the same format can be used for n countries. The pioneering work of Kuroyanagi, Hamada, and Sakurai, reported elsewhere in these proceedings, provides data for this kind of model.

CHAPTER 2

An overview of (older) exchange rate theory

RICHARD N. COOPER

I take as my starting point, the title of Paul Krugman's lecture at the Third Sanwa Conference, "Exchange Rates and External Balances: Do the Old Rules Still Apply?" That piqued my curiosity. What does Krugman mean by the "old rules"? This is one of those questions that dates economists. One can judge their vintage by what they mean by the old rules. I thought back to my graduate school education and what we read on the question of exchange rates and external balances. We read first of all Joan Robinson (1947) and Fritz Machlup (1939), who independently rediscovered what Marshall had already discovered a generation earlier, the conditions under which currency devaluation would improve the trade balance. That is what we still call the Marshall-Lerner condition, that the sum of the elasticity of demand for our country's exports and our country's elasticity of demand for imports must exceed unity for a currency depreciation to produce an improvement in the trade balance, starting with initial balance. Gottfried Haberler (1949) suggested that that result had to be qualified if supply was not perfectly elastic. We therefore learned some complicated formulas involving supply elasticities as well as demand elasticities and the influence of an initial imbalance on the outcome. Sidney Alexander (1952) came along and pointed out that a country will not get any trade balance improvement at all unless there is some room in the economy to permit it, and that led to the so-called "absorption approach" to exchange rate changes, an approach still with us.

In the meantime, off to one side, so to speak, Milton Friedman (1953) argued that we should not be concerned with the consequences of a discrete devaluation, that it would be far more sensible to move to a regime of flexible exchange rates. He argued that flexible exchange rates would insulate our country fully from monetary disturbances coming from overseas; in particular, we would not have to import inflation. Interestingly, he also argued that flexible exchange rates would help to insulate our country from real disturbances coming from abroad, such as rearmament.

In other words, he did not assume the perfect neutrality of money when it came to exchange rates; that came later, with Mundell (1971).

So this was the fare to which graduate students were exposed in the late 1950s. I want to underline several key assumptions of that analysis. The first is that the law of one price – i.e., that the same good everywhere would command the same price, after adjustment for tariffs and transport costs – was assumed to apply. The second is that, at least as originally conceived, currency devaluation was coterminous with changes in the terms of trade. Before one worried about secondary effects, one assumed a devaluation to change the prices of our exports (relative to our imports) by the full amount of the devaluation. That was later qualified. The third assumption is that the focus was exclusively on the market for goods and services. Virtually no discussion (and I only add the "virtually" as a courtesy) of the impact on capital transactions occurred.

Finally, aggregate demand had to be adjusted to make room for any improvement that was to take place in the balance on goods and services consequent upon devaluation. That could be achieved either if the economy had a lot of slack in it, as was originally assumed, or if, as James Meade (1951) assumed in his great synthetic volume on the balance of payments, monetary and fiscal policy are adjusted to ensure that capacity became available to accommodate any improvement in the current account, in effect simulating perfect elasticity of supply.

One by one, these assumptions have been critically questioned and have been substantially qualified. Let me take them in reverse order. The assumption that a successful devaluation would necessarily be expansionary and therefore would require some reduction in aggregate domestic demand was brought into question. I contributed to that debate in 1971, and Paul Krugman (1978) contributed as well. Under certain conditions, mostly applying to developing countries, successful devaluation may be contractionary in its overall impact on aggregate demand.

The most significant of the qualifications from a theoretical point of view concerned the introduction of assets and the observation that the exchange rate was also – or could be thought of as, or was related to – an asset price. That led to some new theory. It led to jumping exchange rates. There was a time when an analyst who got a positive root in the system of differential equations threw it out on the grounds that the system was unstable and therefore could not obtain in the real world. We then discovered that with forward-looking expectations, discrete jumps in prices are not only possible but likely: systems of equations can have a positive root and still converge to equilibrium on the stable manifold, as it is called. Under those circumstances the ultimate movement in a flexible exchange rate might reverse the direction of its initial movement, a manifestation of overshooting, something that earlier would have been considered a perverse case.

Third, the link between devaluation and the terms of trade was questioned. This is most obviously so in the case of a small country, where the terms of trade by the very assumption of smallness cannot be changed by the country's own actions. The analysis shifted in those cases from the commodity terms of trade – the price of exports in terms of imports – to the relative price of tradables versus nontradables. An extensive literature on the small country case now exists, and unfortunately it has introduced some confusion in terminology because the old language is used to apply to the new concepts. In particular the expression "real exchange rate" is now often applied to the relative price of tradables in terms of nontradables, even though that relative price does not in any way resemble an exchange rate between currencies.

Apart from the extreme case of a small economy, many feedbacks can be allowed for. Thus the impact of a change in an exchange rate on the terms of trade can be reduced to some extent or even, in extreme cases, completely nullified, thus establishing, in this domain, the classical dichotomy between money and real side of the economy, in which money is just a veil and changes in exchange rates cannot have any real effect. This view was first propounded by Mundell and picked up in somewhat modified form more recently by McKinnon (1981).

That leaves on my list of original assumptions just the law of one price. It is an absolutely key assumption for much economic analysis. Happily, two of the three papers in this book bring into question the law of one price. Anyone who does serious comparative shopping knows that the law of one price does not, in fact, obtain, even though it is routinely assumed in most if not all economic theorizing. We rationalize the observations with our theory on the grounds that there are special factors associated with the price differentials that persist not only month after month but year after year. There are locational advantages. There are services implicitly bundled with the goods that are being sold, part of an informal contract or handshake. In short, we get imperfect competition, which permits price differentials to persist for long periods of time on what looks and feels like the same good.

No doubt much of that rationalization is valid. But the need to rationalize should at least raise questions about the viability of the law of one price as a central operating assumption applied to the goods market. Yet it has done so. I suppose the grounds would be that, while it is true that price differentials exist and persist, we do not observe them changing substantially over time. While price levels are not homogeneous, movements in prices are homogeneous, the argument could run.

In the 1980s, we have put that proposition to a test with exchange rate changes. As two of our papers point out, changes in exchange rates have led to quite marked changes in price differentials on tradable goods. These observations seem to me a very fertile field for further development. One of the papers mentions in passing that marked price differentials on tradable goods can persist only if something prevents arbitrage from taking place. A key question that we therefore have to ask is why arbitrage did not take place. The contrast with other papers at the conference, reflecting what we know in general about financial markets, is striking. Arbitrage in financial markets is almost palpable. Arbitrage differentials get eliminated relatively quickly, sometimes almost instantaneously. Yet apparently in the goods market they certainly do not get eliminated instantaneously and indeed in some cases seem to take years.

The phenomenon is not limited to exchange rate changes. We should have been aware of it before. Three examples that predate the big changes in exchange rates will make the point. The first has to do with the extremely turbulent oil market in 1979–80. By that time the United States was collecting detailed statistics on oil imports by price, by quality, by origin, by contract, by time, and by port of import. About 50,000 observations on oil imports from 1973–1984 have been analyzed [see Anderson (1988) and Cooper (1988)]. One of the striking results is that the variance of oil prices (controlling for all of the variables for which data are available) rose dramatically from 1977–78, to 1979, 1980, and early 1981, and then receded back to more or less the 1977–78 levels in 1983–84. For a period of 3 to 4 years, arbitrage – in the sense of rapid elimination of price differentials – was not working in the oil market. The market was sufficiently turbulent during the Iranian revolution that price differences could persist for some period of time.

A second example concerns the U.S. embargo on sales of grain of the Soviet Union in 1980. Because wheat and corn are relatively homogeneous commodities, economists predicted the embargo could not work, not being entirely clear what "working" meant. When the embargo was imposed, the United States leaned on Canada, Australia, and the European Community not to undermine it, but Argentina was in a period of economic liberalization and declined to cooperate. Sure enough, Argentine grain started to move to the Soviet Union. It had already been contracted for, however. In order to buy out the contracts, the Soviet Union had to pay a premium of 20 to 25%, and this premium lasted as long as the Argentine grain crop lasted (essentially for northern winter and spring 1980). There arbitrage was visible; Italians and others cancelled their Argentine contracts and bought U.S. grain, while the Soviet Union acquired Argentine grain. But it only worked at a substantial price differential, and even so the Soviet Union was unable to satisfy all of its demand.

A third example concerns electrolytic copper, far more homogeneous than either grain or oil. For nearly two decades the U.S. producer price for copper differed consequentially – sometimes lower, more often higher – from the price of copper on the London Metal Exchange, even after allowing for transfer costs. Eventually the U.S. producer price system collapsed in favor of the LME price, but the possibility for arbitrage took two decades to eliminate the differential.

Those examples should have been warnings about what could happen, but at least the first two episodes were of such a peculiar and transitory nature that we could perhaps dismiss them as being idiosyncratic, even though oil price differentials lasted for several years, the time frame referant for analyzing currency devaluation.

The large run-up of the dollar followed by the large decline in the dollar in the 1980s provides a powerful experiment on the law of one price. This kind of experience poses an acute tension for businesses that sell identical or even modestly differentiated products in different markets. For a variety of reasons, firms like to keep prices stable for their customers, who like stable prices. That is true both in the home market and in the foreign market. A fluctuating exchange rate between those two markets poses a marketing problem. A firm must decide whether to allow its prices to fluctuate in both markets, or in one market but not the other, or – as many of them seem to elect – to try to separate the markets in some way and maintain stable prices in both. To achieve the last option, firms must assume that the arbitrage will not take place quickly, or if it does, that they can stop it in some way. In this setting the informal trade barriers of Japan become very important. The papers focus mainly on the U.S. market, but it would also be interesting to know how much arbitrage took place back in the Japanese market.

In the U.S. market, to be very concrete (although this can be generalized to many products) BMW and Mercedes elected to stabilize their prices in dollars, and in Germany to stabilize their prices in marks, even in 1984 and early 1985, the period during which the dollar was exceptionally strong. The mark actually reached 3.50 DM per dollar briefly, and for many months it was above 3 marks to the dollar, compared with the 1.80 it was before (in 1980) and later became (in 1987).

Automobiles must meet somewhat different standards in different markets, and it took a while for somebody to develop the kit (which sold for a few thousand dollars) to convert a European car to an American car (the amber lights had to be replaced with red lights and so forth). For a period the price differential was about a factor of 2 on the identical car, apart from these adjustments to meet American standards. Sure enough, arbitrage began to take place. A "gray market" developed in the United States in BMWs, Mercedes, Sony products, and in a host of other products. So arbitrage occurred, but it was insufficient to eliminate the price differentials. Then the exchange rate situation changed and we did not run the experiment, so to speak, long enough to find out how long it would have taken for these price differentials to be arbitraged away.

What we did see was the formation of a trade association in Washington of firms with branded products who were concerned with what they called "gray markets." In the United States there is nothing illegal whatsoever about these sales, but in their public statements and their congressional testimony the spokesmen for the firms implies that this was an illegal activity and was somehow cheating the public. Draft legislation was prepared (fortunately it never got out of committee) to stop this kind of arbitrage.

The low point, in my view, was reached in the Duracell battery case. Duracell brought a trademark infringement case against its own product, made in a Belgian plant, 100% owned by Duracell. Duracell was dual pricing, like many other firms with branded products. Some jobbers began to buy up Duracell batteries in Europe and ship them across the Atlantic for sale at wholesale in the United States. Duracell first asked U.S. Customs officials to block these imports on grounds of trademark infringement. Customs quite correctly (after the proper inquiries) declined to do so on the grounds that these were Duracell batteries being sold as Duracell batteries and therefore seemed to infringe no trademark. Duracell took the matter to court, arguing that any branded product involves an implicit set of services that goes along with it, covered by the trademark: controlled transportation conditions, assurances about how long it takes to get from the factory to the store, and so on. Duracell lost the case. Again, we did not run the experiment long enough to learn how long it would have taken for the arbitrage to have eliminated the price differential, perhaps by leading firms such as Duracell to change their pricing strategies.

These differentials lasted for 2 years, or longer in some cases, that is to say, about the same period to which our business cycle theory applies, about the same time horizon within which we frame macroeconomic stabilization policy. So the empirical evidence raises fundamental questions about the viability of the assumption, of the law of one price, at least in the branded goods market, within the time frame of macroeconomics. This is extremely troubling for theory, but it may in fact help explain a number of the conundrums that arise in trying to match our macro-economic analysis with what we actually observe in economies.

The academic literature has a tendency these days to emphasize the real exchange rate. That is what economists think is appropriate, that is what they are comfortable with, that is a relative price with which we think we know how to deal. Paul Krugman's paper, for example, is drawn entirely in terms of real exchange rates.

The public is really interested in the nominal exchange rate. Noneconomists are interested in the rate at which one currency changes for another. We should therefore ask ourselves, what do economists have to say about nominal exchange rates? The answer, turns out, is embarrassingly little. Kareken and Wallace (1981) put their finger on the problem explicitly a decade ago. They pointed out that an exchange rate is a rate of exchange between two nominal variables. Since two nominal variables are involved, the rate of exchange can be anything. We do not have anything in which to ground it. Yet actual monetary economies are not completely arbitrary. They have a given set of institutions, a process for framing monetary policy, and so on. In groping for an anchor for the nominal exchange rate between actual currency areas, economists are led naturally to think there ought to be some relationship to purchasing power parity. Yet when we look at that empirically, at least among countries with relatively low inflation rates (less than 10 or 15% a year), purchasing power parity does not do very well as an explanatory variable, either in the relatively short run of 1 or 2 years or in the intermediate time frame of 5 to 10 years.

The economics profession is somewhat at sea on that question, and yet the decision-making public, those who make business decisions, is troubled by changes in nominal exchange rates.

That leads me to my final thought, which is that the economics profession has treated the exchange rate primarily as an adjusting variable. It is a relative price that adjusts to clear markets, as all prices do. Exogenous disturbances occur, and inside the economic system the various endogenous variables adjust to absorb the disturbances. Exchange rates act as a kind of a shock absorber. That is the way economists think of exchange rates, and surely economists are, at least in part, right in thinking of them that way.

I would suggest, though, that volatility in nominal variables may also be a *source* of disturbance, a genuine additional source of uncertainty to the economic system, while even at the same time playing the role of adjusting variable and permitting other variables to adjust less than they would otherwise do. That leads us back to financial markets and how they work, and in particular whether financial markets can have rational bubbles or even irrational bubbles. In other words, are financial markets, including foreign-exchange markets under floating rates, a *source* of disturbances to the real economy? That is an important topic for further research.

References

Alexander, Sidney S. (1952), "Effects of a Devaluation on a Trade Balance," IMF *Staff Papers*, 2, 263–78.

Anderson, Joseph M. (1988), "Empirical Analysis of World Oil Trade, 1967–1984," *in* G. Horwich and D. Weimer (eds.), *Responding to International Oil Crises*, Washington: American Enterprise Institute.

Cooper, Richard N., "An Analysis of the International Energy Agency: Comments of a Sometime Practitioner," *in* Horwich and Weimer, op. cit.

Cooper, Richard N. (1971), "Devaluation and Aggregate Demand in Aid-Receiving Countries," *in* J. Bhagwati et al. (eds.), *Trade, Balance of Payments, and Growth*, Amsterdam: North-Holland.

Friedman, Milton (1953), "The Case for Flexible Exchange Rates," *Essays in Positive Economics*, Chicago: University of Chicago Press.

Haberler, Gottfried (1949), "The Market for Foreign Exchange and the Stability of the Balance of Payments: A Theoretical Analysis," *Kyklos*, 3, no. 3, 193–218.

Karaken, John, and Neil Wallace (1981), "On the Indeterminacy of Equilibrium Exchange Rates," *Quarterly Journal of Economics*, 96 (May).

Krugman, Paul R., and Lance Taylor (1978), "Contractionary Effects of Devaluation," *Journal of International Economics*, 8 (Aug.), 445–56.

Machlup, Fritz (1950), "The Theory of Foreign Exchanges," reprinted in American Economic Association, *Readings in the Theory of International Trade*, Philadelphia: Blakiston; first published in *Economica* in 1939–40.

McKinnon, Ronald I. (1981), "The Exchange Rate and Macroeconomic Policy: Changing Postwar Perceptions," *Journal of Economic Literature*, 19 (Jun.), 531–57.

Meade, James E. (1951), *The Balance of Payments*, Oxford: Oxford University Press.

Mundell, Robert A. (1971), *Monetary Theory*, Pacific Palisades, CA: Goodyear Publishing Co.

Robinson, Joan, "The Foreign Exchanges," reprinted in AEA *Readings*, op. cit., originally published in 1947 in *Essays in the Theory of Employment*.

CHAPTER 3

Second thoughts on EMU*

PAUL KRUGMAN

Remarkably, it appears at the time of writing that a monetary union of Europe might still happen. The prospect is, admittedly, far from certain. There may well be a significant one-time exchange realignment to deal with the consequences of German reunification, and a subtlety in the rules allows for a final realignment before currency union. Britain and Denmark have insisted on clauses that effectively allow them to stay out if they choose. The convergence criteria established at Maastricht allow for "variable geometry," under which some nations will join EMU faster than others. At this point, however, it is still possible that all of these will turn out to be mere technicalities, that by the year 2000 or a little later, all of Western Europe will use ECU as the medium of exchange.

This momentous event raises two questions. First, is it a good thing? That is, will monetary union actually be beneficial to Europe? Second, if it is going to happen, how should the transition be managed? That is, does the plan for "stage 2" laid out at Maastricht make sense?

The purpose of this paper is to offer some thoughts about these two questions. Obviously they have been heavily discussed, and one cannot expect to break a lot of new ground. [Kenen (1992) provides a thorough summary of the issues and, in a more guarded way, offers a similar perspective to that of this paper]. Most European discussion has, however, been rather cautious and respectful. This paper is written from the stance of an outsider and therefore raises questions in a somewhat harsher and more irreverent way. As I will argue, the economics of EMU are by no means as favorable as widely assumed. More important, perhaps, the logic of the transition is very unclear, and the elements of the Maastricht agreement can and should be criticized quite severely.

---

*Reprinted with permission from *Japan and the World Economy*, 4:3, 1992.

Is EMU a good idea?

General principles

The basic economic logic for EMU is the same as that for any currency area. By unifying their currencies, the European nations will save the transactions costs and uncertainty that having a multiplicity of currencies imposes. At the same time they will sacrifice the flexibility and ability to adjust that come with independent monies.

The theory of optimum currency areas, in its classic exposition by McKinnon (1963), suggests that the terms of the tradeoff depend on how much trade there is between a pair of countries. If the countries trade very little, the efficiency gains from monetary union will be modest relative to the increased difficulty of adjustment. One can thus carry out a thought experiment. First, imagine a world with very many tiny currency areas. For such tiny areas the benefits of merging with their neighbors will be large relative to the costs; so they will benefit from assembling into somewhat larger currency areas. These areas in turn may benefit from merging into still larger areas – but not as much. At some point the benefits of merging currency areas may be outweighed by the costs. At that point the world will have been partitioned into optimal currency areas.

It is possible to add other factors to this story. As Mundell (1961) argued, regions with high mutual factor mobility will tend to make better candidates for monetary union than those without. As many authors, e.g., Eichengreen and Bayoumi (1992), have pointed out, the usefulness of exchange rate flexibility and hence the costs of monetary union depend on how asymmetric the shocks hitting nations are. Much discussion of the EMS has focused on the special role of a monetary zone in creating credibility for disinflationary monetary policy. The basic story, however, remains the same: There is a tradeoff between macroeconomic flexibility and microeconomic efficiency, which leads to some optimum size of currency area.

But what is that optimal size? The presumption behind EMU is that a continent-sized area is about right, which is a plausible guess. But there are other plausible guesses. To many economists it seems natural to suppose that a single world currency must be optimal – and if we had one, there is little doubt that we would find it hard to imagine living in our current fragmented world. On the other hand, there is a quite reasonable economic (if not political) case to be made for independent currencies at the level of metropolitan areas, which are really the largest units for which labor is highly mobile over the course of a normal business cycle.

The question is: Has new information become available in recent years that would increase our belief that European nations will be better off giving up their monetary independence? It is hard to argue that any convincing new evidence has been provided. That is, there is little in recent developments either in economic analysis or real world experience that makes the economic case for EMU look any stronger (or weaker) than it did 10 or 20 years ago.

Basically, while the optimal currency area theory is a very useful intellectual organizing device, it is just not operational in the current state of economic knowledge. We can make some estimate of the cost of currency union by looking at the macroeconomics of adjustment, but we have no effective way of measuring the benefits. This was true a decade ago, and remains true now.

Europe vs. the U.S.

The usual route taken by those who want to have *something* empirical to say about EMU is to draw comparisons with the U.S. The U.S. is a roughly Europe-sized economy that is, among other things, a currency union. It works, and if Europe looks sufficiently similar to the U.S. in terms of the fundamental issues raised by optimal currency area theory, currency union should work there too.

It is worth pointing out, however, that while the U.S. is a successful currency union, there is no particular reason to believe that it is an optimal currency area. The decision to unify the currency was, after all, undertaken more than two centuries ago, by a small agricultural nation. All one can say is that since then the union has worked well enough to survive.

Indeed, there have undoubtedly been times when U.S. regions would have welcomed the flexibility that multiple currencies bring. It is worth reviewing, as a spectacular case in point, the problems experienced by New England during the late 1980s.

New England is a region of about 10 million people. Like other regions in the U.S., it is highly specialized. Its "export" base, those industries that sell primarily to customers outside the region, is concentrated in several narrow high-technology sectors: minicomputers, advanced medicine, precision military hardware. During most of the 1980s, these sectors thrived. As computing power grew, many businesses shifted from the large mainframe computers made by IBM to the minicomputers manufactured by Massachusetts firms like Digital Equipment. The large Reagan-era defense budgets concentrated on high-tech hardware like the Patriot missile manufactured by Massachusetts-based Raytheon, and so on. This export boom had both a multiplier and an accelerator effect on the local economy: Employment grew in nontraded sectors like retailing, and a commercial real estate boom led to a surge in construction employment. In late 1987, Massachusetts had an unemployment rate of only 2.5%, less than half the national average.

But then the bottom fell out. Demand shifted away from New England products. Personal microcomputers began to displace office minicomputers. Pentagon spending fell. The construction boom collapsed as it became apparent that the state was overbuilt. Within the space of 3 years the unemployment rate nearly quadrupled.

It is clear that during the crisis the New England region paid a heavy price for its membership in the U.S. currency union. Imagine that there had been an independent New England currency (the Yankee dollar?). Arguably the boom of the 1980s might have been reined in by monetary policy, with an appreciation of the currency rather than the soaring real estate prices and labor costs that happened in practice, and the overbuilding would have been much less. Even if this had not happened, New England would now be able to ameliorate its slump via currency depreciation.

So it is not always easy and pleasant to be a part of a currency union, even one as long-established and credible as the U.S. And it is easy to make the case that the problems of currency union will be larger in Europe, for at least three reasons.

First, some evidence suggests that asymmetric shocks are larger in Europe than in the U.S. This is a disputed point. A broad econometric analysis by Eichengreen and Bayoumi (1992) finds substantially larger asymmetric shocks in Europe, but in some of my own work (Krugman 1991, 1992) I have argued that in principle the greater specialization of U.S. regions exposes them to larger shocks, and some casual empiricism seems to support the case (as in the New England example). At least arguably, however, the greater economic diversity of Europe means that there will be more occasions when European nations would benefit from exchange rate flexibility.

Second, there is no question that interregional labor mobility is now and will for the foreseeable future remain vastly less in Europe than in the U.S. Part of this is the result of language barriers, but for a variety of reasons Europeans seem to be much less mobile even within their countries than are U.S. residents. What this means is that the Mundell criterion for optimal currency areas – that they be characterized by extensive labor mobility – is much less well satisfied by Europe than by the U.S. We may note that very recent work on U.S. regional employment behavior by Blanchard and Katz (1992) suggests that U.S. regions adjust to adverse shocks primarily through out-migration rather than wage adjustment. Thus the absence of a comparable mechanism in Europe represents a serious liability.

Finally, Europe is trying to move to currency union without full political union. This has serious fiscal consequences. In the U.S., massive fiscal federalism provides a cushion against adverse regional shocks: The federal funding of most social insurance, defense, and a variety of aid programs, financed by proportional or progressive taxation, means that a distressed region automatically receives a large increase in net transfers from luckier regions. In Europe the Community budget is too small to provide such automatic stabilization. While the EC has been, by American standards, relatively generous about making explicit resource transfers to poorer regions, such long-term development aid does not fulfill the stabilizing role that would make it an aid to Europe as a currency area. (New England is a relatively rich region; it is the distress relative to its own norm, not relative to the national average, that the federal budget helps relieve.)

A comparison of Europe and the U.S., then, does not suggest that Europe is especially well fitted to be a currency union.

The microeconomics of money

In the classic analysis of optimal currency areas, the microeconomics of money plays a key role. Floating or adjustable exchange rates always make macroeconomic policy easier (except for issues of credibility, discussed below). The reason for forsaking this advantage has traditionally been assumed to lie in a compensating microeconomic advantage.

The arguments are familiar. A flexible exchange rate creates uncertainty and may raise transaction costs, inhibiting economic integration. A fixed exchange rate, by contrast, facilitates trade and capital flows. A common currency, by eliminating foreign-exchange transactions altogether, yields even more transaction cost gains.

The microeconomic argument for fixed rates/common currencies is often argued to include some more diffuse gains than those associated with measurable transaction costs. There are, it is alleged, subtle costs of information and decision making associated with multiple currencies and unpredictable future exchange rates. Unfortunately, these alleged costs are pretty much unmeasurable given any known methods.

What seems clear is that the microeconomic gains from fixed exchange rates and common currencies depend in large part on the extent of trade and investment relations between the relevant countries. A country with a very large share of trade in national income, like the Netherlands, will have more to gain from common currencies than one with a smaller share, like the U.S.

It may also be worth noting that to the extent an independent exchange rate imposes transaction costs on trade, the incentive to join a currency area will be greater the more of one's trading partners are already part of the area. On one side, pegging to, say, the Deutsche mark will have a greater effect in reducing uncertainty if other major trading partners are also pegged to the mark; and of course a common currency is more attractive, the wider the area over which it serves as medium of exchange. On the other side, the decision by trading partners to form a currency area, like formation of a customs union, tends to encourage trade among the members of the union at the expense of external trade, and can therefore impose a terms of trade loss on nations that do not join.

Traditionally, however, economists have assumed that for large countries these microeconomic advantages of abandoning currency flexibility are fairly small. Have we learned anything in the last decade to suggest that they are larger than we used to think? It is hard to make the case that we have. Estimates of the direct transaction cost savings that would be achieved by full currency union are on the order of 3% of trade value – not a trivial sum, but not enough to make joining a currency union (and still less a simple currency area) crucial even if other countries do become members. A strong case for fixed exchange rates/common currencies must rest either on more diffuse and debatable gains from enhancing the unit of account function of money or from alleged gains in monetary discipline and credibility.

We might even make the argument that the microeconomic advantages of a common currency have fallen rather than risen in the last decade or two. Suppose that we accept that the key issue is not the role of money as a medium of exchange but that of money as a unit of account. This role is essentially one that makes it easier for firms and individuals to process information: It provides a common ruler for measuring seemingly disparate quantities. But if there is one thing that has become radically cheaper in recent years, it is information processing.

Consider the following Kindleberger-like analogy. There was a time when there was strong agitation in the U.S. for adoption of the metric system. Metric measures have two advantages: They are easy to compute and compare with each other, and the rest of the world uses them, so using them would make it easier for us to do international business. As the years go by, however, metric conversion has been losing its point. Computers (which themselves operate in base 2 rather than base 10) can more or less effortlessly handle both the idiosyncracies of English measurement and conversions between English and metric measures. So why not stick with our quirky system and avoid the costs of changing over?

Similarly, it could be argued that it has never been easier to do business in a world of multiple currencies. I can cheerfully use my Visa card to pay my Japanese hotel bill, knowing that the Citibank computer will calculate the appropriate exchange rate. There is less need either to carry around a variety of cash or indeed even to calculate equivalences in my head than ever before.

I have already argued that there is no good reason to suppose that the macroeconomic costs of EMU will be low. I have now argued that there is no good reason to suppose that the microeconomic benefits will be high.

The success of the EMS and the credibility issue

It is clear that the current enthusiasm for EMU has a great deal to do with the unexpected durability of the European Monetary System (or, to be more precise, with the Exchange Rate Mechanism of that system). The success of the EMS shows that Europe can manage to live with nearly fixed rates for extended periods. It has also allowed economists to turn their attention away from deep, intractable issues like the microeconomics of money to seemingly easier, and certainly trendier, issues like time consistency and credibility.

The success of EMS had a great deal to do with fears of inflation. These fears led to widespread acceptance both by theorists and practitioners of a new argument for fixed exchange rates – as a way of establishing a monetary anchor in inflation-prone nations.

The monetary anchor argument for fixed rates can usefully be thought of as involving three main, somewhat distinct parts. A currency peg is argued (1) to provide monetary *discipline*; this discipline in turn gains the country valuable *credibility* with both (2) financial markets and (3) wage and price setters. Discipline and credibility are not the same thing; while one cannot achieve credibility without discipline, one might achieve discipline without any valuable gain in credibility.

The discipline argument is essentially political. It is argued that an announcement by a country that it is pegging its currency to that of a larger country with a reputation for low inflation (such as Germany) is a more binding promise than a less transparent monetary target. A devaluation represents an unambiguous abandonment of previous policies in a way that, say, exceeding an M3 target does not; so the temptation to engage in inflationary monetary policies may be reduced by exchange rate pegging.

To the extent that a fixed rate is perceived to create monetary discipline, it also gains the government credibility with financial markets. This may be useful to break what could otherwise be a vicious circle in which financial markets, expecting inflationary policies, set nominal interest rates high. Given these high interest rates, the central bank is then under pressure to ratify inflationary expectations lest debtors, perhaps including the government itself, find themselves in financial distress.

More controversially, a fixed rate may also help prevent a self-fulfilling inflationary process in the goods and labor markets. If wage and price setters expect that the central bank will be willing to accept some inflation in order to limit unemployment, they will raise prices and wages in anticipation. The central bank then finds that it must fulfill expectations by inflating or face a recession. The argument is that by committing itself to a fixed rate, a central bank can avoid this inflationary trap.

It should be noted that the credibility argument for fixed exchange rates, although very influential, does not have strong evidence in its support. Exchange rate policy does have a strong influence on interest rates, but only governments that have large amounts of outstanding short-term debt denominated in domestic currency are likely to find this a crucial policy issue. The effects of exchange rate policy on wage and price behavior, by contrast, is of vital concern; but there is at best modest evidence that such moves as joining the EMS actually improve the output-inflation tradeoff (see, for example, Giavazzi and Giovannini 1989).

Let us, however, put these doubts on one side and accept as a working hypothesis that the EMS has played a crucial role in getting European inflation rates down. Does this success for fixed rates then constitute a persuasive additional argument for EMU?

It is not obvious that it does. The success of the EMS rested on a very special set of circumstances. First, it depended on a policy context in which controlling inflation was seen as the first priority, and in which the credibility argument was itself seen as highly credible. Second, it depended on the lucky coincidence that Europe's largest economy also contained its most determinedly anti-inflationary central bank. Third, the EMS has depended on a nice distinction between manifest and latent function: formal symmetry with a *de facto* monetary hegemon.

EMU will have none of these characteristics. Although controlling inflation will always be an issue, it is unlikely to dominate the monetary policy agenda in the future the way it did in the 1980s (indeed, in the U.S. it has evidently receded substantially already). And EMU will end the sleight of hand that allows non-Germans to place their monetary policy under German control without any formal oath of fealty. In EMU, Italy and the U.K. will have votes in determining monetary policy – whether they like it or not.

My own view is that credibility for EMS was always overstated. But that is a moot point when it comes to EMU, which will reflect, not the monetary preferences of the most disinflationary, but some kind of collective average. There is no obvious reason to suppose that this collective will be more credible or less inflationary than the average of its parts.

Concluding thoughts

This section has not argued that EMU is necessarily a bad idea. What it does argue is that there has been no accumulation of new evidence over the past decade that makes it look like a better idea than it did in the past.

A few years back, discussing the inflationary problems of the U.K. before it entered the exchange rate mechanism of the EMS, *The Economist* opined that "if Britain had joined the ERM, it would not have its current problems. It would have different problems." Precisely. EMU will solve some problems and create others; we have basically no idea whether the problems it creates will be better or worse than the ones it solves. In fact, even in hindsight we may never know whether it was actually a good idea.

The enthusiasm for EMU, then, cannot be justified on economic grounds. It can perhaps be best justified as a political gesture. After all, the reason that multiple currencies within the U.S. are basically unthinkable has little to do with economic logic; it is more a matter of the political symbolism that links a unified currency with a unified polity.

Suppose, then, we accept that EMU is either a good thing or at any rate something that is going to happen. The next question is how to get there from here.

The transition to EMU

How should a group of economies with separate currencies go about moving to a single currency? One answer is that of a popular commercial for athletic shoes: just do it. Exchange all your currencies for some common unit at some parity as soon as it is technically feasible, and you have a monetary union. This is what Germany did with its newly acquired East. The only degree of freedom in this Big Bang strategy is the choice of merge parity. Arguably the Germans got this wrong, although the surge in East German wages after reunification suggests that it would not have made much difference if Ostmarks had been abolished at a lower parity.

The architects of EMU have, however, been unwilling to jump in all at once. Instead they have sought a transition period, stage 2, that is intended to establish the preconditions for a more successful monetary union.

As the Eurocrats themselves freely admit, it has been hard to establish principles for stage 2. Indeed, some of them admit, not too privately, that they are not sure what purpose stage 2 serves. But whatever the doubts in theory, the EMS has now gotten together in Maastricht and established a set of criteria. Let us review Maastricht and consider its logic.

Maastricht

I will not go into numerical detail here but instead summarize the qualitative features. Maastricht sets five criteria that must be passed by a country if it is to enter EMU (together with ways to waive the rules; but let's focus on the rules themselves). They are the following:

Exchange rates: A country must keep its EMS exchange rate within a narrow band for an extended period.

Interest rates: Long-term interest rates in the country must be close to those with the lowest rates.

Inflation: Inflation must not be much higher than that in the lowest inflation nations.

Budget deficit: The budget deficit must be low, measured as a share of GDP.

Debt: The debt of the central government must be an acceptable ratio to GDP.

The official view is that a country must satisfy these criteria in order to be economically ready for EMU. But do the criteria actually make sense?

Thinking about Maastricht

Let us consider each of the criteria in turn. First, adherence to a narrow exchange rate band essentially tests the discipline and effectiveness of each country's central bank. This is fine, but it seems somewhat peculiar as a criterion for entry into EMU, since it tests the ability of governments to do precisely the one thing that they will never need to do again.

The criterion on long-term interest rates is really not a direct test of government policy, but instead one of market expectations. After all, if a country were viewed as certain to join EMU, its long-term bonds should command the same interest rate as those of other nations that are also expected to join. (There is a small qualification: If a country is expected to make one last realignment before entry, this might be reflected in an interest differential, but the basic point stands.) So in essence a country will pass this test, and be allowed to join EMU, if the market expects it to join.

This looks more than a little circular. It is reminiscent of some of the proposals circulated a few years ago about returning the U.S. to the gold standard, which were of the form "Announce that 2 years from now we will peg the dollar to gold at the then-prevailing market price" – proposals that provided a nice classroom exercise in the issue of multiple equilibria.

The criterion on inflation is also somewhat dubious. Under stage 2 countries will in effect have no independent monetary policies, so their inflation rates will have nothing to do with monetary policy. What is then being tested? The obvious concern is that countries will be penalized for success: Take the not-at-all abstract example of a country whose booming economy attracts large voluntary capital inflows, leading to a real appreciation that under fixed exchange rates is manifested as higher inflation. Should this be regarded as punishable behavior?

Indeed, such concerns are already leading to some strange policies. For example, Portugal is currently viewed as a very attractive place to invest. It is also maintaining an approximately fixed rate against the ecu. This means that there are inflationary pressures on the Portuguese economy, inflationary pressures that are exactly the same as those that might occur in any region under EMU. Yet in an effort to preserve their inflation record, the Portuguese are imposing controls on capital inflows, in effect distorting microeconomic forces in pursuit of a dubious macroeconomic goal.

Finally, the last two criteria, both of which relate to fiscal policy, make somewhat more sense. But it remains obscure why fiscal probity is a key issue for monetary union. Some people have pointed to the adverse effects of Germany's reunification deficit as a demonstration that fiscal policy carries strong externalities. But the German case is a very special one, because the Bundesbank is in the peculiar position of making European monetary policy while serving only German interests. Under EMU nobody will be in that position, so the case for collectively policed fiscal policy will be much weaker.

The question is, will a country be better prepared for EMU after several years of adherence to the Maastricht criteria? It is hard to see why. One might offer other convergence criteria, relating to such nonmonetary issues as structural flexibility and labor mobility, issues that relate ultimately to the optimal currency area argument. But making any significant progress on these issues will take a great deal of time, putting them essentially beyond the event horizon of current negotiations.

Making sense of Stage 2

I have argued that the criteria established at Maastricht do not seem to make a lot of economic sense. But then what is Maastricht – an agreement concluded by very intelligent men – about?

One uncharitable interpretation is that it represents stalling for time.

European nations are not actually sure that they want EMU, which is reasonable, since it is unclear whether it is really a good idea. But they don't want to make the decision yet. So Stage 2 gives a chance to delay matters, under the guise of achieving convergence.

A slightly more charitable interpretation would see Stage 2 as not so much a preparation as an extended test. I would like to suggest an analogy. In U.S. colleges, in order to join a select fraternity one must submit to a process known as "hazing." This involves performing a number of moderately unpleasant and humiliating acts as a condition for entry. The acts do not, by themselves, make you a better member of the fraternity, but they force you to prove both that you really want to join and that you are the fraternity's kind of guy. In effect, the Maastricht criteria should be seen more as a hazing than as an economically relevant transition path. They test the determination and character of nations that want to join, rather than their actual readiness in economic terms.

Is there anything wrong with this male-bonding exercise? I think there is, because it takes time, and delaying the move to full EMU looks to me like tempting fate.

The fragility of the EMS

The reason for concern about a protracted Stage 2 is that the continuing success of the EMS is not guaranteed. The EMS as now constituted is a kind of lucky accident. Originally designed as a system with few teeth, it has fortuitously evolved into an effective device for monetary coordination. Originally a system without a clear mechanism for decision making, it has evolved into a *de facto* Deutsche mark area in which a stern-willed Bundesbank exerts control. But this success and effectiveness do not rest on firm foundations.

As everyone now concedes, the symmetry of the EMS in principle has given way to German monetary hegemony in practice. But German monetary leadership in Europe is not a natural consequence of German size. True, Germany is the largest economy, by a margin that will have been slightly increased once the East has been absorbed. But its size advantage is not huge. It is worth remembering that even at the end of the Bretton Woods system, U.S. gross national product was larger than the combined GNPs of the rest of the G5 combined – and yet these nations did not feel that pegging their currencies to the dollar was a necessary policy. By contrast, Germany has a GNP that is only about 25% larger than that of France, only about 30% of the total for the EC. German dominance of European monetary policy is by no means preordained by sheer economic weight.

Why, then, has Europe become a mark area? Because of a triple coincidence of factors: At a time when Europe has been preoccupied with inflation, with issues of discipline and credibility, the largest economy has also had the most hard-money central bank. This made ceding monetary policy to Germany seem natural.

But this is not a durable basis for running Europe's money. Only in an environment in which all nations are essentially preoccupied with the common problem of inflation is it true that what is good for Germany is good for Europe. In a lower-inflation environment, subject to other shocks, conflicts of interest can and do arise. The consequences of German unification are the most immediate and obvious. From Germany's point of view, a high-interest-rate policy to offset the expansionary impact of huge reconstruction costs seems natural. For the rest of Europe, compelled to share that policy, the result is a pointless recession at a time when inflation in some of the countries is already quite low.

The EMS may or may not make it through this shock without a major realignment. But there will be other shocks: perhaps an Italian budget crisis, an investor loss of confidence in Britain or Spain, even an inflationary surge in German wages. The golden age of the EMS, in which the common concern over inflation and the iron virtue of the Bundesbank made the political equation easy to solve, is now behind us.

What this means is that an extended Stage 2 is simply giving bad things a chance to occur. As the bumper stickers don't quite say, "Stuff happens." After 5 or 10 years of Stage 2, countries will be no more ready economically for EMU than they are now, but the EMS may have cracked apart in the meantime.

Given the discussion in the first half of this paper, this would not be an economic tragedy: The benefits of EMS would be lost, but so would its costs. But the *political* blow to the idea of Europe would be terrible. Even though it is not clear whether EMU is really a great idea, it is too late to stop now without severe damage.

Conclusions

This paper has offered two arguments challenging the conventional wisdom about EMU. The conventional wisdom holds that a monetary union in Europe is a wonderful idea but that it must be achieved via a gradual transition. I argue that it is not clear whether EMU is actually such a great idea, at least from an economic point of view – but that if it will be done, it should be done quickly.

The economics of EMU are straightforward in principle: They involve a tradeoff of macroeconomic flexibility for microeconomic efficiency. The problem is that the macroeconomic costs of EMU are hard to quantify, and the microeconomic benefits impossible to quantify. Is EMU a good idea? We don't know, and we may never know.

But whether or not EMU is a good idea, 5 or more years of transition will not improve the tradeoff. All that they will do is allow the weaknesses of the current system chances to display themselves. Europe has fortuitously stumbled into a system of voluntary acceptance of German monetary leadership, which has made the EMS a surprise success. But Germany is neither large enough nor representative enough to play that role indefinitely. As time goes by, the chance of a breakdown of the EMS grows (more or less literally, if bad news is Poisson!) exponentially.

So this paper offers two second thoughts on EMU. Is it a good idea? Maybe not. If EMU is coming, how fast should it be done? Immediately.

References

Blanchard, O., and L. Katz (1992), "Regional Evolutions," *Brookings Papers on Economic Activity* 1.

Eichengreen, B., and T. Bayoumi (1992), "Shocking Aspects of European Monetary Integration," NBER Working Paper # 3949.

Giavazzi, F., and A. Giovannini (1989), *Limiting Exchange Rate Flexibility*, Cambridge: MIT Press.

Kenen, P. (1992), *EMU after Maastricht*, Washington: Group of Thirty.

Krugman, P. (1991), *Geography and Trade*, Cambridge: MIT Press.

Krugman, P. (1992), "Lessons of Massachusetts for EMU," mimeo.

McKinnon, R. (1963), "Optimum Currency Areas," *American Economic Review* 53, 717–24.

Mundell, R. (1961), "A Theory of Optimum Currency Areas," *American Economic Review* 51, 657–64.

PART II

Capital flows and exchange rates in the open economy

Investment flows and performance: evidence from mutual funds, cross-border investments, and new issues

JAYENDU PATEL

RICHARD J. ZECKHAUSER

DARRYLL HENDRICKS

Introduction

What determines the magnitude of investment flows to and from securities? To specific mutual funds? To new issues of bonds and stocks? From one nation to another? Unfortunately, modern financial theory provides little guidance in answering such questions. For instance, the Capital Asset Pricing Model (CAPM) implies that an efficient individual's mix of holdings should be in the same proportions, namely, proportional to the total market values of the securities.[1] When combined with the efficient markets hypothesis (EMH), this view leads to a passive, that is, nontrading, portfolio strategy. Yet in practice we observe active trading by investors, frequently driven by recent relative performance, both at the microlevel and at the level of international security flows. Equally perplexing from the standpoint of theory is the willingness of investors to pay for active portfolio management and advice, or for security issuers' to alter the timing of their trips to the capital market to take advantage of market conditions believed to be favorable. Finally, few individuals hold a well-diversified portfolio; most have invested far too little in foreign securities.

Since theory provides little direction – although it predicts much lower levels of trading than we observe – it is perhaps not surprising that there has been relatively little empirical documentation and analysis of investment flows and the phenomena that correlate with them. Our purpose in this chapter is to sketch some hypotheses that could explain investment flows and then take some preliminary empirical steps to assess them using price and volume data from financial markets.

---

[1] The recently introduced multifactor Arbitrage Pricing Theory (APT) is no better than the CAPM in explaining investor flows. Moreover, the factors that APT posits to underlie security pricing remain to be identified, though Chen, Roll, and Ross (1986) have made a first cut at this important task.

Financial markets are an especially interesting arena in which to investigate nonrational behavior, for at least four reasons:

1. The efficient markets hypothesis, which has proved an effective paradigm, provides a natural benchmark of investor rationality.
2. There is poaching potential in many financial markets; that is, players can take advantage of poor decisions made by others. Even if a substantial number of participants are not rational, sophisticated arbitrageurs can bring the market outcomes into conformance with finance theory.
3. Financial markets are liquid and individual motivations are relatively straightforward, in accord with wealth-maximizing hypotheses (possibly modified by risk aversion).
4. The operation of these markets is well documented; rich price and volume data are readily available.

Beyond these scientific advantages, the performance of financial markets is of interest in its own right since its outcomes profoundly influence the operation of economies and the welfare of participants and nonparticipants alike.

Street wisdom posits a significant relationship between the recent performance of specific instruments and investment flows to those instruments. We explore such a relation with empirical evidence at three levels. At the microlevel, we study flows to open-end mutual funds, which are demand determined (since funds expand and contract to accommodate investor preferences); the interpretation of results is relatively clear. We identify a significant relation between annual flows to specific no-load equity funds and past performance, fund size, and past flows. Related work provides some justification for such behavior.[2]

On a more macrolevel, we examine net flows to U.S. securities (equities and corporate/Treasury bonds) from Japan, the United Kingdom, Canada, and West Germany. Investment flows to the United States have increased dramatically since 1984, when the U.S. trade deficit first became large and persistent.[3] These flows have significant policy consequence, affecting macroeconomic planning, international competitiveness, and international diversification of risk (and, consequently, the interdependence of nations).

---

[2] The cross-sectional flow correlation with past performance, at first blush, may appear inappropriate or at best an inconsequential quirk. However, it is consistent with rationality, for we have separately shown [Hendricks, Patel, and Zeckhauser (1991)] that *ex ante* gains can be realized by selecting top-performing mutual funds. Maybe street smarts appropriately refuse to be swayed by a possibly incorrect academic consensus!

[3] Of course, the offsetting reaction between capital flows and balance of trade is a near identity.

Observers have viewed these foreign flows with mixed emotions: Though they symbolize foreign influence on the U.S. economy, their termination could require wrenching adjustments in the dollar-exchange rates, international trade, and world growth.[4]

International flows, of course, may be influenced by goals beyond mere maximization of risk-adjusted return. Purchases of international securities may be a prelude to takeovers, friendly position taking, accessing technology, and so on. And the equilibrating processes are not instantaneous. There may well be a shallow learning curve in international investments.[5]

We consider the relative strengths of conventional variables (such as trade deficits, bilateral exchange rates, relative stock market performance, interest rate differentials) in explaining the behavior of foreign flows into the United States. For the post-1984 period, we find that the most significant variables explaining foreign flows are measures of security performance. Other variables add little: Measures of exchange rate risk, relative interest rates, and trade deficits have insignificant marginal correlations.

Finally, we examine the quarterly series on net U.S. issues of stocks and bonds during the period 1952–88. We focus on short-run fluctuations in net issues and relate them to stock- and bond-market conditions. Here interpretation and results are cloudy. Clearly, supply as well as demand considerations are likely to be important; also, substantial institutional shifts have occurred during the four-decade period.

The next section outlines some behavioral hypotheses that motivate our examination of flows and performance. The following sections report on investment flows to mutual funds, examine foreign purchases of United States securities, and report on net U.S. issues of stocks and bonds.

---

[4] Since this paper was presented in spring 1990, the Japanese stock market has experienced a sustained decline. In 1989, Japanese investors had purchased U.S. equity worth $3.33 billion, U.S. corporate bonds worth $6.29 billion, and U.S. treasury bonds and notes worth $1.68 billion. In 1990, the flows changed: Japanese investors were net sellers to the tune of $2.89 billion in U.S. equity and of $14.78 billion in U.S. government bonds and notes. In U.S. bonds though, they continued purchases but only of $0.73 billion. In 1991, there was a pickup in the acquisition of U.S. securities by Japanese investors, though well below 1989 levels: Net purchases of U.S. equities were $1.18 billion and of U.S. corporate bonds, $5.73 billion; the sell-off in U.S. government bonds and notes continued, with net sales of $4.05 billion.

[5] Consider the rational foreign investor's need to account for xenophobic policy reactions, strategic macroeconomic behavior, and so on. Such features are likely to be important since otherwise it is hard to explain why, contrary to considerations of efficient diversification, portfolios of most Americans include a minuscule position in Japanese assets and vice-versa. This puzzle is especially relevant since the market value of Japanese equities is now roughly comparable to that for U.S. equities.

Behavioral hypotheses

As is conventional, we posit a null hypothesis of rational behavior. Our alternative hypothesis is that investors fall prey to a variety of behavioral anomalies. That is, they fail to make optimal portfolio choices, systematically selecting alternative actions that would be expected *ex ante* to reduce their own welfare.[6] We break down our behavioral alternatives into several categories.

Null hypothesis of efficient markets and efficient diversification

Our benchmark is the efficient markets hypothesis, which implies that investors cannot find opportunities to secure above-market returns (except through access to nonpublic information). Of course, we may observe persistent suboptimal decisions and outcomes if some financial anomalies arise that are not poachable. For example, if investors from certain countries diversify insufficiently, or individuals purchase inferior open-end mutual funds, there is no way for more knowledgeable players to capitalize on this nonrational behavior. Our null hypothesis also posits that investors diversify appropriately. This implies, for example, that all investors would generally hold shares roughly in proportion with the portfolio of securities available in the world.

Alternative behavioral hypothesis

For a variety of reasons, the null hypothesis of rational behavior in efficient markets may need to be modified.[7] We outline five alternate hypotheses:

Impediments to investment: Some assets cannot be arbitraged. For example, if institutions are prohibited from trading or offering securities overseas, then cross-border assets may not be tightly related to each other [see Gultekin et al. (1989) and references therein. Observers have suggested that the recent rash of financial innovations has been brought about by (1) government responses to pressures to open up markets and (2) lower costs to exploit arbitrage opportunities among different assets.[8] However, there may still be impediments to investment. This would be the case, for

---

[6] An alternative interpretation of such anomalous behavior is that individuals seek to maximize the quality of the experience associated with their choices. See Kahneman and Snell (1990).

[7] See Zeckhauser, Patel, and Hendricks (1992) for a more extensive discussion on the value for nonrational considerations in finance.

[8] See Miller (1986) for a provocative argument along these lines.

example, if differences in interest rates for mortgages across nations were not fully compensated for by expected currency value movements as indicated by forward exchange rates. The existence of impediments need not indicate any behavioral anomalies, though it would imply that markets are not efficient.

Propensity to ride the winners: Investors seek to reproduce past investment successes by continuing to invest in the same way; that is, they believe that the future is bright for investments that have done well in the past. (In efficient markets, by contrast, prevailing asset prices capture all rational expectations about future prospects.) If this behavioral trait is significant, investors might be slow to reenter the stock market after a plunge (e.g., the 1987 crash) and foreign investors might withhold investment flows to the U.S. after periods in which the dollar depreciated rapidly.

Status quo bias: Investors tend to stick with strategies because of a fondness for the *status quo*, a widely observed human tendency [Samuelson and Zeckhauser (1988)]. *Status quo* bias would be reinforced by transactions costs incurred in getting out of a position (brokerage fees, exit charges, and taxes). *Status quo* bias may be promoted by reliance on rules of thumb, which is an outgrowth of bounded rationality. It is also stimulated by concerns about regret, which tend to make errors of omission (failing to sell a stock that goes down) much less serious than errors of commission (switching stocks only to see the recently divested security perform spectacularly). A period of learning how to function in changing financial markets – a phenomenon not acknowledged in conventional finance theory – could also explain *status quo* bias. Most United States investors, for example, may not know how to go about investing in Japan.[9]

Window dressing: Professional market participants often engage in behavior that amounts to window dressing. For example, managers of mutual funds may sell stocks in which they have losses, or that have recently lost value, just before the holdings of the portfolio are publicly reported. Here as elsewhere, asymmetric information is a key feature of the agency problem. Because principals cannot readily review, access, or understand the whole record, they will judge the manager-agent on the basis of the identified portfolio.

---

[9] If the Japanese stocks that issue ADRs in the United States, or the U.S. stocks that are traded on the Tokyo Exchange, turn out to have much higher levels of cross ownership, that might be considered evidence for a learning factor contributing to *status quo* bias. Causality could flow in the opposite direction, if stocks desired by foreign investors are made available through ADRs.

Exchange rate illusion and framing: Investors ignore some of the implications of changes in the exchange rate. For example, if they are well diversified and the pound doubles against the dollar, this change should double the amount of incremental dollar-flows put into sterling-denominated assets. However, since U.S. investors deal mainly in dollar transactions, they pay insufficient attention to exchange rate fluctuations and their implied consequence; this is a framing error.[10] Exchange rate illusion arises in another form when investors conclude that certain currencies are weak or strong and that fundamental forces will move them more than is implied by prices in futures markets.

Net investments in mutual funds

We begin by examining investment flows into U.S. no-load open-end mutual funds that invest primarily in U.S. equities and that announce their goal as capital growth. By selecting a narrowly specified class for our analysis of net investment flows, we avoid confounding variables (such as changing investor preferences for safety and cash flows). Also, we steer clear of supply-demand interactions (and the econometric perils they entail), since open-end funds have no intrinsic supply-size constraints: Each mutual fund's growth is demand driven.

Our explanation of mutual fund flows will relate to the alternate behavioral hypotheses set forth in the previous section.

Description of data

The data on individual mutual funds for 1975 to 1987 are compiled from three sources. For 1975 to 1982, annual figures for per-share values and fund size are taken from the Weisenberger Investment Survey.[11] Net fund returns for this perod were provided by CDA Investment Technologies. Data on all variables for the 1982–87 period are from Barron's quarterly publications of data collected by Lipper Analytical Services. The overlap in our sources enabled us to cross-check the data satisfactorily. We collected data for a total of 96 no-load mutual funds. No-load funds were selected to minimize the influence of both initial purchase (or exit) fees and securities brokers. Since the funds in our sample are growth oriented,

---

[10] See Kahneman and Tversky (1984).
[11] While relevant data are available quarterly, we use annual data for convenience. This procedure bypasses any problems of seasonal flows; for many investors, moreover, a less-than-annual horizon for mutual fund selection appears unlikely.

they will not attract investors who desire significant cash dividends, and so cash payout policies are unlikely to be important. (Income-oriented funds also invest in a different class of assets from growth-oriented funds.)

For each fund in the sample, three variables were collected: share price (P), fund size (S), and net returns (R). For open-end funds, P is the per-share market value of the underlying assets held by the mutual fund. Fund size, S, is simply the per-share net asset value multiplied by the number of shares outstanding. Net returns, R, are calculated as the total pretax percentage gain that would accrue to an investor in the mutual fund during the year. R includes consideration of dividends and is net of all management fees and costs; intrayear dividends are assumed to be immediately and fully reinvested in the fund.[12]

Construction of investment flow measures

Changes in the size of a mutual fund arise from three sources:

Unrealized capital gains of assets of shareholders who remain with the fund,

Realized capital gains (i.e., dividends distributed to mutual fund shareholders) that are reinvested (either by automatic reinvestment or explicit choice),

Net new share purchases.

We focus on the second and third sources. We construct two measures of investment flows:

1. The first hypothesis is that investors' basic strategy is to buy and maintain. In this case, the existing shareholders reinvest all distributions in the fund. For fund i during period t, the size fluctuations identifiable as net new fund flows would be

$$I_{it} = S_{i,t+1} - S_{it}(1 + R_{it}) \tag{4.1}$$

2. The second hypothesis is that any strategy changes on the part of investors apply to all incremental investments, including dividends received from existing investments. In this case, an appropriate flow measure is

$$J_{it} = S_{i,t+1} - S_{it} \frac{NAV_{i,t+1}}{NAV_{it}} \tag{4.2}$$

Note that J_{it} is greater than I_{it} by the amount of dividends declared by

---

[12] All mutual funds in our sample allow investors to do so automatically.

Table. 4.1. *Summary statistics on variables relevant to mutual fund flows, 1975–87 ($ millions)*

Panel A: *Statistics from annual cross sections*

Variable	Average over cross sections Mean	Std. deviation	First–order autocorrelation in means
Flow 1 (I_{it})	$17.57	$60.04	0.82
Flow 2 (J_{it})	$-0.92	$47.96	0.48
Returns (R_{it})	17.37%	12.24%	-0.12
Size (S_{it})	$152.39	$247.17	0.68
Alpha (A_{it})	-0.08	2.80	0.37
Sharpe's Measure (SM_{it})	0.26	0.37	-0.11

Panel B: *Distribution of mean values across funds*

Variable	25th percentile fund	Median fund	75th percentile fund
Flow 1 (I_{it})	$5.60	$20.59	$43.27
Flow 2 (J_{it})	$-7.12	$-1.16	$2.73
Returns (R_{it})	14.41%	16.66%	20.32%
Size (S_{it})	$30.30	$80.64	$176.84
Alpha (A_{it})	-0.70	0.00	0.59
Sharpe's measure (SM_{it})	0.18	0.24	0.34

Notes: Panel A reports summary statistics based on 13 sets of cross-sectional means, one set per year. Panel B shows selected percentiles of the distribution of the time-series means of the 96 mutual funds. As discussed in the section on investment flow measure, flow 1 (I_{it}) measures reinvested dividends as positive flows, and flow 2 (J_{it}) measures nonreinvested dividends as negative flows.

the mutual fund.[13] In the interest of brevity, we report below regression results only for the second measure of net investment flows, J_{it}. In all cases, the unreported results with the first measure are similar. Table 4.1 provides summary statistics for both investment flow measures, as well as for performance measures.

[13] We also hope to investigate the effect of dividends on flows. A buy-and-maintain strategy suggests that its coefficient should be 1.0 [see discussion surrounding Eq. (4.1)]. A belief that "dividends don't matter" suggests a coefficient of 0.0 or more generally a diffuse prior over all possible values.

Since mutual-fund dividends are unlikely to be positive signals (though capital gains dividends may indicate churning, a negative signal) and since dividends entail tax liabilities (assuming, reasonably, that investors in a mutual fund are not all in the same tax status), theory predicts that the coefficient, if nonzero, should be negative. Though we do not have the data to construct it, a third, interesting measure of investment flow would account for the fraction of investors in a fund who have selected automatic dividend reinvestment.

Hypotheses explaining flows to mutual funds

The mutual funds in our sample are sufficiently similar that the efficient markets hypothesis provides little theoretical basis to explain cross-sectional differences in flows to funds. In Hendricks, Patel, and Zeckhauser (1991), the beta measures (relevant under the capital asset pricing model) of the 96 funds are found to be scattered closely about unity. Further, the funds are not consistently mispriced relative to multifactor benchmarks (which account for multiple factors of the APT and anomalies like the small-firm effect). However, a casual examination of investor behavior – as reported in the press and as reflected in mutual fund practice – and advertising suggests that past performance is likely to be an important influence on flows. For instance, *Consumer Guide* (1988) reports, "Loads, fees, and expenses can be considerable, but most financial professionals suggest that the performance of the fund, not the costs, should be the primary consideration when choosing a fund."[14] Mutual fund performance rankings are compiled on a regular and timely basis and are widely followed.

Mutual funds that do relatively well tout their performance prominently in their advertising. Those that lag behind search for the measure that puts them in the best possible light. Directly or indirectly, investors are willing to act on such relative performance information. Hendricks, Patel, and Zeckhauser (1991) show that a superior-performance *ex ante* strategy can be based on recent (last year's) performance. Investor reliance on past performance may thus represent rational behavior that has flourished in spite of academic consensus to the contrary – a form of super-rationality?

We conjecture that investors' consideration of past performance is likely to focus on widely reported ranks rather than on cardinal measures indicating absolute or risk-adjusted performance, which are not so easily interpreted. Such behavior is consistent with psychological evidence that people follow simple rules. Samuelson and Zeckhauser (1988) have documented substantial *status quo* bias in individual behavior, in investment situations among others. For no-load funds in which switching incurs no transactions costs (we ignore taxes), this behavior can be explained as a reflection of learning costs. Alternatively, it may simply be a psychological propensity that does not fit into the rational model of *homo economicus*, arising, for example, from severe regret avoidance, which is an attempt to avoid a mistaken act of commission. *Status quo* bias suggests

---

[14] In contrast, academics, as in Brealey's (1983) chapter on "Can Professional Investors Beat the Market?", advise that most of the differences between *ex post* performances of individual funds are due to chance.

that the previous level of flows will be of substantial relevance in explaining current flows.

We also expect the size of the fund to be an important variable. Factors that influence investors, such as advertising levels, are positively associated with fund size. Investors may also perceive a signal of reliability in fund size.

In sum, we posit three variables to explain cross-sectional variation in flows to mutual funds: past performance, size, and past flows. The empirical analysis will support a behavioral approach if the coefficients are not merely statistically significant but economically significant. Besides performance measured by net returns, we also consider risk-corrected measures such as Jensen's alpha[15] and Sharpe's measure,[16] which are both grounded in financial theory [for instance, see Brealey and Myers (1988, pp. 868–71)].

Empirical results

The linear model[17] that we use to explain cross-sectional flows to mutual funds is

$$J_{it} = \beta_{0t} + \beta_1 J_{i,t-1} + \beta_2 R_{i,t-1} + \beta_3 S_{it} + e_{it};$$

$$i = 1,\ldots,96;\ t = 76,\ldots,87 \quad (4.3)$$

Here e_{it}, the error, is likely to be heteroscedastic across funds, and thus ordinary least squares may give incorrect standard errors for the parameter estimates. We estimate Eq. (4.3) by weighted least squares, with the weights based on the variances of the ordinary-least-squares residuals associated with each fund. The results are presented in Table 4.2.[18] The residuals are uncorrelated over time and reasonably homoscedastic, indicating that the

---

[15] We use returns data from previous years to estimate, by ordinary least squares (OLS), the market model:

$$(R_{it} - R_{ft}) = \alpha_i + \beta_i(R_{mt} - R_{ft}) + \varepsilon_{it}$$

Here $R_{it} \equiv$ the return by fund i over quarter t, net of all fees and assuming dividend reinvestment; $R_{ft} \equiv$ the risk-free return over quarter t (which we proxy by the yield on 90-day U.S. Treasury bills); $\alpha_i \equiv$ Jensen's alpha, which measures superiority of fund i in period t; relative to the benchmark portfolio m in a mean-variance framework; $\beta_i \equiv$ "beta" of fund, which measures systematic risk of fund i within the Capital Asset Pricing Model; $R_{mt} \equiv$ the return to the market (benchmark) portfolio over quarter t; and $\varepsilon_{it} \equiv ex\ post$ idiosyncratic component (error) of the return, which would be unpredictable under a joint hypothesis of the CAPM and EMH.

[16] Sharpe's measure is the ratio of the mean to the standard deviation of excess returns.

[17] A log-linear model would be an equally interesting specification. Since residuals diagnostics did not indicate any misspecification, we did not explore this alternative in the regressions that follow.

[18] Separate regressions for each cross section that were estimated by ordinary least squares gave results similar to those reported with the pooled data.

Table 4.2. *Determinants of flows to mutual funds, 1976–87*

Estimates of Eq. (4.3): $J_{it} = \beta_{0t} + \beta_1 J_{i,t-1} + \beta_2 R_{i,t-1} + \beta_3 S_{it} + e_{it}$; $i = 1, \ldots, 96$; $t = 76, \ldots, 87$.

	β_1	β_2	β_3	$\bar{R}^2$	ρ_1
OLS estimates	0.56	0.76	0.07	0.50	-0.05
	(16.91)	(5.76)	(8.25)		
Feasible GLS estimates (allowing for fund-specific heteroscedasticity)	0.75	0.20	0.05	0.76	-0.17
	(27.07)	(5.10)	(11.05)		

Notes: Variables are as defined in Table 4.1; t statistics are shown in parentheses. $\bar{R}^2$ denotes the adjusted R-squared for the regression; ρ_1 denotes the first-order autocorrelation of the residuals.

Table 4.3. *Fund performance and flows to mutual funds (Sample period: 1976–1987)*

A: Ordinal versus cardinal measures of performance

Regression: $J_{it} = \beta_{0t} + \beta_1 J_{i,t-1} + \beta_2 R_{i,t-1} + \beta_3 S_{it} + \beta_4 Rank_{i,t-1} + e_{it}$

where $Rank_{i,t-1} \equiv$ rank of the annual return of mutual fund i in year $t-1$ (96 is best performer and 1 is worst performer).

	β_1	β_2	β_3	β_4	$\bar{R}^2$	ρ_1
GLS estimate	0.70	-0.18	0.05	0.21	0.73	-0.15
	(24.63)	(-2.13)	(10.93)	(5.43)		

B: Risk-adjusted performance

Regression: $J_{it} = \beta_{0t} + \beta_1 J_{i,t-1} + \beta_3 S_{it} + \beta_4 Rank_{i,t-1} + \beta_5 Alpha_{i,t-1} + \beta_6 SM_{i,t-1} + e_{it}$

where *Alpha* (Jensen's alpha) and *SM* (Sharpe's measure) are two common gauges of risk-adjusted performance.

	β_1	β_3	β_4	β_5	β_6	$\bar{R}^2$	ρ_1
GLS estimate	0.71	0.05	0.12	0.13	0.07	0.72	-0.15
	(24.77)	(10.64)	(4.34)	(0.45)	(1.03)		

Notes: See variable definitions in Table 4.1. The t statistics are shown in parentheses. $\bar{R}^2$ denotes the adjusted R-square for the regression; ρ_1 denotes the first-order autocorrelation of the residuals.

regression is well specified and that tests are reliable. Each of the included variables is statistically significant. The regression explains 76% of the cross-sectional time-series variation in flows. We observe remarkable persistence: Other things equal, a \$1 flow in the past year implies a 75-cent flow in this period. Past performance also matters: A return 1% above the cross-sectional mean return in the previous period implies a $200,000 increased flow in this period. Finally, being $1 bigger in size at the beginning of the period induces a 5-cent increased flow.

In Table 4.3, we consider whether alternative measures of past performance do better in explaining flows to mutual funds. Risk-adjusted performance measures offer no additional explanatory power. However, if investors are influenced by data packaging, flows should be better related to performance ranks, which are widely available, than to raw returns. The evidence on the data-packaging effect is somewhat cloudy because, quite naturally, ranks and raw returns have a high correlation of 0.86. Statistically, the inclusion of ranks drives out the statistical significance of other performance measures, though it does not increase the R-squared measure of total explanatory power. In sum, simple behavioral considerations explain a large portion of the variation in flows across mutual funds for the 1975–87 period. We extend these conjectures to explain flows at a more aggregate level in the next sections.

Foreign purchases of U.S. securities

In the latter half of the 1980s, Japanese investment flows to the United States increased dramatically. Several researchers – Kawai and Okumura (1988), Koo (1989), and references therein – have proposed specific bilateral features to explain the flows, such as Japanese financial deregulation, burgeoning bilateral balance-of-trade imbalances, or the U.S./Japanese agreement calling for an expanded international role for Japanese financial institutions. Koo (1989) also argues that the Japanese continue to invest during periods when there is little portfolio rationale to do so, because of an altruistic motivation to help the United States finance its deficits, a Marshall plan in reverse. (Cynics might counter that the Japanese flows were motivated in part by a large player trying to protect past investments.)

In this paper, we do not evaluate or speculate on institutional explanations of this genre, important though they may be. We stick with basic time-series analysis comparing purchases of U.S. securities by the Japanese, Germans, Canadians, and British. We seek to explain these foreign-investment purchases on a behavioral basis as a function of past flow levels and past performance.

Data sources and preliminary transformations

The data on investment flows, the variables to be explained, are taken from Tables 3.24 and 3.25 in the Bulletin of the Federal Reserve Board of Governors (various issues). U.S. financial security returns are from

Ibbotson and Sinquefield (1988). The equity returns series is based on a portfolio of the Standard and Poor's 500 stocks (S&P500). And the bond returns series is based on a high-grade long-term corporate bond portfolio (Salomon Brothers index). All other explanatory variables – financial, macroeconomic, and international – are from the OECD Main Economic Indicators (various issues).

During the 1980s, the monthly net purchases of U.S. securities (equities, government and corporate bonds) from investors in the four countries display, not surprisingly, a slowly moving trend. We decompose the series into low-frequency (smooth, i.e., local trend) and high-frequency (rough, i.e., deviations from smooth) components. The smooth series is a 13-month-centered moving average; the rough series is the contemporaneous deviation from the smooth series.[19] The results are shown in Fig. 4.1, which gives total flows by country. (Disaggregated plots are similar.) The smooth series captures the trend that meanders slowly; the rough is the high-variance component that fluctuates around zero. Examining the first panel, we observe clearly the widely commented upon 1984 shift in the level and variability of investment flows from Japan to the United States. What is not well known is that the same shift occurs in the panels of flows from Canada and the United Kingdom (though not from West Germany). Excluding a sheer coincidence, we infer that the Japanese shift is part of a broader phenomenon that is not principally bilateral. The abolition in July 1984 of the U.S. withholding tax on interest earned by foreign investors could be such a causal factor. Since the 1984 shift applies to the variability of the flows as well as the levels, the series are fundamentally nonhomogeneous, and reliance on conventional time-series econometrics with data from the entire period is inappropriate.[20]

Hereafter, we restrict our analysis to the post-1984 period for Japan, Canada, and the United Kingdom. Given the short period in which we have a homogeneous time-series behavior, we cannot undertake analysis of the smooth component, which accounts for trends such as long-run adjustments toward equilibrium in error-correction models. Analyzing

---

[19] A more formal decomposition can be achieved following the algorithm in Beveridge and Nelson (1981). The Beveridge-Nelson approach exploits the decomposition of a homogeneous linearly regular first-order integrated process into a random walk component (smooth) and a stationary component (rough). A suitable parametric model has to be adopted to implement the method. Alternatively, a frequency-domain filter could achieve the desired decomposition after suitable detrending [see Engle (1974) on band spectral methods]. For our exploratory purposes, we adopt the simple (naive) decomposition approach noted in the text.

[20] Relations among homogeneous time series with stochastic trends can be analyzed within a cointegration framework [see Granger (1986)]. Patel and Zeckhauser (1990) applied these methods to study inter-country price indices.

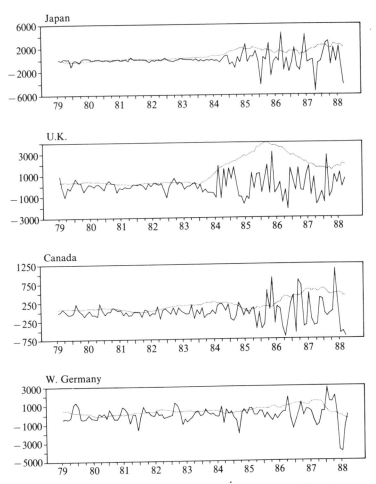

Fig. 4.1. Monthly purchases of U.S. securities ($ millions): rough (solid line) and smooth (dashes) components, 7/79–8/88.

levels of security holdings instead of flows cannot overcome the problems; indeed, since levels are integrated of one order higher than flows, the inapplicability of conventional econometrics is even clearer in that case. We focus on the short-run flow deviations, denoted F and identified as rough in Fig. 4.1. F, in the post-1984 period, appears stationary. This is confirmed by unreported small and statistically insignificant autocorrelations.

Explaining international flows

We study the four countries' security purchases, disaggregated into bonds and equities. Summary statistics of the central variables are shown in Table 4.4. Except for the equity purchases of Canadians and Germans, which are small ($60 million dollars per month or less) and thus may have a large component of measurement error, the other flows exceed $150 million per month. Initially, let us ignore macroeconomic and international variables, which have been the focus of earlier studies. Consider a

Table 4.4. *Summary statistics on foreign purchases of U.S. securities, 1/85–9/88 ($ millions)*
Purchases of bonds

	Total		Rough component	
Purchaser	Mean, $	Std. dev., $	Mean, $	Std. dev., $
Japan	$1294	2239	-40	2093
United Kingdom	2450	1311	-20	1174
Canada	233	431	-18	388
West Germany*	317	993	-38	880

Purchases of stocks

	Total		Rough component	
Purchaser	Mean, $	Std. dev., $	Mean, $	Std. dev., $
Japan	395	582	21	468
United Kingdom	160	699	9	603
Canada	57	123	6	125
West Germany*	25	99	0	82

Benchmark performance measures (percent per month)

	Mean, %	Std. dev., %
S&P 500	1.5	5.6
Corporate bonds	1.2	2.8

Source: Ibbotson and Sinquefield (1988).
Notes: West German data begin from 1/80. Total denotes the total net purchases; the rough components denote the difference between the total and a 13-month-centered moving average.

regression that is parallel to Eq. (4.3), which was used to explain mutual fund flows. We posit as well that international flows are likely to be driven by recent securities performance. Since bonds and equities may in some sense be substitutes, we include the performance measures of both variables. The regression for each country's purchases by security type is

$$F_t = \beta_0 + \beta_1 F_{t-1} + \beta_2 B_{t-1} + \beta_3 E_{t-1} + e_t \qquad (4.4)$$

Here B_{t-1} is the net return on a portfolio of corporate bonds in period $t-1$, and E_{t-1} is the net return on the equity portfolio comprising the Standard and Poor's 500 stocks. The two act as benchmark measures.

Table 4.5. *Explaining "rough" flows to U.S. securities, 1/85–9/88*

Estimates of Eq. (4.4): $F_t = \beta_0 + \beta_1 F_{t-1} + \beta_2 B_{t-1} + \beta_3 E_{t-1} + e_t$

F_t = the "rough" investment flow into the U.S. in month t. The "rough" flow is the difference between the actual flow and a centered, 13-month, moving average of the raw investment flow.

B_{t-1} = the total return on a portfolio of long-term, high-grade, U.S. corporate bonds in month $t-1$.

E_{t-1} = the total return on the S&P 500 index in month $t-1$.

Purchaser	β_1	β_2	β_3	$\bar{R}^2$	Mean absolute purchase ($ millions)
Bonds					
Japan	−0.07	18176	8532	0.08	1492
	(−0.44)	(1.58)	(1.47)		
U.K.	−0.18	9558	−4152	0.07	973
	(−1.21)	(1.48)	(−1.27)		
Canada	0.20	2230	−1581	0.01	298
	(1.21)	(1.01)	(−1.41)		
West Germany*	0.48	1353	−4241	0.24	552
	(5.72)	(0.68)	(−2.63)		
Stocks					
Japan	0.28	−4269	2648	0.11	312
	(1.93)	(−1.73)	(2.09)		
U.K.	0.05	−5939	7726	0.50	351
	(0.45)	(−2.39)	(6.17)		
Canada	−0.13	−214	−345	0.00	95
	(−0.81)	(−0.30)	(−0.93)		
West Germany*	0.14	−256	272	0.01	59
	(1.39)	(−1.20)	(1.58)		

Notes: West German data begin from 1/80. We show t statistics in parentheses. In each of the above cases, the residual autocorrelations are consistent with a white-noise process.

(The corresponding benchmark for the mutual fund return was provided by the cross-sectional mean fund return.)

The results of estimating Eq. (4.4) by ordinary least squares are shown in Table 4.5. For bond purchases, the previous month's return on the bond portfolio index has the expected positive sign. The stock returns measure has a negative sign (as expected if bonds and stocks are investment substitutes) for the United Kingdom, Canada, and Germany, and is statistically significant for Germany. Japanese bond purchasers may not be viewing stocks as substitutes; if anything, they interpret good stock returns as indicating a healthy bond investment climate. The lagged bond purchase is significant with the conjectured positive sign for Germany only. This absence of a significant dependence on previous flows is not surprising since the prefilter used in constructing the "rough" flow series removes long-term autocorrelation. For equity purchases, the large-flow countries (Japan and the United Kingdom) have significant coefficients with the expected sign. For the U.K., 50% of the high-frequency variation in monthly flows is explained, and for Japan 11%. For Canada and Germany, whose flows are small, the performance-based explanation is uninformative. Might these four countries respond differently to past performance?

While considerable variation remains unexplained in Table 4.5, success is relative: We have found (in results not reported here) that no further explanatory power results from addition of conventional relative macroeconomic performance measures (GNP growth differentials, inflation differentials, real return differentials, etc.) or conventional international variables (e.g., exchange rate risk, proxied by the usual coefficient of variation estimated with daily exchange rates from the prior month,[21] changes in exchange rates, balance of trade). The explanation of investment flows, we conclude, is less likely to rest in traditional macroeconomic or international investment variables than in whatever forces stir the animal spirits of investors.

Net flows of bond and equity issues

In this section, we briefly explore net flows of bond and equity issues in the United States. The interpretation of our analysis proves complicated, unfortunately, since net issues clearly reflect both supply and demand factors. Unlike the market for open-end mutual funds, where supply is infinitely elastic, net issues of bonds and equities are influenced by issuers'

[21] Exchange rates display autoregressive conditional heteroscedasticity (ARCH), which has led other investigators of international flow behavior to consider varying exchange rate risk as a potential explanatory variable. We employed the usual exchange rate risk measure, though an ARCH-model-based measure might be better justified.

needs and opportunities. Our simple framework cannot distinguish between demand and supply effects. Our analysis, as in preceding sections, relates net issues to recent performance and past flows, variables that are consistent with behavioral explanations.

Data sources and preliminary transformation

The quarterly data on flows of net issues (new issues less redemption) were obtained from the Federal Reserve Board of Governors for the period 1952–88. The Federal Reserve also collects data on the purchases of the net issues by sector (including such categories as life insurance companies, private pensions, and public pensions, and a residual category labeled households). However, the sectoral purchases are nearly impossible to interpret outside the context of global portfolio changes by sector, which we are researching separately.

Before examining the relation of net issues and lagged performance, we have to control for basic trends such as inflation and real growth in the economy, which naturally induce a substantial long-term rise in net new issues of bonds and equities. As in the preceding section, we focus on short-term fluctuations in the flow series. We prefiltered the flows data by a three-stage process as follows. In the first stage, the series of net issues and a series representing fixed investment in the U.S. economy were normalized by the nominal gross national product. This normalization controls for the effects of both inflation and real growth in the economy. In the second stage, we followed the decomposition method described under data sources; that is, we removed a nine-quarter-centered moving average from the normalized series. This step filters any remaining trends. In the last stage, we cumulated the quarterly series up to a calendar year basis, to avoid dealing with seasonality and to reduce measurement error and random noise. The net results provide detrended annual series (high-frequency components) of flows of net issues and net economywide investments. The returns series on stocks and bonds are the same ones described above.

Relation of net issues to recent performance

Both the exploratory regressions employ five explanatory variables: 1-year lags of net issues of bonds and equities, bond and equity performances, and a 2-year lag of prefiltered net fixed investment, which measures the need for raising funds.[22] To interpret the coefficients on lagged equity

---

[22] We included four lags in preliminary regressions. Only the second lag was statistically significant.

Table 4.6. *Explaining annual "rough" flows of bond and equity issues, 1954–84*

Regression: $Issues_t = \beta_0 + \beta_1\ Bond\ issues_{t-1} + \beta_2\ Equity\ Issues_{t-1} + \beta_3 B_{t-1} + \beta_4 E_{t-1} + \beta_5$
$Fixinv_{t-2} + error$

Issues = new issues less redemptions of either *bonds* or *equities*. This variable is created by a three-stage process. First, the quarterly series of raw net issues is divided by GNP. Second, a "rough" series is extracted from this by subtracting a centered, nine-quarter moving average. Third, this "rough" series is cumulated into an annual series representing the total annual deviation from the moving average.

B = the total return on a portfolio of long-term, high-grade U.S. corporate bonds.

E = the total return on the Standard & Poor's 500 Index of equities.

Fixinv = gross fixed investment in the U.S. This series is transformed in the same way as the *issues* series (i.e., it represents a 2-year lag of the deviation of fixed investment from a 2-year trend).

Issues	β_1	β_3	β_4	β_5	β_6	$\bar{R}^2$	ρ_1
Bonds	0.03	0.12	−4.46	−3.70	5.90	0.17	0.02
	(0.14)	(0.98)	(−1.55)	(−2.32)	(0.19)		
Equities	−0.36	−1.06	17.54	1.89	87.15	0.74	−0.35
	(−1.43)	(−7.29)	(5.17)	(1.01)	(2.39)		

Notes: The t statistics are shown in parentheses. $\bar{R}^2$ denotes the adjusted R-squared for the regression; ρ_1 denotes the first-order autocorrelation of the residuals.

and bond portfolio returns, note that since market conditions are considered good when equity values are high and interest rates are low, a good market condition is associated with positive returns on both the bond and equity portfolios. The regression results are reported in Table 4.6.

The equity regression is quite successful, explaining 74% of the variance of the high-frequency equity flows. The coefficients on recent performance variables confirm a relation between the type of issues brought to market and perceived market conditions. We have a significant positive coefficient on bond portfolio returns as well as a positive coefficient on equity returns. Issuers behave as if they followed the conventional wisdom that stocks are best issued when market conditions are good. In light of the bond issue results, discussed below, the increase of equity issues in perceived favorable market conditions substitutes for contemporaneous bond issues. The significant negative coefficient on the lagged equity issues hints that there is substitution across periods for equity issues.

The bond regression explains 17% of the variance of the high-frequency bond flows. The only significant variable is equity performance, which has a negative coefficient. This is consistent with the view that "good market conditions" lead to fewer bond issues and more equity issues. Stock issues and bond issues are substitutes for one another. Finally, as we might expect, the coefficient on lagged investment is positive in both regressions. It is significantly so for equities. This result is consistent with securitization of fixed investments with a 2-year lag. Of course, this inference, like the ones above, is only suggestive: Sharper testing and more explicit models of alternative hypotheses are needed. For now, we have at least identified a significant prediction relation for variations in stock issues.

Several questions arise from our analysis. For example, why are bond issues less well explained than stock issues? Could it be that they are a residual class of securitizing investments?[23] Questions about asset mix are relevant to current policy deliberations in the wake of the 1989–90 collapse of the junk-bond market. More broadly and indirectly, such examinations address capital structure issues in an expanded framework, going beyond the classic rational market framework of Modigliani and Miller (1958), Miller (1977), or the agency literature approach following Jensen and Meckling (1976), which though rational recognizes information asymmetries.

Concluding remarks

Investment flows are significantly influenced by the recent returns offered by particular assets, although efficient markets theory suggests that the current asset price should completely reflect future prospects. A simple behavioral model based solely on past performance, when combined with considerations of *status quo* bias, can explain more than 70% of the variance in cross-sectional flows to mutual funds over the 1975–87 period. Mutual fund flows appear better related to performance ranks than to absolute performance. Since funds and fund raters regularly tout relative rankings, this finding is consistent with investors responding to the readily available information format. Risk-adjusted performance measures, which are more complicated to construct and are not advertised, have no marginal explanatory power in accounting for relative flows to mutual funds, even though they may be more appropriate benchmarks from the perspective of finance theory or expected utility maximization.

Our regressions explain less of the variation of international purchases of U.S. equities and bonds. The analysis is complicated by changing trends in the flows during the 1980s. For the homogeneous post-1984 period, a

---

[23] In Myers' (1984) pecking order theory of capital structure, equity is posited to be the last resort means of financing by firms.

simple performance-based explanation for the high-frequency component of monthly international flows to U.S. securities performs as well as more complex conventional models that allow for macroeconomic or international variables. We also provide some evidence, for the period 1953–84, on the relation of net new issues of bonds and stocks to market performance. Here the timing considerations of issuers may be more significant than purchasers' motivations. We are quite successful in explaining net stock issues on the basis of recent stock and bond market performances and past fixed investments.

We have considered departures from rational behavior – due to *status quo* bias, framing distortions, or adoption of rules of thumb – as an approach to better understanding financial markets. We find that models with limited poaching and incompletely rational participants generate rich hypotheses; flows of funds data yield insights into investors' behavior; and accepting departures from the EMH paradigm facilitates robust prediction about financial market behavior.

References

Beveridge, S., and C. Nelson (1981), "A New Approach to Decomposition of Economic Time Series into Permanent and Transitory Components with Particular Attention to Measurement of the 'Business Cycle'," *Journal of Monetary Economics*, 7, 151–74.

Brealey, R. A. (1983), "Can Professional Investors Beat the Market," Chap. 3 in *An Introduction to Risk and Return for Common Stocks* (2d edition), Cambridge: M.I.T. Press.

Brealey, R. A., and S. C. Myers (1988), *Principles of Corporate Finance*, New York: McGraw-Hill Book Co.

Chen, N., R. Roll, and S. Ross (1986), "Economic Forces and the Stock Market," *Journal of Business*, 59, 383–403.

Consumer Guide (1988), "Top Performing Mutual Funds," 483.

Engle, R. (1974), "Band Spectrum Regression," *International Economic Review*, 15, 1–11.

Gultekin, M., B. Gultekin, and A. Penati (1989), "Capital Controls and International Capital Market Segmentation: The Evidence from the Japanese and American Stock Markets," *Journal of Finance*, 44, 849–70.

Granger, C. (1986), "Developments in the Study of Scintillated Economic Variables," *Oxford Bulletin of Economics and Statistics*, 48 (3), 213–28.

Hendricks, D., J. Patel, and R. Zeckhauser (1991), "Hot Hands in Mutual Funds: The Persistence of Performance, 1974–1988," working paper, John F. Kennedy School of Government, Harvard University, appeared in *Journal of Finance*, 28 (1), 93–130.

Ibbotson, R., and R. Sinquefield (1988), *Stocks, Bonds, Bills, and Inflation*, Chicago: Ibbotson Associates.

Jensen, M., and W. Meckling (1976), "Theory of the Firm: Managerial Behavior, Agency Costs and Capital Structure," *Journal of Financial Economics*, 23, 371–407.

Kawai, M., and H. Okumura (1988), "Japan's Portfolio Investment in Foreign Securities," *JCIF Policy Studies Series*, 9, 1–29.

Kahneman, D., and A. Tversky (1984), "Choices, Values and Frames," *American Psychologist*, 39, 341–50.

Kahneman, D., and J. Snell (1990), "Predicting Utility," in R. Hogarth (ed.), *Insights in Decision Making*, Chicago: University of Chicago Press.

Koo, R. (1989), "Japan and International Capital Flows," mimeograph, Nomura Research Institute.

Miller, M. (1977), "Debt and Taxes," *Journal of Finance*, 32, 261–76.

Miller, M. (1986), "Financial Innovation: The Last Twenty Years and the Next," *Journal of Financial and Quantitative Analysis*, 21, 459–70.

Modigliani, F., and M. Miller (1958), "The Cost of Capital, Corporate Finance, and Theory of Investment," *American Economic Review*, 48 (Jun.), 261–91.

Myers, S. (1984), "The Capital Structure Puzzle," *Journal of Finance*, 39 (Jul.), 575–92.

Patel, J., and R. Zeckhauser (1990), "Shared Price Trends: Evidence from U.S. Cities and OECD Countries," *Journal of Business & Economic Statistic*, 8, 179–89.

Samuelson, W., and R. Zeckhauser (1988), "Status Quo Bias in Decision Making," *Journal of Risk and Uncertainty*, 1, 7–59.

Weisenberger A. (1974–1987), *Investment Company Survey*, New York, A. Weisenberger & Co.

Zeckhauser, R., J. Patel, and D. Hendricks (1991), "Nonrational Actors and Financial Market Behavior," *Theory and Decision*, 31, 257–87.

CHAPTER 5

Accumulation of net external assets in Japan

MASAHIRO KAWAI

Introduction

Japan experienced large and persistent current account surpluses through-out the 1980s and accumulated considerable amounts of net external assets. Based on the external asset-liability data, it became the world's largest *net* creditor country in 1986 and the world's largest *gross* creditor country in 1991, surpassing the United Kingdom and the United States, respectively. Japan's ascendance to creditor country status was accom-panied by a rapidly declining net external asset position in the United States. According to the same stock data, the United States became a net debtor country in the mid-1980s for the first time since the end of World War I, and it is now the world's largest net debtor country (although its net investment income data indicate that the United States is still a large net creditor country). Figure 5.1 demonstrates not only the dramatic changes in the two countries' net external asset positions but also their contrasting movements in the 1980s. (Net investment income exhibits similar, though less striking, movements.) Japan's creditor status poses the important question of what Japan can and will do with these substantial external assets.

This paper examines the causes of accumulation of net external assets in Japan. The next section reviews recent developments in Japan's net external asset position by focusing on both external asset-liability (stock) data and net investment income (flow) data in the balance of payments. Japan's net external asset position is compared with those of the major industrial countries. Subsequent sections (1) analyze the causes of rapid accumulation of Japan's net external assets by examining current account and capital account transactions, and saving-investment balances, and (2) specifically focus on the determinants of long-term net capital outflows, a dominant vehicle through which Japan accumulated its net external assets in the 1980s. These two sections will argue that both factors of a long-term structural nature and factors specific to the 1980s contributed

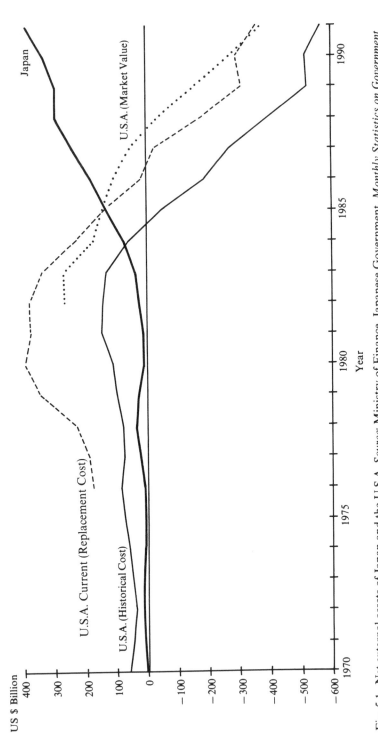

Fig. 5.1. Net external assets of Japan and the U.S.A. *Source:* Ministry of Finance, Japanese Government, *Monthly Statistics on Government Finance and Banking,* various issues.
Department of Commerce, U.S. Government, *Survey of Current Business,* June 1988, June 1991, June 1992.

to the expansion of net external assets. Long-term, structural factors include (a) Japan's rapid productivity growth in key manufacturing sectors and (b) high household saving. Factors specific to the 1980s include (c) Japan's liberalization of capital controls and (d) U.S. and Japanese macro-economic conditions and the consequent behavior of real domestic demand, real interest rates, real exchange rates, and real stock and share prices. A last section presents concluding remarks and some international impli-cations of Japan's ascendance to a leading creditor country.

Japan's net external asset position

Stock data and flow data

Several statistical measures are used to express a country's net external asset position (NEAP). A direct measure is the difference between a country's gross external assets and liabilities; an indirect measure is a country's net income generated from investment abroad. The stock balance between gross external assets and liabilities is readily available in official publications; Japan's Ministry of Finance has been publishing external asset and liability data (and its composition) annually since 1971, and the Economic Planning Agency has published some pre-1971 data. Net invest-ment income is reported as part of the current account of Japan's balance of payments (Table 5.1). Since net investment income is the fruit of past investments abroad, it can be postulated that the capitalized value of net investment income presents another measure of the NEAP.

Figure 5.2 plots these two measures of Japan's NEAP as a ratio of Gross National Product (GNP). Net external assets, represented by the solid curve, are the stock data constructed as the difference between gross external assets, excluding official gold holdings, and gross external liabilities, expressed as a ratio of GNP. The dotted curve represents the flow data constructed by capitalizing net investment income using 3-month U.S. Treasury bill interest rates as a discount factor and expressing the capitalized value as a ratio of GNP. The reason official gold holdings are excluded from the stock data is that gold does not bear interest and the data must be made comparable with the flow data. (Official gold holdings, valued at the official price, relative to GNP are small anyway.)

Not surprisingly, the two data series move together in a parallel fashion with a correlation coefficient of 0.96 for the 1970–91 period. Both data sets show that Japan's NEAP was stable as a trend throughout the 1970s, when oil price increases plagued the economy twice, and started to rise in the beginning of the 1980s. The pace of the rise in the 1980s was rapid and much faster than in any preceding period. The NEAP reached a plateau toward the end of the 1980s.

Table 5.1. *Japan's balance of payments*

(U.S. $ million)

	1965	1970	1975	1980	1981	1982	1983	1984	1985	1986	1987	1988	1989	1990	1991
Current account	932	1,970	-682	-10,746	4,770	6,850	20,799	35,003	49,169	85,845	87,015	79,631	57,157	35,761	72,901
Merchandise trade	1,901	3,963	5,028	2,125	19,967	18,079	31,454	44,257	55,986	92,827	96,386	95,012	76,917	63,528	103,044
Services	-884	-1,785	-5,354	-11,343	-13,573	-9,848	-9,106	-7,747	-5,165	-4,932	-5,702	-11,263	-15,526	-22,292	-17,660
Net investment income	-189	-209	-273	854	-763	1,718	3,082	4,231	6,840	9,473	16,670	21,032	23,442	23,204	26,724
Other	-695	-1,576	-5,081	-12,197	-12,810	-11,566	-12,188	-11,978	-12,005	-14,405	-22,372	-32,295	-38,968	-45,496	-44,384
Unrequited transfers	-85	-208	-356	-1,528	-1,624	-1,381	-1,549	-1,507	-1,652	-2,050	-3,669	-4,118	-4,234	-5,475	-12,483
Capital account (a)	-881	-2,241	1,266	13,861	-5,263	-11,577	-22,854	-38,746	-53,160	-88,303	-83,122	-82,427	-35,149	-14,884	-65,070
Long-term capital account	-415	-1,591	-272	2,324	-9,672	-14,969	-17,700	-49,651	-64,542	-131,461	-136,532	-130,930	-89,246	-43,586	37,057
Direct investments	-30	-261	-1,537	-2,107	-4,705	-4,101	-3,196	-5,975	-5,810	-14,254	-18,354	-34,695	-45,184	-46,271	-29,358
Securities investments (b)	12	234	2,729	9,360	4,443	2,117	-1,876	-23,601	-43,032	-101,432	-93,838	-66,651	-28,034	-5,028	40,978
Loans	-97	-548	-1,129	-2,784	-5,269	-8,083	-8,462	-11,999	-10,502	-9,315	-16,309	-15,293	-4,682	16,930	25,027
Trade credits	-252	-780	-55	-733	-2,746	-3,245	-2,581	-4,934	-2,788	-1,876	-536	-6,957	-4,011	671	3,926
Other	-48	-236	-280	-1,412	-1,395	-1,657	-1,585	-3,142	-2,410	-4,584	-7,495	-7,334	-7,335	-9,888	-3,516
Short-term capital account, private	-346	358	742	16,285	8,651	-1,544	-3,547	13,265	9,912	56,897	95,666	63,981	29,403	7,835	-119,212
Private nonbanking	-61	724	-1,138	3,141	2,265	-1,579	23	-4,295	-936	-1,609	23,865	19,521	20,811	21,468	-25,758
Authorized foreign-exchange banks	-285	-366	1,880	13,144	6,386	35	-3,570	17,560	10,848	58,506	71,801	44,460	8,592	-13,633	-93,454
Short-term capital account, official (c)	-120	-1,008	796	-4,748	-4,242	4,936	-1,607	-2,360	1,470	-13,739	-42,256	-15,478	24,694	20,867	17,085
Changes in foreign-exchange reserves	-108	-903	703	-4,905	-3,171	5,141	-1,234	-1,817	-197	-15,729	-39,240	-16,183	12,767	7,842	8,073
Errors and omissions	-51	271	-584	-3,115	493	4,727	2,055	3,743	3,991	2,458	-3,893	2,796	-22,008	-20,877	-7,831

Note: (a) Minus sign indicates capital outflows, (b) Gensaki transactions are entered as short-term capital, (c) constructed as the negative of current account + long-term capital account + private short-term capital account + errors and omissions.

Source: Bank of Japan, *Balance of Payments Monthly*, various issues.

Though moving closely with each other, the two data series exhibit some discrepancy. First, the stock data show that Japan has been a net creditor country since 1968 (not shown in the figure), while the flow data indicate that Japan was never a persistent net creditor until 1982. According to the flow data, Japan became a net creditor country in 1972 but moved back to be a net debtor in 1974–76 and 1981.[1] That is, each time the economy was hit by an oil price shock (in 1973–74 and 1979–80), its net investment income recorded a deficit 1 or 2 years after the shock. Second, the flow data exhibit a smaller NEAP than do the stock data, until the beginning of the 1980s when such a relationship disappeared.

There are several reasons for a discrepancy between the stock data and flow data. One obvious reason is that neither data set is completely reliable. It is known that the data for external assets and liabilities do not reflect true economic values because most of them are eveluted at historical costs. The Ministry of Finance makes valuation adjustments every year when it publishes annual data, but the adjustments are far from complete. The data for investment income, which is considered more accurate because of the reporting requirements imposed by the Foreign Exchange Law, may not capture all the investment income flows. For example, reinvestment by Japanese firms abroad is not treated as part of investment income, so the data tend to be underestimated.

Another possible reason for a discrepancy between the stock and flow data is that the rates of return on external assets and liabilities are different. The *ex post* rates of return, reported in Table 5.2, reveal that the return on external assets was lower than that on external liabilities until 1981, but that this trend has been completely reversed since then. It is argued, therefore, that although Japan became a net creditor country on the stock basis in 1968, it never recorded a persistent surplus on net investment income until the beginning of the 1980s due to the low rate of return on external assets relative to external liabilities. Only after 1982 did a persistent and rising surplus on net investment income start to emerge, and Japan became a net creditor country on the basis of both stock and flow data.

Composition of Japan's net external assets

To analyze the causes of the rise in the NEAP, one must understand what type of net external assets Japan accumulated in the 1980s. Let us examine changes in the composition of Japan's NEAP over time.

Table 5.3 summarizes the composition of Japan's NEAP based on the

[1] The IMF's data on net investment income show that Japan was a net debtor country until 1981, except in 1979 when net investment income was positive; see Table 5.5 to be discussed later.

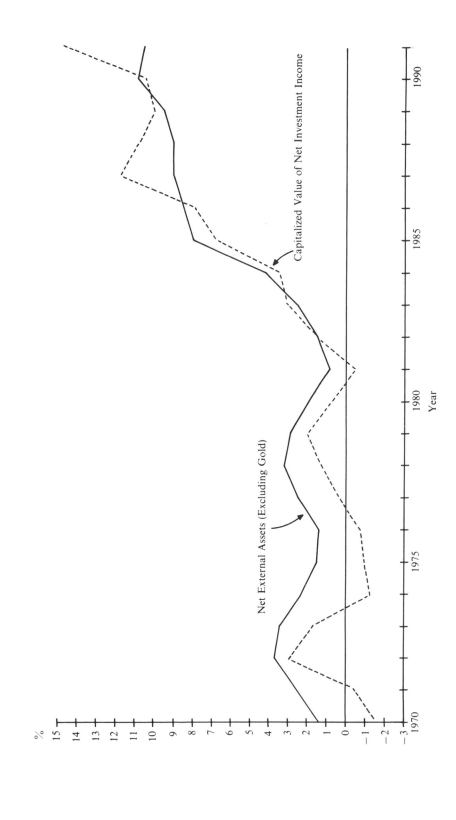

Table 5.2. *Ex-post rates of return on external assets and liabilities*

| Year | Direct investment | | Indirect investment | | Total | |
	Assets	Liabilities	Assets	Liabilities	Assets	Liabilities
1972	7.6	11.5	4.1	4.4	4.3	4.8
1973	6.3	18.2	5.9	6.1	5.9	6.7
1974	6.3	16.7	7.1	9.5	7.0	9.8
1975	6.8	15.1	6.4	7.6	6.4	7.9
1976	6.9	15.1	5.3	6.3	5.6	6.7
1977	7.6	17.0	4.7	5.8	5.1	6.2
1978	5.9	16.0	5.3	5.9	5.4	6.2
1979	5.9	18.7	7.3	7.0	7.1	7.4
1980	7.3	15.9	7.6	7.8	7.6	8.1
1981	6.5	17.4	8.9	9.4	8.6	9.5
1982	5.9	15.1	8.8	8.1	8.4	8.3
1983	6.7	16.4	6.2	5.5	6.3	5.7
1984	6.3	17.5	6.1	5.6	6.1	5.8
1985	6.2	18.0	5.6	5.1	5.7	5.3
1986	5.2	22.4	5.0	4.4	5.0	4.6
1987	5.3	19.9	5.5	4.6	5.5	4.7
1988	4.0	20.6	6.0	5.2	5.9	5.4
1989	3.5	23.3	6.5	5.8	6.3	5.9
1990	2.7	23.7	7.2	6.5	6.7	6.6
1991	2.9	18.7	7.8	7.1	7.3	7.2

Note: The *ex-post* rate of return is calculated as investment income received (or paid) divided by the average asset (liability) stock, where average asset (or liability) stock is the average of the end-of-the-year stocks of the year concerned and the previous year. The average asset stock data exclude official gold holdings.
Source: Bank of Japan, *Balance of Payments Monthly*, various issues.

Ministry of Finance's stock data. Net external assets are broken down into those of the private sector and the government sector. Each sector's net external assets are further broken down into long-term and short-term net external assets. Private long-term net external assets include direct investments and securities investments among others.

Fig. 5.2. Two measures of Japan's net external asset position (relative to GNP). *Note*: Net external assets refer to the average of net external assets (excluding official gold holdings) of the year concerned and the previous year, expressed as a ratio of GNP. Capitalized value of net investment income is constructed as net investment income divided by the 3-month U.S. Treasury bill interest rate, expressed as a ratio of GNP. *Source*: Ministry of Finance, *Monthly Statistics on Government Finance and Banking*, various issues; Bank of Japan, *Balance of Payments Monthly*, various issues; IMF, *International Financial Statistics*, various issues.

Table 5.3. Composition of Japan's net external assets

(U.S. $ million)

	1971	1975	1980	1981	1982	1983	1984	1985	1986	1987	1988	1989	1990	1991
Private sector	-7,088	-10,302	-16,659	-18,537	2,046	11,928	47,069	104,450	138,541	146,494	147,571	158,839	218,835	285,545
Long term	-495	12,931	31,760	39,531	56,928	61,500	108,208	172,682	272,512	386,290	459,737	496,238	565,542	524,810
Direct investments	514	6,238	16,342	20,591	24,971	27,814	33,463	39,231	51,557	68,004	100,364	145,207	191,591	219,494
Securities investments	-3,490	-3,591	-8,305	-12,444	-7,006	-13,833	10,497	60,901	114,322	173,471	172,332	159,791	229,292	188,308
Loans	-1,620	3,282	13,216	17,466	21,903	27,946	39,335	45,659	68,012	96,368	122,602	118,169	72,059	41,542
Trade credits	4,853	6,734	9,752	13,220	15,905	18,094	22,800	23,472	31,959	37,154	48,768	52,870	47,134	47,290
Other	-752	268	755	698	1,155	1,479	2,113	3,419	6,662	11,293	15,671	20,201	25,466	28,176
Short term	-6,593	-23,233	-48,419	-58,068	-54,882	-49,572	-61,139	-68,232	-133,971	-239,796	-312,166	-337,399	-346,707	-239,265
Monetary movements	-1,471	-13,471	-32,816	-39,545	-38,986	-35,221	-52,536	-61,265	-127,450	-209,901	-262,909	-266,833	-254,367	-162,693
Other	-5,122	-9,762	-15,603	-18,523	-15,896	-14,351	-8,603	-6,967	-6,521	-29,895	-49,257	-70,566	-92,340	-76,572
Government sector	16,861	17,320	28,193	29,455	22,636	25,331	27,277	25,371	41,810	94,250	144,175	134,376	109,224	97,527
Long-term	2,211	5,823	8,832	7,224	4,878	6,611	7,754	6,287	11,288	23,710	61,307	75,508	66,521	75,635
Loans	1,809	5,083	15,282	19,758	20,287	22,349	24,388	23,209	33,492	43,098	55,544	60,464	60,927	77,285
Other	402	740	-6,450	-12,534	-15,409	-15,738	-16,634	-16,922	-22,204	-19,388	5,763	15,044	5,594	-1,650
Short term	14,650	11,497	19,361	22,231	17,758	18,720	19,523	19,084	30,522	70,540	82,868	58,868	42,703	21,892
Monetary movements	14,877	12,103	21,790	25,330	20,444	21,791	23,671	23,093	36,191	78,253	92,725	68,115	50,894	30,408
Other	-227	-606	-2,429	-3,099	-2,686	-3,071	-4,148	-4,009	-5,669	-7,713	-9,857	-9,247	-8,191	-8,516
Total net external assets	9,773	7,018	11,534	10,918	24,682	37,259	74,346	129,821	180,351	240,744	291,746	293,215	328,059	383,072

Source: Ministry of Finance, Monthly Statistics on Government Finance and Banking, various issues.

The table demonstrates that the government sector was always a net creditor (at least in the 1970s and 1980s), while the private sector was a net debtor until 1981 (except in 1979 – not shown in the table). This means that Japan's net creditor position for the 1968–81 period, based on the stock data, was made possible by the official holding of net external assets that exceeded private net external liabilities. (Since the rate of return the government sector faced was likely lower than that of the private sector, this perhaps explains why Japan's overall rates of return on external assets were lower than those on external liabilities until the beginning of the 1980s.) In the 1980s, however, the private sector became a net creditor and increased its net external assets substantially, contributing to the rapid expansion of Japan's total NEAP. Out of the rise in total NEAP between 1980 and 1991 (US\$ 371.5 billion), the private sector accounted for 81% and the government sector accounted for only 19%.

Among the private NEAP, long-term net external assets such as securities and direct investments rose substantially, while short-term net external assets declined at least until 1990. An important compositional shift is observed in long-term net external assets in the 1980s. The net position of securities investments rose rapidly between 1980 and 1991 (US\$ 196.6 billion), with most of the rise occurring in the 1984–87 period. It declined, however, in 1988–89 and in 1991. The net position of direct investments saw the biggest rise between 1980 and 1991 (US\$ 203.2 billion), and most of the rise occurred in the 1987–91 period when net accumulation of securities investments was slowing down. Several explanations for such a compositional shift will be offered in a later section.

It must be pointed out that as private long-term net external assets grew, private short-term net external assets, particularly those of monetary movements, experienced a substantial decline (a decline of US\$ 190.8 billion between 1980 and 1991). Private monetary movements represent short-term capital transactions by authorized foreign-exchange banks, which include all city banks as well as some large regional banks. These commercial banks had large net external debts in the 1970s because of the need of their nonbanking customers to finance export, import, and other business activities; they borrowed short-term funds externally and lent them domestically to their nonbanking customers. The commercial banks also borrowed short-term funds abroad to finance their own purchases of foreign long-term securities. Due to the increased demand for such external short-term funds by the nonbanking sector as well as by commercial banks themselves, their net external debts rose substantially in the 1980s. Since the decline in short-term net external assets was accompanied by the rise in long-term net external assets, Japan was effectively engaged in large-scale international financial intermediation by borrowing short and lending long. (However, such international financial intermediation disappeared suddenly in 1990 and was reversed in 1991.) This was also the time when Japanese commercial banks expanded their international operations and emerged as one of the most powerful financial institutions in the world.

The government sector also played a role in accumulating net external assets in the 1980s. Its role was conspicuous in 1987 when it increased short-term external assets through monetary movements. Government monetary movements represent official short-term capital transactions, mostly in the form of intervention in the foreign-exchange market. The year 1987 was the time when serious fears of a free fall of the dollar mounted due to persistent current account deficits in the United States [see Marris (1987), Krugman (1988), and papers in Bergsten (1991)]. As autonomous private capital outflows became small, thereby putting downward pressure on the value of the U.S. dollar, the Bank of Japan (together with the central banks of other major industrialized countries) had to step in to support the dollar. The resulting accumulation of foreign-exchange reserves contributed to a rise in Japan's overall NEAP.

To summarize, rapid expansion of Japan's NEAP in the 1980s was essentially private-sector driven, though it was supplemented by official intervention in the foreign-exchange market when private capital outflows were drying up. The private sector accumulated net external assets in the form of securities investments particularly during the 1984–87 period and in the form of direct investments thereafter. As will be explained in the two following sections, such developments were brought about largely by Japan's liberalization of exchange and capital controls and by the macroeconomic events in the United States and Japan. The latter include the divergent fiscal policies of the two countries and the subsequent change in their macroeconomic variables, such as real domestic demand and real asset prices.

International comparisons

It is useful to compare Japan's NEAP data with those of other major industrial countries. Tables 5.4 and 5.5 summarize two measures of external assets and liabilities of four major industrial countries, using stock and flow data.

Table 5.4 compares Japan, the United States, the United Kingdom, and Germany regarding their stock measures of gross external assets and liabilities and net external assets. The data are taken from each country's

Table 5.4. Gross external assets and liabilities, and net external assets of Japan, the U.S.A., the U.K., and Germany

(U.S. $ million)

	Japan			United States			United Kingdom			Germany		
	Assets	Liabilities	Net Assets	Assets	Liabilities	Net Assets	Assets	Liabilities	Net Assets	Assets	Liabilities	Net Assets
1970	n.a.	n.a.	4,674	165,385	106,912	58,473	49,130	40,517	8,613	50,870	34,673	16,197
1971	32,753	22,980	9,773	179,004	133,493	45,511	62,662	52,343	10,319	62,518	44,892	17,626
1972	43,595	29,728	13,867	198,694	161,658	37,036	73,585	57,810	15,775	69,000	51,026	17,974
1973	47,551	34,535	13,016	222,430	174,536	47,894	71,503	58,902	12,601	92,376	68,569	23,807
1974	55,942	46,999	8,943	255,719	196,988	58,731	180,435	175,034	5,401	114,677	81,145	33,532
1975	58,334	51,316	7,018	295,100	220,860	74,240	199,507	193,989	5,518	122,906	85,914	36,992
1976	67,990	58,416	9,574	457,636	281,713	175,923	222,388	214,181	8,207	152,320	108,547	43,774
1977	80,060	58,080	21,980	519,032	328,484	190,548	273,602	261,389	12,213	182,575	134,046	48,530
1978	118,725	82,511	36,214	627,261	398,840	228,421	340,179	312,886	27,293	234,883	178,970	55,912
1979	135,365	106,588	28,777	792,908	449,979	342,929	443,281	415,688	27,593	262,384	213,153	49,231
1980	159,580	148,046	11,534	936,275	543,728	392,547	550,830	507,671	43,159	256,627	223,436	33,191
1981	209,257	198,339	10,918	1,004,162	629,908	374,254	630,319	568,036	62,283	250,126	220,970	29,156
1982	227,688	203,006	24,682	1,119,178	740,245	378,933	671,764	601,550	70,214	254,342	223,441	30,900
1983	271,956	234,697	37,259	1,169,162	831,786	337,376	705,655	625,050	80,605	242,828	209,885	32,943
1984	341,208	266,862	74,346	1,177,532	944,680	232,852	721,038	629,217	91,821	242,746	200,652	42,093
1985	437,701	307,880	129,821	1,252,535	1,113,585	138,950	857,790	751,136	106,654	341,751	288,554	53,197
1986	727,306	546,955	180,351	1,410,190	1,391,455	18,735	1,065,111	912,291	152,820	501,787	404,786	97,001
1987	1,071,631	830,887	240,744	1,564,748	1,591,378	−26,630	1,299,691	1,174,426	125,265	665,925	496,462	169,463
1988	1,469,347	1,177,601	291,746	1,654,582	1,838,297	−183,715	1,415,950	1,269,437	146,513	689,655	479,739	209,916
1989	1,771,003	1,477,788	293,215	1,794,727	2,107,013	−312,286	1,557,969	1,423,555	134,414	863,633	594,393	269,270
1990	1,857,862	1,529,803	328,059	1,884,199	2,179,035	−294,836	1,760,197	1,703,394	56,803	1,113,165	738,770	374,395
1991	2,006,521	1,623,449	383,072	1,960,301	2,321,804	−361,503	n.a.	n.a.	n.a.	n.a.	n.a.	n.a.

Note: The exchange rates used to convert the U.K. and German data are their respective rates at the end of the year, obtained from IMF, *International Financial Statistics.* The Japanese data are expressed in U.S. dollars. The U.S. data are based on "historical costs" for the 1970–75 period and on "current replacement costs" for the 1976–91 period.

Sources: Ministry of Finance, *Monthly Statistics on Government Finance and Banking,* various issues. Department of Commerce, U.S. Government, *Survey of Current Business,* June 1988, June 1991, and June 1992; Central Statistical Office, U.K. Government, *United Kingdom Balance of Payments (Pink Book),* 1982–1984, 1986–1991; Deutsche Bundesbank, released data.

Table 5.5. *Investment income of Japan, the U.S.A., the U.K., and Germany*

(U.S. $ billion)

Year	Japan Received	Japan Paid	Japan Net Received	United States Received	United States Paid	United States Net Received	United Kingdom Received	United Kingdom Paid	United Kingdom Net Received	Germany Received	Germany Paid	Germany Net Received
1970	760	1,310	−550	14,080	5,730	8,350	3,926	2,438	1,488	2,450	2,960	−510
1971	1,030	1,490	−460	15,260	5,670	9,590	4,097	2,699	1,398	3,030	3,800	−770
1972	1,670	1,790	−120	17,550	6,870	10,680	8,927	7,360	1,567	3,530	4,340	−810
1973	2,720	2,830	−110	25,010	10,050	14,960	12,562	9,206	3,356	4,820	5,720	−900
1974	3,670	4,740	−1,070	31,430	12,470	18,960	15,096	11,458	3,638	5,910	7,100	−1,190
1975	3,760	4,570	−810	29,670	13,060	16,610	15,172	13,133	2,039	6,240	6,790	−550
1976	3,620	4,450	−830	33,670	13,800	19,870	15,781	12,826	2,955	6,950	7,180	−230
1977	4,020	4,750	−730	37,310	15,180	22,130	16,136	15,512	624	7,490	9,310	−1,820
1978	5,690	5,710	−20	48,360	22,830	25,530	22,356	20,627	1,729	10,690	10,080	610
1979	9,450	8,420	1,030	70,560	34,280	36,280	38,241	35,440	2,801	13,630	14,280	−650
1980	11,600	11,810	−210	78,720	43,820	34,900	56,200	56,408	−208	15,790	16,160	−370
1981	16,430	18,470	−2,040	92,360	54,810	37,550	76,044	73,244	2,800	15,490	16,760	−1,270
1982	19,090	18,680	410	90,610	58,330	32,280	78,580	75,871	2,709	16,040	18,730	−2,690
1983	16,350	14,820	1,530	87,330	55,900	31,430	65,457	60,900	4,557	16,240	16,190	50
1984	19,670	17,100	2,570	98,660	71,210	27,450	69,590	63,668	5,922	17,120	15,170	1,950
1985	23,040	17,940	5,100	88,350	67,760	20,590	68,316	64,625	3,691	17,700	15,890	1,810
1986	30,160	23,180	6,980	88,340	71,880	16,460	71,155	63,462	7,693	25,730	23,470	2,260
1987	50,810	36,960	13,850	99,710	85,240	14,470	80,524	73,908	6,616	33,900	32,370	1,530
1988	76,750	59,520	17,230	121,630	108,420	13,210	103,092	94,065	9,027	38,650	36,470	2,180
1989	104,210	84,520	19,690	140,770	129,160	11,610	123,609	116,773	6,836	48,470	40,180	8,290
1990	125,130	106,180	18,950	145,560	121,910	23,650	146,810	140,483	6,327	68,550	55,420	13,130
1991	143,940	121,240	22,700	131,760	110,490	21,270	141,495	138,388	3,107	76,800	64,580	12,220

Source: IMF, *International Financial Statistics*, in tape.

national statistics and expressed in US$ million.[2] The stock data in the table indicate that Japan had the smallest *net* external assets among the four countries until 1982, but that, as a result of rapid accumulation in the 1980s, it surpassed Germany in 1983 and both the United Kingdom and the United States in 1985–86.[3] In terms of the size of *gross* external assets, though Japan was the smallest among the four countries until 1982, it exceeded Germany in 1983, the United Kingdom in 1988, and the United States in 1991. Although Japan is still the third after the United States and the United Kingdom in terms of the size of *gross* external *liabilities*, it also grew fast in the 1980s. Japan became a world-leading net creditor country while rapidly accumulating both gross external assets and liabilities. This reflected the portfolio expansion and diversification on both sides of external balance sheets, a feature of Japan's rapid internationalization of finance [see Shinkai (1988)].

Table 5.5 compares for the same four countries, investment income received from and paid to the rest of the world, which represents an indirect measure of external assets and liabilities. The data are taken from the IMF's balance of payments statistics for international comparison.[4] On the basis of net investment income received, Japan became a larger net creditor country than the United Kingdom and the United States in the late 1980s. However, the data show that the United States has always been a net creditor country, and, in fact, it was one of the world's largest net creditors even in the 1990s. The divergence between the stock and flow

---

[2] U.S. data are taken from Department of Commerce, *Survey of Current Business*, June 1988, June 1991, and June 1992. U.K. data are taken from Central Statistical Office, *United Kingdom Balance of Payments* (The Pink Book), 1982–1984, 1986–1991. German data are obtained from Deutsche Bundesbank, released data. All data are end-of-the-year data, converted into the U.S. dollar using the end-of-the-year exchange rate. The published Japanese data are expressed in U.S. dollars.

   Sinn (1990) estimates the stock of external assets and liabilities for 145 countries using flow transactions data. Although they differ from individual countries' national data, his estimates are useful for international comparisons of a larger number of countries.

[3] According to Sinn's (1990) estimates for the end of 1987, countries with large net external assets were, in descending order, Japan (US $322.9 billion), Switzerland (US $178.1 billion), West Germany (US $177.0 billion), the United Kingdom (US $166.3 billion), and Saudi Arabia (US $116.9 billion). As a percentage of GDP (Gross Domestic Product), Luxembourg (407%) was by far the largest net creditor among the industrial countries, followed by Switzerland (104%), the Netherlands (35%), the United Kingdom (24%), West Germany (16%), and Japan (14%). On the other hand, countries with large net external liabilities were, in descending order, the United States (US $367.6 billion), Canada (US $154.4 billion), Brazil (US $121.1 billion), and Australia (US $82.6 billion). As a percentage of GDP, large net debtor countries in the industrialized world included New Zealand (50%), Denmark (44%), Australia (42%), Ireland (38%), and Canada (37%). The net liability/GNP ratio of the United States was 8%.

[4] The IMF's statistics are internationally more comparable than national statistics.

data is significant for the United States. A similar divergence is observed for other countries, but to a much smaller degree. Investment income data also indicate that Japan's internationalization of finance progressed rapidly in the last half of the 1980s and is now more advanced than that of the United States, if measured as a ratio of GNP.

While it is not possible to obtain accurate statistics of Japan's net external asset position because of the lack of truly reliable data, we can safely conclude from the available stock and flow data that Japan accumulated huge amounts of net external assets and established itself as a world-leading net creditor country in the 1980s. When accumulating net external assets, Japan experienced rapid internationalization of finance.

Current account, capital account, and saving and investment balances

That Japan accumulated considerable amounts of net external assets and became a world-leading creditor country in the 1980s suggests that its causes must be found specifically in the 1980s. However, this does not mean that the underlying conditions behind the remarkable expansion of Japan's NEAP emerged suddenly in the 1980s. It will be argued that both factors of a long-term structural nature and factors specific to the 1980s played important roles in the rise of Japan's NEAP. Long-term structural factors include (a) rapid growth of Japanese labor productivity and the consequent improvement of international competitiveness in key manufacturing sectors and (b) high rates of saving by the Japanese household sector. Factors specific to the 1980s include (c) Japan's liberalization of exchange and capital transactions and (d) fiscal expansion in the United States, fiscal contraction in Japan, and the consequent macroeconomic developments, such as fast growth of U.S. real domestic demand, a rise in real long-term interest rates in the United States, real yen rate depreciation and appreciation, and an increase in Japan's real stock and share prices.

A change in a country's NEAP is identical to the current account or the negative of the capital account, which in turn is the same as the saving-investment balance:

$$NEAP - NEAP_{-1} = \text{Current Account} = -\text{Capital Account}$$
$$= \text{Saving} - \text{Investment}$$

Hence, to examine causes of the rise in Japan's NEAP, we must focus on factors affecting its current account, capital account, and saving and investment balances. This section considers each of these in turn.

Current account

Japan has been running current account surpluses since 1981 when the economy recovered from the second oil-price shock. Accumulation of persistent current account surpluses led to a massive buildup of net external assets.

Table 5.1 demonstrates that current account surpluses in the 1980s were caused principally by merchandise trade surpluses. The merchandise trade account has been in surplus since the mid-1960s, even at times of oil-price shocks. In the 1980s trade surpluses widened considerably until 1987 and remained large during the rest of the 1980s. The services and transfers accounts were stable and in deficit in the same decade, so that they cannot be judged as an element contributing to persistent current account surpluses.

Table 5.6 summarizes the net exports of major commodity categories. It is observed that Japan's large merchandise trade surpluses in the 1980s were brought about primarily by increases in the net export of machinery and equipment and by decreases in the net import of crude materials and mineral fuels. Japan has long maintained the trade pattern of importing raw materials and mineral fuels while exporting manufactured products. In the 1980s imports of foreign raw materials and mineral fuels declined, and exports of manufactured products, particularly those of machinery and equipment, exploded. Dependence on foreign raw materials and mineral fuels was reduced partly due to declines in their international prices and partly due to the increased efficiency in the use of intermediate inputs and development of energy-saving technologies.

Over the years, Japan has been shifting the weight of manufacturing exports from low value-added products with high labor intensity to high value-added products with high technology and human-capital intensity. Starting with textile and other light-industry products, the weight of exports shifted over time to iron and steel products, color TV sets, motor vehicles, machine tools, and semiconductors. Such a shift reflected dynamic changes in the Japanese industrial structure and the consequent changes in its comparative advantage. Keen competition among firms in the domestic market and scale economies due to growing domestic demand made the Japanese manufacturing industry one of the most efficient producers of high value-added and highly income-elastic manufactured products. This process was fueled by continuous growth of labor productivity in key manufacturing sectors. Japan quite successfully exploited the dynamically changing comparative advantage and thus increased exports of key manufactured products.[5]

[5] Such explosive and aggressive export behavior, however, has generated trade conflicts with the United States and EC countries.

Table 5.6. Exports, imports, and net exports of selected commodity categories

(U.S. $ million)

Exports	1960	1965	1970	1975	1980	1981	1982	1983	1984	1985	1986	1987	1988	1989	1990	1991
Foodstuff	256	344	648	760	1,588	1,739	1,401	1,389	1,440	1,316	1,476	1,546	1,695	1,687	1,646	1,822
Crude materials and fuels	112	156	215	629	1,271	1,269	1,039	1,100	1,244	1,256	1,398	1,649	1,718	2,115	2,435	2,474
Textile products	1,223	1,582	2,408	3,719	6,296	7,174	6,240	6,613	6,753	6,263	6,874	6,917	6,908	6,862	7,195	7,943
Chemical products	181	547	1,234	3,889	6,767	6,841	6,365	6,983	7,626	7,698	9,484	11,662	13,964	14,776	15,872	17,475
Iron and steel products	388	1,290	2,844	10,176	15,454	16,669	15,645	12,843	13,852	13,566	12,706	12,610	15,321	14,789	12,509	13,612
Machinery and equipment	1,035	2,975	8,941	30,004	81,481	100,163	90,514	99,560	119,809	126,179	155,027	171,077	196,965	205,471	215,097	236,641
Others	860	1,558	3,028	6,576	16,950	18,175	17,627	18,439	19,390	19,360	22,186	23,760	28,346	29,475	32,194	34,558
Total exports	4,055	8,452	19,318	55,753	129,807	152,030	138,831	146,927	170,114	175,638	209,151	229,221	264,917	275,175	286,948	314,525

Imports	1960	1965	1970	1975	1980	1981	1982	1983	1984	1985	1986	1987	1988	1989	1990	1991
Foodstuff	548	1,470	2,574	8,815	14,666	15,913	14,575	14,896	16,027	15,547	19,186	22,395	29,120	31,012	31,572	34,473
Crude materials and fuels	2,951	4,846	10,528	37,301	93,752	92,597	84,529	77,136	79,862	73,834	54,423	61,122	66,330	73,649	85,102	81,807
Textile products	19	57	314	1,310	3,180	3,430	3,434	2,987	3,875	3,886	5,027	7,624	10,631	13,283	12,804	13,660
Chemical products	265	408	1,000	2,057	6,202	6,487	6,824	7,207	8,346	8,073	9,733	11,845	14,830	15,948	16,045	17,412
Iron and steel products	88	141	276	189	894	1,067	1,216	1,349	1,912	1,479	1,762	2,484	4,625	5,068	4,584	5,503
Machinery and equipment	435	760	2,298	4,286	9,843	10,240	9,112	10,409	12,066	12,372	14,699	19,123	26,661	32,376	40,863	42,851
Others	185	487	1,891	3,905	11,991	13,556	12,241	12,409	14,415	14,348	21,578	24,922	35,157	39,511	43,829	41,031
Total imports	4,491	8,169	18,881	57,863	140,528	143,290	131,931	126,393	136,503	129,539	126,408	149,515	187,354	210,847	234,799	236,737

Net exports	1960	1965	1970	1975	1980	1981	1982	1983	1984	1985	1986	1987	1988	1989	1990	1991
Foodstuff	-292	-1,126	-1,926	-8,055	-13,078	-14,174	-13,174	-13,507	-14,587	-14,231	-17,710	-20,849	-27,425	-29,325	-29,926	-32,651
Crude materials and fuels	-2,839	-4,690	-10,313	-36,672	-92,481	-91,328	-83,490	-76,036	-78,618	-72,578	-53,025	-59,473	-64,612	-71,534	-82,667	-79,333
Textile products	1,204	1,525	2,094	2,409	3,116	3,744	2,806	3,626	2,878	2,377	1,847	-707	-3,723	-6,421	-5,609	-5,717
Chemical products	-84	139	234	1,832	565	354	-459	-224	-720	-375	-249	-183	-866	-1,172	-173	63
Iron and steel products	300	1,149	2,568	9,987	14,560	15,602	14,429	11,494	11,940	12,087	10,944	10,126	10,696	9,721	7,925	8,109
Machinery and equipment	600	2,215	6,643	25,718	71,638	89,923	81,402	89,151	107,743	113,807	140,328	151,954	170,304	173,095	174,234	193,790
Others	675	1,071	1,137	2,671	4,959	4,619	5,386	6,030	4,975	5,012	608	-1,162	-6,811	-10,036	-11,635	-6,473
Total net exports	-436	283	437	-2,110	-10,721	8,740	6,900	20,534	33,611	46,099	82,743	79,706	77,563	64,328	52,149	77,788

Source: Bank of Japan Economic Statistics Annual various issues.

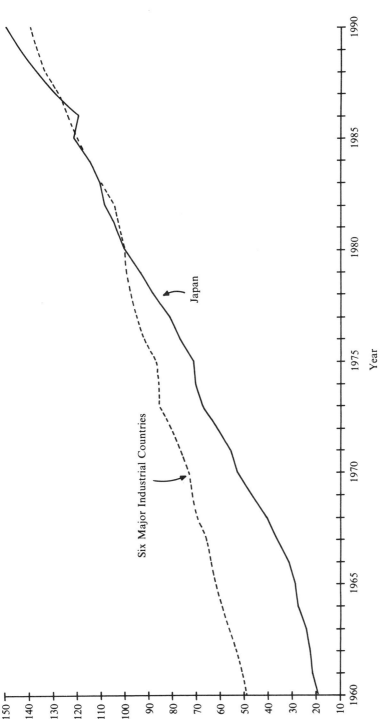

Fig. 5.3. Manufacturing productivity of Japan and six major industrial countries (1980 = 100). *Note*: The index of manufacturing productivity for six major industrial countries is constructed as the geometric weighted average of the indices for the U.S., Germany, France, the U.K., Italy, and Canada. The weight used is the share of GNP in 1980. *Source*: Data for 1960–80, Department of Labor, U.S. Government, *Handbook of Labor Statistics*, August 1990. Data for 1980–90, Department of Labor, U.S. Government, *Monthly Labor Review*, January 1993.

Figure 5.3 depicts labor productivity in the manufacturing sector for Japan and an aggregate of six major industrial countries: the United States, Germany, France, the United Kingdom, Italy, and Canada.[6] Between 1960 and 1990, Japanese labor productivity rose almost 700%, while a weighted average of six major industrial countries' labor productivities increased only less than 200%. Even before entering the 1980s Japan had established highly competitive industrial capacity with rapidly rising labor productivity, and it was ready to export key manufacturing products whenever and wherever foreign demand rose. (Foreign demand indeed rose in the United States during the first half of the 1980s.) Although the high rate of growth of Japanese labor productivity and the consequent improvement of its international competitiveness was not the direct cause of large merchandise trade surpluses in the 1980s, it was definitely a fundamental, underlying factor. Without it, Japan would not have experienced such explosive net export behavior in key manufactured products.

To identify the major determinants of Japan's net exports, a simple OLS regression has been run.[7] The explanatory variables are the real effective exchange rate, relative levels of real domestic demand in six major industrialized countries and Japan, a time trend, and the lagged dependent variable. The following is the result, using quarterly data from 1975.I through 1990.III, with standard errors in parentheses:

$$\frac{X}{Y} = 6.76 - 2.25 \log E + 26.68 \log \frac{D}{D^*} + 0.114 TIME + 0.64 \left(\frac{X}{Y}\right)_{-1}$$

$$(3.67)\ (0.90)\qquad (6.87)\qquad\quad (0.028)\qquad\quad (0.11)$$

$$\bar{R}^2 = 0.92,\ \text{Standard error} = 0.693,\ DW = 2.15$$

Here, $\frac{X}{Y}$ is nominal Japanese exports in the national income accounts as a percentage of nominal GNP, E is a distributed lag of the IMF's relative normalized unit labor costs, and $\frac{D^*}{D}$ is a distributed lag of relative real domestic demand between six major industrialized countries (U.S., Germany,

---

[6] The aggregate labor productivity index for the six industrialized countries is constructed as the geometric weighted average of labor productivities of the United States (0.4958), Germany (0.1502), France (0.1227) the United Kingdom (0.0992), Italy (0.0835), and Canada (0.0486). Numbers in parentheses are the nominal GNP share of the respective countries in 1980. In what follows, these six countries are assumed to represent the rest of the industrial world and the same weights are used to construct other aggregate variables for these countries.

[7] See Corker (1989) for econometric analyses of Japan's export and import behavior in disaggregated levels.

France, U.K., Italy, and Canada) and Japan.[8] The number of distributed lags chosen is two for both E and $\dfrac{D^*}{D}$; the choice is made on the basis of the explanatory power of the regression, such as $\bar{R}^2$.[9]

The regression shows that the real exchange rate and relative real demand are significant determinants of net exports. A 44% real depreciation of the yen or a 4% rise in the level of real foreign demand relative to Japan's real demand increases Japan's net exports by 1 percentage point of GNP in the short run. In the long run a 13% real depreciation or a slightly more than 1% rise in relative real foreign demand would increase net exports by 1 percentage point of GNP. The upward time trend indicates that net exports rise by 1% of GNP in every nine quarters. Thus, relative real domestic demand is quantitatively the most important variable affecting Japan's net exports/GNP ratio.

The regression equation allows a simple, partial-equilibrium simulation exercise to highlight the important impact the high growth of U.S. real domestic demand may have had on Japanese net exports. The exercise is to simulate dynamically Japan's net exports/GNP ratio on the counter-factual assumption that U.S. real domestic demand grew at a rate identical to other industrialized countries (including Japan) between 1983.I and 1985.IV and that all other variables took on historically observed values.[10] It is easy to find that Japan's net exports/GNP ratio would have been smaller by more than 3 percentage points after 1983.I if U.S. real domestic demand had grown at a rate comparable to its trading partners in the

---

[8] Here D^* is constructed as the geometric weighted average of the real domestic demand indices for the United States and Europe-Canada, with the respective weights being 0.4958 and 0.5042. The real domestic demand index for Europe-Canada is in turn constructed as the geometric weighted average of the real domestic demand indices for Germany (0.2978), France (0.2433), U.K. (0.1968), Italy (0.1657), and Canada (0.0963).

[9] The distributed lags for $\log E$ and $\log\dfrac{D^*}{D}$ are, respectively, given by

$$-1.87\log E - 0.32\log(E)_{-1} - 0.06\log(E)_{-2}$$
$$\quad(2.28)\qquad\;(3.61)\qquad\qquad(2.44)$$
and
$$-88.46\log\frac{D^*}{D} + 80.46\log\left(\frac{D^*}{D}\right)_{-1} - 18.68\log\left(\frac{D^*}{D}\right)_{-2}$$

where numbers in parentheses are the estimated standard errors.

[10] More precisely, the counterfactual growth rates of U.S. real domestic demand are assumed to be the same as those of the geometric weighted average of real domestic demand for Japan (with the weight of 0.2794) and Europe-Canada (with the weight of 0.7206) during the 1983.I–1985.IV period and return to its own historically observed growth rates thereafter, with the level of real domestic demand for 1986.I permanently lower.

1983.I–85.IV period.[11] The implied quantitative impact of U.S. economic growth on Japanese net exports/GNP ratio is large because (1) the ups and downs of the U.S. economy strongly affect Japan's external demand and (2) the rapid growth of the U.S. economy during 1983.I–85.IV maintained U.S. real domestic demand at substantially higher levels even after 1985.IV. This simulation exercise clearly demonstrates the importance of relative real domestic demand in determining Japan's net exports.

Capital account

As has been summarized in Table 5.1, Japan's capital account recorded large deficits (net outflows) throughout the 1980s. This led to the accumulation of net claims against the rest of the world.

The long-term net capital outflow moved in a parallel fashion with the current account surplus. This is demonstrated clearly in Fig. 5.4, which depicts the movements of current account surpluses and long-term and short-term (private) net capital outflows expressed as a percentage of GNP. The rise and fall in the current account has been accompanied by a rise and fall in long-term net capital outflows throughout the 1970s and 1980s. The current account movement had also been accompanied by a rise and fall in short-term net capital outflows until the early 1980s, but they started to exhibit divergent movements from the historical pattern thereafter.

This fluctuation in long-term net capital outflows was associated with a remarkable expansion and contraction in the net outflows of securities investment (Table 5.1). The share of net securities investment outflows in total long-term net capital outflows, which was only 11% in 1983, rose rapidly over the next 3 years, reaching a peak of 77% in 1986, and then started to decline. The share continued to decline to 12% in 1990 and became negative in 1991. During the latter half of the 1980s the net outflow of direct investment grew steadily from a mere 9% of the total long-term net capital outflow in 1985 to 106% in 1990. Although the long-term capital account turned into surplus (net inflow) in 1991, the net outflow of direct investment remained positive and large. Other components of long-term capital flows, such as loans and trade credits, were less important in magnitude than securities and direct investment at least in the second

---

[11] Since this exercise is partial equilibrium in that all other variables (including the exchange rate) are assumed unaffected by slower growth of the U.S. economy, it is likely to understate the important role U.S. real domestic demand may have played in determining Japan's net exports. Given that the real value of the yen tends to depreciate less (or even appreciate) with slower growth of the U.S. economy, Japan's net exports would probably be smaller than simulated here if the response of the yen value were appropriately taken into account.

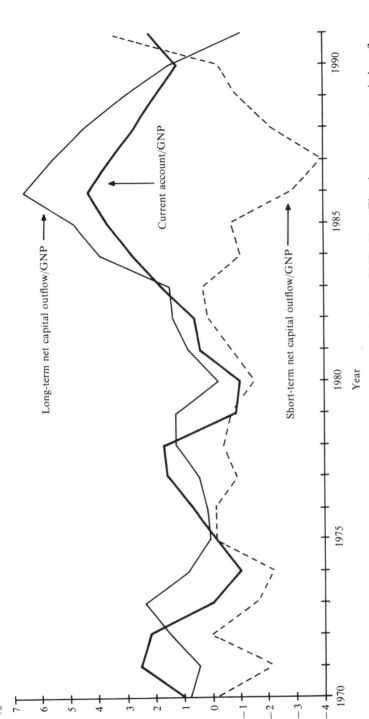

Fig. 5.4. Current account, long-term and short-term net capital outflow (relative to GNP). *Note:* The short-term net capital outflow excludes official transactions. *Sources:* Bank of Japan, *Balance of Payments Monthly*, various issues; IMF, *International Financial Statistics*, in tape.

half of the 1980s and the beginning of the 1990s. Thus, securities investment was clearly the principal vehicle through which Japan accumulated net external assets between 1984 and 1988, while direct investment has recently assumed this role.

Private short-term net capital outflows started to move in the opposite direction to that of long-term net capital outflows in 1984. When Japan's long-term net capital outflows expanded rapidly between 1984 and 1986, private short-term net capital inflows also expanded quickly. As long-term net capital outflows started to decline rapidly after 1987, short-term net capital inflows also started to shrink. Essentially, Japan played the role of international financial intermediary by borrowing short and lending long until 1989. During this period Japan's long-term net capital outflows were financed not only by current account surpluses (domestic excess saving over investment) but also by short-term net capital inflows. However, such an international financial intermediary role disappeared suddenly in 1990 and 1991.

The official sector at times generated net capital outflows in the 1980s. As has already been mentioned, when strong downward pressure on the value of the U.S. dollar came to bear in 1986–87, the Bank of Japan intervened heavily to support the value of the U.S. dollar and added to its foreign-exchange reserves, thus generating large net outflows of official short-term capital. In 1988 when long-awaited improvements in the U.S. current account finally occurred and the confidence in the dollar was restored, autonomous private capital flows increased and net official dollar purchases dropped.

Detailed information about the composition of long-term capital transactions is given in Table 5.7. The rise and fall in net outflows of long-term capital in the 1980s and the early 1990s was principally the result of a big surge and decline in net outflows of securities investment. The rapid rise and the high level of securities investment abroad until 1989 was through bonds; Japanese investment in stocks and shares abroad was relatively small throughout the 1980s.[12] When the net outflow of long-term capital declined in 1990 and switched to a net inflow in 1991, all types of long-term capital, with the exception of direct investment, registered net inflows.

Table 5.8 provides information about the composition and geographical

---

[12] One reason for the large volume of investment in bonds and the small volume of investment in stocks and shares is that bonds are a more standardized and less information-specific financial asset and, hence, more easily managed than stocks and shares. Management of foreign stocks and shares, on the other hand, requires highly specialized knowledge, experience, and information, which Japanese investors have yet to acquire to become global fund managers.

Table 5.7. *Japan's long-term capital transactions*

(U.S. $ million)

	1970	1975	1980	1981	1982	1983	1984	1985	1986	1987	1988	1989	1990	1991
Japanese capital	-2,031	-3,392	-10,817	-22,809	-27,418	-32,459	-56,775	-81,815	-132,095	-132,830	-149,883	-192,118	-120,766	-121,446
Direct investment	-355	-1,763	-2,385	-4,894	-4,540	-3,612	-5,965	-6,452	-14,480	-19,519	-34,210	-44,130	-48,024	-30,726
Securities investment	-62	-24	-3,753	-8,777	-9,743	-16,024	-30,795	-59,773	-101,977	-87,757	-86,949	-113,178	-39,681	-74,306
Stocks and shares	n.a.	7	213	-240	-151	-661	-51	-995	-7,048	-16,874	-2,993	-17,887	-6,256	-3,630
Bonds	n.a.	41	-2,996	-5,810	-6,076	-12,505	-26,773	-53,479	-93,024	-72,885	-85,812	-94,083	-28,961	-68,202
Yen-denominated external bonds	n.a.	-72	-970	-2,727	-3,516	-2,858	-3,971	-5,299	-1,905	2,002	1,856	-1,208	-4,464	-2,474
Export credits	-787	-29	-717	-2,731	-3,239	-2,589	-4,937	-2,817	-1,836	-535	-6,939	-4,002	681	3,928
Loans extended	-628	-1,295	-2,553	-5,083	-7,902	-8,425	-11,922	-10,427	-9,281	-16,190	-15,211	-22,495	-22,182	-13,097
Others	-199	-281	-1,409	-1,324	-1,994	-1,809	-3,156	-2,346	-4,521	-8,829	-6,574	-8,313	-11,560	-7,245
Foreign capital	440	3,120	13,141	13,137	12,449	14,759	7,124	17,273	634	-3,702	18,953	102,872	77,180	158,503
Direct investment	94	226	278	189	439	416	-10	642	226	1,165	-485	-1,054	1,753	1,368
Securities investment	296	2,753	13,113	13,220	11,860	14,148	7,194	16,741	545	-6,081	20,298	85,144	34,653	115,284
Stocks and shares	n.a.	596	6,546	5,916	2,549	6,126	-3,610	-673	-15,758	-42,835	6,810	6,998	-13,276	46,779
Bonds	n.a.	922	5,331	5,936	5,030	2,359	3,454	4,524	-2,109	6,675	21,628	2,400	16,991	21,241
External bonds	n.a.	1,235	1,236	1,368	4,281	5,663	7,350	12,890	18,412	30,079	35,116	75,746	30,938	47,264
Import credits	7	-26	-16	-15	-6	8	3	29	-40	-1	-18	-9	-10	-2
Loans received	80	166	-231	-186	-181	-37	-77	-75	-34	-119	-82	17,813	39,112	38,124
Others	-37	1	-3	-71	337	224	14	-64	-63	1,334	-760	978	1,672	3,729
Long-term capital account	-1,591	-272	2,324	-9,672	-14,969	-17,700	-49,651	-64,542	-131,461	-136,532	-130,930	-89,246	-43,586	37,057
Direct investment, net	-261	-1,537	-2,107	-4,705	-4,101	-3,196	-5,975	-5,810	-14,254	-18,354	-34,695	-45,184	-46,271	-29,358
Securities investment, net	234	2,729	9,360	4,443	2,117	-1,876	-23,601	-43,032	-101,432	-93,838	-66,651	-28,034	-5,028	40,978
Stocks and shares, net	n.a.	603	6,759	5,676	2,398	5,465	-3,661	-1,668	-22,806	-59,709	3,817	-10,889	-19,532	43,149
Bonds, net	n.a.	963	2,335	126	-1,046	-10,146	-23,319	-48,955	-95,133	-66,210	-107,440	-91,683	-11,970	-46,961
External bonds, net	n.a.	1,163	266	-1,359	765	2,805	3,379	7,591	16,507	32,081	36,972	74,538	26,474	44,790
Trade credits, net	-780	-55	-733	-2,746	-3,245	-2,581	-4,934	-2,788	-1,876	-536	-6,957	-4,011	671	3,926
Loans, net	-548	-1,129	-2,784	-5,269	-8,083	-8,462	-11,999	-10,502	-9,315	-16,309	-15,293	-4,682	16,930	25,027
Others, net	-236	-280	-1,412	-1,395	-1,657	-1,585	-3,142	-2,410	-4,584	-7,495	-7,334	-7,335	-9,888	-3,516
Reference: current account	1,970	-682	-10,746	4,770	6,850	20,799	35,003	49,169	85,845	87,015	79,631	57,157	35,761	72,901

Source: Bank of Japan, *Balance of Payments Monthly*, various issues.

Table 5.8. *Composition and geographical distribution of Japan's long-term net capital outflows*

(U.S. $ million)

		Direct investments	Securities investments	Trade credits	Loans	Others	Total	(Reference) Current account
United States	1970	20	50	26	−43	165	218	587
	1975	545	−439	11	−45	−35	37	−935
	1980	729	−3,001	−15	409	224	−1,654	6,251
	1985	2,043	29,874	587	716	−57	33,163	41,727
	1986	7,774	55,944	334	690	908	65,650	53,782
	1987	9,018	48,223	489	1,663	1,637	61,030	56,678
	1988	19,568	33,320	1,024	2,830	2,518	59,260	51,320
	1989	22,768	22,074	1,255	4,761	3,003	53,861	47,483
	1990	24,986	−19,849	633	2,783	3,166	11,719	37,653
	1991	15,302	−1,045	−314	2,569	1,846	18,358	40,025
EC Countries	1970	42	−237	87	−101	0	−209	−369
	1975	81	−1,217	−59	−150	39	−1,306	500
	1980	195	−4,559	−8	46	106	−4,220	4,959
	1985	1,480	6,639	482	835	192	9,628	7,993
	1986	2,694	29,013	1,087	1,038	554	34,386	14,828
	1987	3,476	26,434	1,066	2,091	1,260	34,327	17,712
	1988	5,693	21,229	4,507	1,768	917	34,114	19,756
	1989	9,419	−24,562	1,625	−1,431	1,713	−13,236	9,875
	1990	9,921	9,409	494	582	1,812	22,218	6,163
	1991	7,344	−45,273	−843	−1,876	1,441	−39,207	25,222

Other OECD Countries							
1970	38	−33	46	81	0	132	−392
1975	10	−430	−53	18	41	−414	−1,587
1980	245	1,719	74	180	7	2,225	−3,117
1985	317	1,705	793	2,163	11	4,989	1,347
1986	635	6,275	108	2,281	145	9,444	3,183
1987	1,705	5,363	−274	3,619	513	10,926	2,060
1988	2,988	−66	1,818	301	1,090	6,131	−948
1989	4,482	5,242	1,828	2,034	1,269	14,855	−1,702
1990	4,084	2,323	778	2,348	1,520	11,053	−2,520
1991	1,712	2,467	−23	195	871	5,222	−2,062
Communist Bloc							
1970	0	0	32	0	0	32	322
1975	0	0	209	208	0	417	2,160
1980	3	1	206	321	0	531	3,477
1985	57	−240	−521	1,086	2	384	9,474
1986	96	−97	−764	783	72	90	7,399
1987	183	−36	−77	−389	264	−55	3,066
1988	604	364	234	1,154	135	2,491	1,732
1989	713	677	616	1,811	211	4,028	−1,110
1990	416	−521	−330	1,743	549	1,857	−5,870
1991	373	574	−271	742	314	1,732	−5,826
Other Countries							
1970	161	−31	589	364	5	1,088	1,555
1975	901	−428	−53	1,051	1	1,472	−884
1980	935	−3,717	476	1,816	47	−443	−21,958
1985	1,913	3,576	1,447	4,825	624	12,385	−12,348
1986	3,055	6,489	1,111	5,151	425	16,231	5,559
1987	3,972	8,855	−668	7,304	544	20,007	5,765
1988	5,842	4,909	−741	8,125	752	18,887	6,509
1989	7,802	10,992	−1,363	−3,406	1,573	15,598	954
1990	6,864	247	−2,246	−24,738	2,894	−16,979	487
1991	4,627	−10,436	−2,475	−26,389	1,392	−33,281	22,163

(continued)

97

Table 5.8. (*Cont.*)

		Direct investments	Securities investments	Trade credits	Loans	Others	Total	(Reference) Current account
International Institutions	1970	0	17	0	247	66	330	−11
	1975	0	−215	0	47	234	66	−18
	1980	0	127	0	12	1,028	1,167	−241
	1985	0	2,246	0	877	883	4,006	922
	1986	0	1,501	0	669	1,176	3,346	1,167
	1987	0	28	0	2,021	1,828	3,877	1,606
	1988	0	2,080	115	1,115	2,054	5,364	1,262
	1989	0	3,469	50	913	1,420	5,852	1,657
	1990	0	2,091	0	352	1,528	3,971	−152
	1991	0	1,363	0	−268	1,176	2,271	−6,621
World Total	1970	261	−234	780	548	236	1,591	1,970
	1975	1,537	−2,729	55	1,129	280	272	−682
	1980	2,107	−9,360	733	2,784	1,412	−2,324	−10,746
	1985	5,810	43,032	2,788	10,502	2,410	64,542	49,169
	1986	14,254	101,432	1,876	9,315	4,584	131,461	85,845
	1987	18,354	93,838	536	16,309	7,495	136,532	87,015
	1988	34,695	66,651	6,957	15,293	7,334	130,930	79,631
	1989	45,184	28,034	4,011	4,682	7,335	89,246	57,157
	1990	46,271	5,028	−671	−16,930	9,888	43,586	35,761
	1991	29,358	−40,978	−3,926	−25,027	3,516	−37,057	72,901

Note: (a) Minus shows net capital inflow into Japan, (b) EC countries include the United Kingdom from 1970, (c) other OECD countries include South Africa in 1970, 1975, and 1980.

Source: Bank of Japan, *Balance of Payments Monthly*, April issues.

distribution of Japan's long-term net capital outflows. Since 1985 net outflow of securities and direct investments has largely been channeled toward the United States and the European Community (EC) countries. Loans have gone primarily to the developing countries ("Other countries" in the table), though they recorded net inflows in recent years. The importance of securities investment in the developed countries has clearly been due to the favorable investment environment – low country risk and a deep capital market in terms of size, instruments, maturity, and liquidity. It is postulated that much of Japan's wealth has been placed in securities and direct investments and in markets where expected yields were high and perceived risks low. However, securities investment outflows stopped rising in 1987 and started to decline fast in subsequent years. The net outflow to the United States became negative in 1990 and 1991. Since 1989 when securities investment outflows declined significantly, direct investment has emerged as the most dominant form of transferring Japanese long-term capital abroad. Direct investment outflows rose persistently in almost all regions until 1990, though they declined somewhat in 1991. The United States, the EC countries, and other countries (particularly Asian countries) are the principal recipients of Japan's direct investments.

Saving and investment balances

That Japan experienced continuous current account surpluses and accumulated large net external assets in the 1980s means that its residents consumed less than what they produced and saved more than what they invested. The excess of saving over investment was transferred abroad in the form of claims against the rest of the world. To fully understand the underlying causes of the rapid expansion of Japan's NEAP, therefore, its saving and investment behavior must be examined.

Figure 5.5 depicts Japan's net saving and net investment as a ratio of GNP. The figure shows that both the saving rate (net saving/GNP ratio) and the investment rate (net investment/GNP ratio) declined over time as a trend, while maintaining a fairly close relationship with each other. The two rates averaged about 22.5% in the 1960s and the first half of the 1970s and declined to the 17% (for the investment rate) and 18% (for the saving rate) range afterward. They moved very closely with each other until the beginning of the 1980s when the relationship became loose. For example, the correlation coefficient between the two rates was 0.90 in the 1970–80 period and declined to 0.50 in the 1980–91 period. The loose relationship between saving and investment in the 1980s is observed because of the increased liberalization of international capital transactions, which will be explained in the next section. Liberalization of capital move-

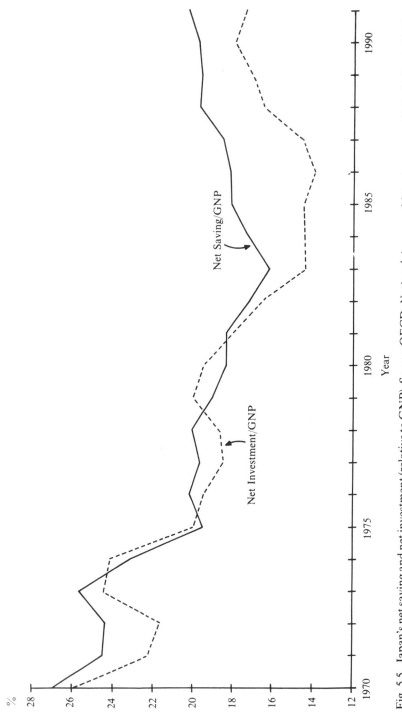

Fig. 5.5. Japan's net saving and net investment (relative to GNP). *Source:* OECD, *National Accounts, Main Aggregates 1960–91* (Paris 1993).

ments made domestic investment less constrained by domestic saving.[13] When the saving rate declined in the late 1970s and the beginning of the 1980s, the investment rate declined faster. When the saving rate started to rise in 1984, the investment rate remained stagnant. The excess saving was transferred abroad mainly in the form of private long-term net capital outflows, such as securities investment and direct investment.

Figure 5.6 breaks down Japan's saving-investment balance by economic sectors as a percentage of GNP. The economic sectors considered here are the household sector (including unincorporated enterprises), the business corporate sector, and the government sector (including the central and local governments as well as the social security account). The negative of the foreign sector equals Japan's current account. It is observed that the household sector maintained a consistently high saving-investment balance without large fluctuations and that the corporate business sector maintained a negative balance while fluctuating over time. The government sector has a close to zero saving-investment balance (i.e., a balanced budget) in the first half of the 1970s but started to experience a negative balance in the mid-1970s as a result of mounting budget deficits. It changed its fiscal stance to reconsolidation in the late 1970s, gradually improved its saving-investment balance in the 1980s, and even reversed the balance from negative to positive in the latter half of the 1980s. The current account moved in parallel with the government's saving-investment balance in the beginning to mid-1980s. Japan's rising current account surpluses in this period were accompanied by improving fiscal balances of the government. The decline in current account surpluses after 1987 was accompanied by a decline in the business corporate sector's saving-investment balance even though the government's balance continued to improve. In other words, active private investment behavior was largely responsible for a reduction in current account surpluses in the late 1980s.

It must be pointed out that, in the United States, the government sector's saving-investment balance worsened rapidly in the first half of the 1980s, and large negative balances persisted throughout the rest of the 1980s. This was noteworthy particularly after 1983; even though the U.S. economy entered the longest expansion in peace time and the private sector increased its spending and reduced saving-investment balance, the budget deficit did not decline, a departure from historical patterns.

Essentially, the United States and Japan adopted fiscal policies that were radically divergent to each other in the 1980s; the United States ran an expansionary fiscal policy by increasing budget deficits, and Japan ran a contractionary fiscal policy by reducing budget deficits. From the view

---

[13] This is the well-known Feldstein-Horioka (1980) effect.

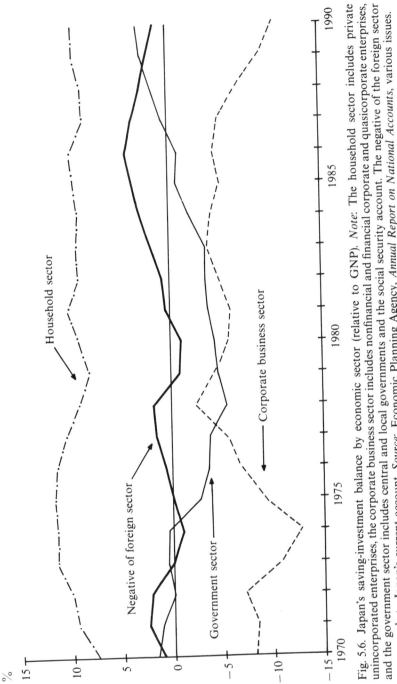

Fig. 5.6. Japan's saving-investment balance by economic sector (relative to GNP). *Note:* The household sector includes private unincorporated enterprises, the corporate business sector includes nonfinancial and financial corporate and quasicorporate enterprises, and the government sector includes central and local governments and the social security account. The negative of the foreign sector corresponds to Japan's current account. *Source:* Economic Planning Agency, *Annual Report on National Accounts*, various issues.

of saving-investment balances, Japan's large current account surplus was attributable to the contrasting fiscal policies between the two countries. Although the high saving-investment balance of the household sector was not the direct cause of the rise in Japan's current account surpluses, it was one of the long-term, structural factors behind it. The household balance, though it slightly declined from the average of 10% in the 1970s to 9% in the 1980s, was high and stable over time. Unlike in the United States, it did not decline even when the economy continued to grow. Without the high saving of the household sector, Japan would not have experienced large saving-investment balances in the 1980s.

Determinants of long-term net capital outflows

Capital account deficits in the 1980s were brought about primarily through private long-term capital outflows. Of private long-term net outflows, securities investment was the most important in 1984–88, and direct investment became of greater importance thereafter.

Figure 5.7 depicts the net outflows of securities investment, direct investment, and loans as a percentage of GNP for the period between 1980.I and 1991.I. Total long-term net capital outflows (the sum of the three components shown in the figure plus trade credits) exhibit a rapid surge until the latter half of 1986 and an equally rapid decline thereafter. Movements of total long-term net capital outflows were clearly the result of the movements of securities investment net outflows. Net outflows of direct investment grew steadily as a trend throughout the 1980s, though they declined slightly in the early 1990s. Net outflows of loans were steady with a declining trend toward the end of the 1980s and the beginning of the 1990s. Net outflows of trade credits (not shown in the figure) were close to zero throughout the period. This section attempts to explain the major determinants of each of these long-term net capital outflows. Our emphasis, however, will be placed on net outflows of securities and direct investments, which were the major components of long-term capital transactions.

Securities investment

It is generally pointed out that the following two factors contributed to the surge of securities investments: (a) Japan's liberalization of capital controls in the 1980s and (b) the high real interest rate abroad (particularly in the United States) relative to Japan [see Fujii and Ueda (1986) and Kawai (1991)]. This paper suggests that a distinction be made between long-term and short-term real interest rates for a proper discussion, and

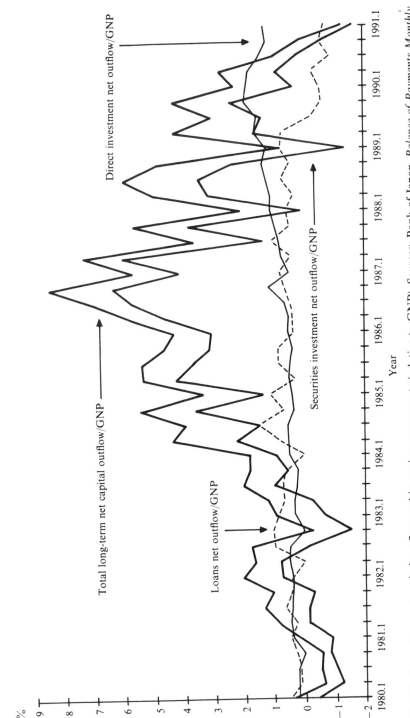

Fig. 5.7. Long-term net capital outflow and its major components (relative to GNP). *Sources*: Bank of Japan, *Balance of Payments Monthly*, various issues; IMF, *International Financial Statistics*, in tape.

that a third factor be added to the list: (c) Japan's rising stock and share prices in the 1980s.

First, there is no doubt that the rapid rise of securities investments abroad was made possible by a series of measures to liberalize government regulation on international capital transactions. Throughout the post–World War II period, the Japanese authorities had maintained tight capital controls to insulate the domestic economy from foreign financial disturbances, thus limiting Japanese investors' ability to diversify their portfolios globally. With slower economic growth and a lower rate of return on domestic investment after the first oil-price shock, Japanese investors began to seek ways to broaden their investment opportunities abroad. As the current account improved and the yen exchange rate rapidly appreciated in the latter half of the 1970s, confidence in the yen rose and pressure for relaxing capital controls mounted. At the same time domestic financial liberalization, a prerequisite for liberalization of international capital restrictions, was progressively under way.

In December 1980, the Ministry of Finance drastically revised the Foreign Exchange and Foreign Trade Control laws to liberalize, in principle, all foreign-exchange and capital transactions. This revision was designed to ensure freer mobility of capital into and out of Japan. Nonetheless, an elaborate system for monitoring capital transactions was retained and regulatory restrictions on foreign-securities investment were still in place, thereby hindering complete integration of the Japanese financial and capital markets with the rest of the world. On the basis of the Yen/Dollar Agreement of May 1984, the Ministry of Finance further implemented additional measures to liberalize international capital transactions and internationalize the Japanese financial system.[14] When the existing restrictions imposed on foreign-securities holdings, such as ceiling limits on the amount of foreign securities held by life and nonlife insurance companies, pension trusts of trust banks, etc., became binding, they were relaxed incrementally. By the latter half of the 1980s, the Japanese financial and capital markets were virtually integrated into world markets. See

---

[14] The United States, while running large trade deficits against Japan, claimed that the deficits were caused primarily by yen rate undervaluation and that the yen was undervalued because Japan's financial and capital markets were closed, thereby limiting capital inflows into Japan. The U.S. Treasury Department and Japan's Ministry of Finance established the so-called Yen/Dollar Committee in November 1983 as a result of the U.S. desire to stimulate capital inflows into Japan and, thus, cause yen appreciation. The committee investigated ways and means to accelerate the liberalization of Japan's financial markets and the internationalization of the yen and reached the May 1984 agreement. The Yen/Dollar Agreement was successful at stimulating net capital outflows and, thus, increasing Japan's integration into world financial and capital markets, but not necessarily at stimulating capital inflows to Japan, at least in the 1980s [see also Frankel (1984, 1988)].

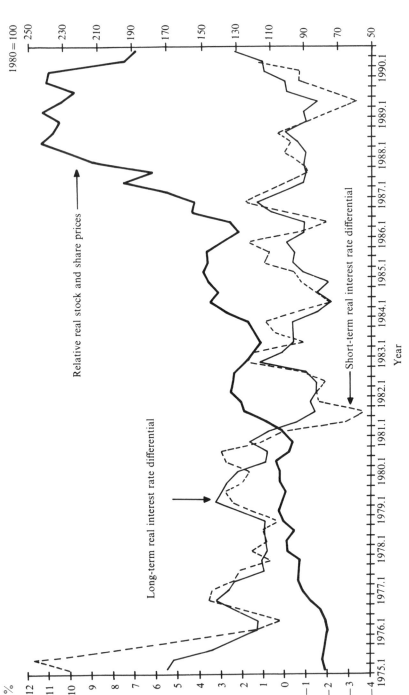

Fig. 5.8. Relative index of real stock and share prices, long-term and short-term real interest rate differentials between Japan and six major industrial countries. *Source*: Constructed from IMF, *International Financial Statistics*, in tape.

106

Table 5.9 for chronological changes in, and relaxation of, capital controls concerning securities investment abroad.[15]

As a result of these liberalization measures, Japanese investors have increasingly been able to pursue new opportunities for global portfolio diversification. They began accumulating foreign securities at a rapid pace to achieve desired stock holdings. This autonomous stock adjustment appears to have taken place over several years, perhaps during the 1983–88 period, which led to a massive buildup of foreign securities.

The second factor that is alleged to have contributed to large net outflows of securities investments is the high long-term real interest rate abroad relative to Japan. Considering the fact that Japan was engaged in large-scale international financial intermediation by borrowing short and lending long until 1989, it is postulated that what caused the big surge and decline in net outflows of securities investments was not only the long-term real interest rate differential between Japan and abroad but also the short-term real interest rate differential. Figure 5.8 plots the long-term and the short-term real interest rate differentials (as well as the relative real stock and share prices, which will be explained below) between Japan and six other industrialized countries.[16] In the first half of the 1980s,

---

[15] See Komiya and Suda (1991) and Fukao (1990) for more detailed explanations and discussions of changes in exchange and capital controls.

[16] The long-term and short-term real interest rate differentials are defined as follows:

$$LTR\text{-}LTR^* = \log\left(\frac{1+LTN}{1+LTN^*}\right) - E[INFD_{+4} + INFD_{+3} + INFD_{+2} + INFD_{+1}]$$

$$STR\text{-}STR^* = \log\left(\frac{1+STN}{1+STN^*}\right) - 4^*E[INFD_{+1}]$$

where LTN and LTN^* are long-term nominal interest rates in Japan and in six industrialized countries, respectively, STN and STN^* are the short-term nominal interest rates in Japan and in six industrialized countries, respectively, $E[\ ]$ is the mathematical expectation conditional on the information available at the time of expectation formation, and $INFD$ is the one-period inflation rate differential between Japan and six industrialized countries so that the terms in the square bracket in the first definition indicate the four-period ahead inflation rate. To construct the long-term and short-term real interest rate differentials, the investors' time horizons are assumed to be four quarters and one quarter, respectively. $1+LTN^*$ or $1+STN^*$ is constructed as the geometric weighted average of 1 plus the nominal interest rate of each of the six countries, the U.S., Germany, France, the U.K., Italy, and Canada. The weight is the same as the one used in footnote 6. Long-term and short-term nominal interest rates are taken from line 61 and line 60b of IMF, *International Financial Statistics*.

The one-period inflation rate differential, $INFD$, is given by

$$INFD = \log\frac{P}{P^*} - \log\left(\frac{P}{P^*}\right)_{-1}$$

where P is Japan's GNP deflator and P^* is the geometric weighted average of GNP

Table 5.9. *Chronological changes in exchange and capital controls and other major events*

Year	Month	Changes and events
1949	12	Foreign Exchange and Foreign Trade Control Law implemented; foreign-exchange transaction prohibited in principle and permitted only in special cases.
1952	8	Japan joined the IMF and accepted the obligation of maintaining 360 yen with plus or minus 1%.
1964	4	Japan moved to an IMF Article VIII status nation. Japan joined OECD.
1970	4	Beginning of the liberalization of foreign-securities investment; securities investment trusts permitted to include foreign securities in their portfolios with an upper limit of US $100 million (subject to prior approval by the MOF).
1971	1	Insurance companies permitted to include foreign securities in portfolios.
	8	Suspension of dollar conversion to gold by the U.S. government (the Nixon shock).
	12	Smithsonian currency realignment.
1972		Yen appreciation pressure prompted policy actions to encourage capital outflows and discourage capital inflows.
	2	Liberalization of the purchase of foreign securities by trust banks.
	3	Japanese banks permitted to buy foreign securities (subject to foreign exposure limit).
1973	10	First oil-price shock; yen depreciation prompted policies to encourage capital inflows and discourage capital outflows.
1977		Yen appreciation prompted policies to encourage capital outflows.
1978		Further yen appreciation prompted more restrictions of capital inflows.
	11	Dollar defense policy by the U.S. and joint intervention in the foreign-exchange market by the U.S., Japan, and Germany.
1979		Second oil-price shock; rapid yen depreciation prompted policies to encourage capital inflows.
1980	12	New Foreign Exchange Control Law enacted; all capital transactions permitted in principle unless explicitly prohibited, and exchange controls to be introduced only in cases of emergency.
1981	10	Postal Life Insurance allowed to purchase foreign securities (Postal Annuities only, limited to 10% of total assets).
1982	4	Introduction of controls on increases in foreign-currency assets of life insurance companies.
	5	Postal Life Insurance fully allowed to purchase foreign securities (limited to 10% of total assets).

1983	11	Yen/Dollar Committee established.
	11	Introduction of controls on increases in foreign-currency assets of pension trusts (until August 1986).
1984	4	Yen/Dollar Agreement.
	6	Overall limits of spot foreign-exchange positions on commercial banks abolished; banks are subject to limits on overall spot-forward positions.
1985	9	Plaza G5 Agreement.
1986	2	Loan trusts and jointly managed money trusts allowed to invest in foreign securities (limited to 1% of total assets).
	3	Relaxation of the upper limit on investment in foreign securities by life and nonlife insurance companies from 10% to 25% (the limit further relaxed to 30% in August 1986). Upper limits of other institutional investors relaxed subsequently.
	4	Relaxation of pension trust's upper limit on foreign currency investment from 10% to 25% of total assets.
	6	Relaxation of loan trusts' and jointly managed money trusts' upper limit on foreign bonds from 1% to 3% (the limit further relaxed to 5% in February 1989).
	10	Commercial banks allowed to invest in foreign securities without hedging; a portion of foreign securities held by banks for more than 1 year without forward cover may be excluded from the overall limit of foreign-exchange positions.
1987	2	Louvre G7 Accord. Japan's discount rate set at 2.5% (until May 1989).
	6	Trust Fund Bureau of the MOF allowed to invest in foreign securities through Postal Savings (limited to 10% of total assets).
	6	Relaxation of Postal Life Insurance's upper limit of foreign bonds from 10% to 20% of total assets.
	10	Worldwide stock price decline (Black Monday).
1990	1	Start of Japan's stock market collapse.

Source: Komiya and Suda (1991), Fukao (1990) and others.

particularly during the 1980–82 and 1983–84 periods, the real interest rate differentials moved generally in favor of six other countries, mainly due to the high real interest rate in the United States. The high U.S. real interest rate resulted from its tight monetary policy, expansionary fiscal policy and growing real domestic demand. It attracted capital from all over the world, and Japanese investors were just beginning to aggressively acquire large quantities of foreign securities in a more liberalized institutional framework. Besides the autonomous rise in the demand for foreign securities, which was prompted by the liberalization measures, the higher real interest rate abroad was the added inducement for further foreign-securities investments. Not only did the long-term real interest rate move in favor of the rest of the world, it also moved favorably against the short-term real interest rate differential. This stimulated Japanese investors to borrow short and lend long.

The third factor to be added here is the effect of Japanese stock and share prices. In the 1980s, the Japanese stock market witnessed one of the biggest booms in its history with an impressive 25% increase (per annum) in the Nikkei Stock Average between 1983 and 1989. It rose even at a higher pace of 29% (per annum) between 1986 and 1989: See Figure 5.8 for the relative index of Japan's real stock and share prices vis-à-vis the six major industrial countries.[17] We can observe a remarkable rise in Japan's relative real index of stock and share prices between 1986 and 1988.

A rise in Japanese stock and share prices tends to stimulate securities investments abroad for two reasons. First is the wealth effect. A rise in stock and share prices raises the value of Japanese investors' overall financial wealth, thereby stimulating demand for various types of financial assets, one of which is foreign securities. The second reason concerns the regulation imposed on the distribution of capital gains. With a continuous rise in stock and share prices, Japanese investors accumulated large capital

deflators of the six industrialized countries. To obtain the conditional mathematical expectation $E[\ ]$, the following AR3 equation for the inflation rate differential is estimated and used as relevant information:

$$INFD = -0.004 + 0.336INFD_{-1} + 0.325INFD_{-2} - 0.133INFD_{-3}$$
$$\quad\quad\quad (0.001)\ (0.131)\quad\quad (0.135)\quad\quad\quad (0.130)$$

$\bar{R}^2 = 0.25$, Standard error $= 0.006$, $DW = 2.02$

[17] The relative index of real stock and share prices is constructed by the following procedure: First, the stock and share prices of Japan and the six industrial countries are divided by their respective GNP deflators. Second, to obtain an aggregate index of real stock and share prices of the six countries, the geometric weighted average of real stock and share prices of the six countries is calculated using the weights described in footnote 6. Third, the ratio of Japan's index of real stock and share prices (SP) to that of the six countries (SP^*) is obtained. The data for stock and share prices are taken from line 62 of IMF, *International Financial Statistics*.

gains, realized or unrealized, in their portfolios. Several important institutional investors, however, were not allowed to distribute current and past capital gains to their clients. For example, article 86 of the Insurance Law prohibits life insurance companies from distributing capital gains to policy holders for prudential reasons; only income gains can be distributed. In the face of fierce competition among financial institutions, induced by the liberalization in the domestic financial system, life insurance companies tried to convert capital gains into income gains in order to offer attractive rates of return to their policy holders. The income gains obtained from holding foreign securities yielding high nominal interest rates, such as those denominated in U.S., Canadian, and Australian dollars, could be distributed to the policy holders, while possible capital losses due to foreign-currency depreciation could be offset by capital gains in the stock market. As long as stock and share prices rise and are expected to rise, Japan's securities investment outflows should increase. This, in turn, suggests that when the stock market starts performing badly, securities investment outflows should start declining.[18]

To find the major determinants of the net outflow of securities investment, a quarterly regression is run for the period 1980.I–1990III. The following is the summary of the result:

$$SEC = 32.43 - 55.82[(LTR\text{-}LTR^*) - (STR\text{-}STR^*)]$$
$$(24.98) \quad (29.32)$$

$$+ 7.42 \log \frac{SP}{SP^*} - 7.23 \log E, \quad \rho = 0.42,$$

$$(3.20) \qquad\qquad (5.5) \qquad\qquad (0.25)$$

$$\bar{R}^2 = 0.56, \text{ Standard error} = 1.138, \, DW = 2.25$$

Here, SEC is the net outflow of securities investment expressed as a percentage of GNP, $(LTR\text{-}LTR^*) - (STR\text{-}STR^*)$ is the long-term real interest rate differential between Japan and six industrialized countries relative to the short-term real interest rate differential, $\frac{SP}{SP^*}$ is the relative index of real stock and share prices between Japan and six industrialized countries, and E is a distributed lag of the real effective exchange rate of the yen. The variable $(LTR\text{-}LTR^*) - (STR\text{-}STR^*)$ essentially represents a measure of the term structure of the real interest rate differential. ρ is the first-order autoregressive coefficient of the residuals. Table 5.10 provides

---

[18] See Kawai (1991) for more detailed discussions.

Table 5.10. *The estimated results of long-term net capital outflow equations (sample period: 1980.I–1990.III)*

	Securities investment		Direct investment		Loans		Trade credits		Total long-term net capital outflow
	A	B	A	B	A	B	A	B	A
Constant	32.43 (24.98)	30.52 (26.30)	−5.83** (2.26)	−6.81** (3.01)	0.66** (0.18)	1.34 (4.20)	1.55** (0.44)	1.55 (1.10)	12.54 (23.72)
Time trend	-----	-----	0.023** (0.007)	0.024** (0.010)	-----	-----	-----	-----	-----
(LTR-LTR*)−(STR-STR*)	−55.82* (29.32)	−57.10* (29.83)	-----	-----	−20.19** (8.68)	−19.51** (9.34)	−9.31** (2.55)	−9.31** (3.38)	−72.51** (28.94)
Sum(LTR-LTR*)	-----	−12.76 (28.50)	-----	1.67 (4.24)	−8.14 (6.85)	−7.93 (6.95)	−7.83** (2.04)	−7.83** (2.08)	−29.71 (27.25)
LTR(0)-LTR*(0)	-----	−12.76 (28.50)	-----	1.67 (4.24)	-----	-----	3.10 (2.65)	3.10 (2.74)	-----
LTR(−1)-LTR*(−1)	-----	-----	-----	-----	−12.04 (7.41)	−11.58 (7.95)	−3.90 (2.62)	−3.90 (2.70)	-----
LTR(−2)-LTR*(−2)	-----	-----	-----	-----	-----	-----	−4.61* (2.65)	−4.61* (2.70)	-----
LTR(−3)-LTR*(−3)	-----	-----	-----	-----	-----	-----	−4.61* (2.65)	−4.61* (2.75)	-----
LTR(−4)-LTR*(−4)	-----	-----	-----	-----	-----	-----	3.93** (1.95)	3.93* (2.13)	-----
Sum[log(SP/SP*)]	7.42** (3.20)	7.26** (3.34)	-----	−0.23 (0.56)	−0.62* (0.36)	−0.56 (0.53)	−0.00 (0.16)	−0.00 (0.16)	6.08** (2.98)

$\log[SP(0)/SP^{*}(0)]$	7.42** (3.20)	7.26** (3.34)	-----	-0.23 (0.56)	-1.20 (0.75)	-1.13 (0.89)	-----	-0.00 (0.16)	6.08** (2.98)
$\log[SP(-1)/SP^{*}(-1)]$	-----	-----	-----	-----	1.84** (0.85)	1.84** (0.85)	-----	-----	-----
$\log[SP(-2)/SP^{*}(-2)]$	-----	-----	-----	-----	-1.26* (0.76)	-1.26 (0.77)	-----	-----	-----
$\mathrm{Sum}[\log(E)]$	-7.23 (5.53)	-6.82 (5.82)	1.28** (0.50)	1.50** (0.67)	-0.15 (0.92)	-0.15 (0.92)	-0.29** (0.09)	-0.29 (0.24)	-2.57 (5.24)
$\log[E(0)]$	1.54 (6.13)	1.60 (6.20)	-1.52* (0.79)	-1.59* (0.82)	-0.15 (0.92)	-0.15 (0.92)	-0.76** (0.36)	-0.76** (0.37)	-0.34 (5.76)
$\log[E(-1)]$	0.12 (8.07)	0.13 (8.09)	1.83** (1.01)	1.84* (1.08)	-----	-----	0.47 (0.36)	0.47 (0.44)	3.99 (7.67)
$\log[E(-2)]$	19.10** (7.63)	18.91** (7.65)	-0.18 (1.01)	-0.11 (1.07)	-----	-----	-----	-----	18.32** (7.32)
$\log[E(-3)]$	-17.87** (7.91)	-17.47** (8.04)	-0.12 (1.02)	-0.05 (1.15)	-----	-----	-----	-----	-24.54 (6.67)
$\log[E(-4)]$	-10.12 (6.27)	-9.98 (6.35)	1.27 (0.81)	1.41* (0.85)	-----	-----	-----	-----	-----
Rho	0.42** (0.15)	0.45** (0.14)	0.39** (0.15)	0.32** (0.15)	0.51** (0.13)	0.52** (0.13)	-----	-----	0.48** (0.14)
R-square adjusted	0.564	0.552	0.874	0.867	0.509	0.495	0.573	0.559	0.623
Standard error	1.385	1.404	0.180	0.185	0.329	0.333	0.093	0.094	1.368
DW	2.25	2.26	2.07	2.05	2.10	2.11	1.73	1.73	2.56

Note: (1) Column A is the result for the best equation, and B is the result when all relevant variables are included on the right-hand side of the equation as explanatory variables. (2) Numbers in parentheses are the estimated standard errors of the coefficients. (3) A single asterisk (*) and two asterisks (**) indicate that the estimates are statistically significant at the 5% and 2.5% levels, respectively.

more detailed and additional information including distributed-lag terms of the real effective exchange rate.

The regression shows that a rise in the Japanese long-term real interest rate, relative to both foreign countries and the short-term interest rate differential, reduces net outflows of securities investment as expected. The term structure of the real interest rate matters in determining securities investment outflows. A rise in the Japanese real stock and share prices or a real depreciation of the yen stimulates securities investment, although the negative effect of the yen rate is statistically insignificant. The positive, significant effect of the relative index of real stock and share prices is quite robust, lending support for the third explanation mentioned above for the rapid rise in securities investment abroad. Placing the long-term interest rate differential alone, instead of the term structure of the real interest rate, or putting it to the above equation as an additional explanatory variable does not improve the explanatory power (see Table 5.10).

The regression equation suggests one reason why net outflows of securities investment declined sharply toward the end of the 1980s. The Bank of Japan started to tighten its monetary policy in mid-1989 and the Japanese interest rate went up, thus reducing the incentive to continue to accumulate foreign securities. In addition, the tight monetary policy started to exert downward pressure on Japanese stock and share prices on the Tokyo exchange. The Nikkei Stock Average declined 38% from ¥ 38,130 at the end of 1989 to ¥ 23,740 a year later, and the market remained stagnant in 1991 and 1992. The relative index of the real stock and share prices reached a plateau already in 1988 and started to decline sharply in 1990 (see Fig. 5.8). In the face of large capital losses in the stock market, the financial institutions and institutional investors no longer had an incentive to purchase high-yielding foreign securities because of the risk of potential exchange losses that could no longer be offset by capital gains elsewhere.

Direct investment

Japan's post–W.W. II direct investment abroad resumed in the first half of the 1950s and accelerated during the second half of the 1960s and early 1970s. The 1973 oil price shock caused a slowdown of direct investment, which remained static throughout most of the 1970s. Since the beginning of the 1980s, direct investment abroad has increased persistently in both developed and developing countries (see Table 5.8 again), and the rise has particularly been remarkable since 1985.[19]

---

[19] See Komiya (1990) for extensive discussions on issues concerning Japan's direct investment.

The recent globalization of business activities has been a natural under-lying factor behind the rise in Japanese direct investment in the 1980s. The most important macroeconomic factor since 1985 has been the yen exchange rate against the major international currencies. As Fig. 5.9 demonstrates, the real effective exchange rate of the yen, measured as the IMF's relative normalized unit labor costs, appreciated abruptly and drastically between late 1985 and 1988. The sharp yen rate appreciation stimulated direct investment from two channels.

First, steep yen rate appreciation meant a dramatic shift in Japan's international price competitiveness. The real effective value of the yen appreciated by 59% between 1985.I and 1988.II. To cope with the new international relative prices, firms in the tradables sector had only three options: They had to either (1) reallocate their productive resources (capital, labor, managerial resources, and R&D stocks) away from the tradables toward nontradables sector, (2) improve productivity while staying in the tradables sector and increase the weight of high value-added, more income-elastic products, or (3) move their production base from the home market to foreign countries where production costs are lower. These were part of the industrial structural adjustment the economy had to go through under the steep yen rate appreciation. Many firms producing goods with high labor contents and low value-added chose to invest directly in countries where production was considered profitable. They invested particularly in growing Asian countries.

The second channel through which the yen rate had a positive impact on Japan's direct investment abroad was the "liquidity" or "wealth" effect [Froot and Stein (1991)]. Insofar as yen appreciation made Japanese firms relatively more "wealthy" in the sense of the increased collateral and liquidity, it enabled them to finance direct investment relatively cheaply compared to their foreign competitors. The Bank of Japan also injected abundant liquidity into the economy between 1986 and early 1989 to cope with the high yen rate. Such a rise in liquidity may have caused the dramatic rise in Japan's direct investment abroad.

Econometric estimation is attempted to explain the movement in the net outflow of direct investment, using quarterly data for 1980.I through 1990.III. The major explanatory variables include the real effective exchange rate and a time trend. The following result is obtained:

$$DIR = -5.83 + 1.28 \log E + 0.023 TIME, \quad \rho = 0.39$$
$$\quad\quad (2.16) \quad (0.51) \quad\quad\quad (0.007) \quad\quad\quad\quad (0.15)$$
$$\bar{R}^2 = 0.87, \text{ Standard error} = 0.180, DW = 2.07$$

where DIR is the net outflow of direct investment expressed as a percentage

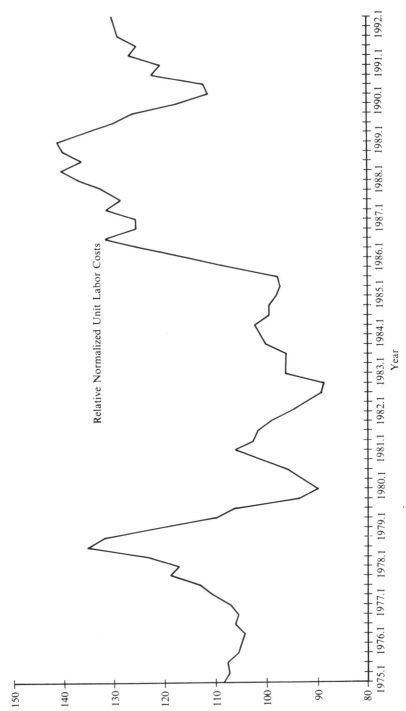

Fig. 5.9. Real effective exchange rate of the yen (1985 = 100). *Source:* IMF, *International Financial Statistics*, in tape.

of GNP, E is a distributed lag of the real effective exchange rate, and $TIME$ is a time trend. ρ is the first-order autoregressive coefficient of the residuals. The number of lags for E is chosen as 4.

The regression clearly supports the view that real appreciation of the yen induced net outflows of direct investment. The positive impact of the real exchange rate, though small in magnitude, is extremely robust regarding specification changes. Other possible explanatory variables, such as the real interest rate differential and relative real share prices, were tried but no significant improvement was made (see Table 5.10 for more information). Direct investment also had a significant upward time trend.

Loans and trade credits

Loans and trade credits are other components of long-term capital transactions. Although their magnitudes are small, similar econometric estimations are attempted to explain the movements of these two types of long-term net capital outflows.

The estimation result of the net outflow of loans is summarized as follows:

$$LOAN = 0.66 - 20.19(LTR\text{-}LTR^*) - 0.62 \log \frac{SP}{SP^*}, \quad \rho = 0.51$$

$$(0.18) \quad (8.68) \qquad\qquad (0.36) \qquad\qquad\qquad (0.13)$$

$$\bar{R}^2 = 0.51, \text{ Standard error} = 0.329, DW = 2.10$$

where $LOAN$ is the net outflow of loans as a percentage of GNP, LTR-LTR^* is a distributed lag of the long-term real interest rate differential between Japan and the six industrial countries, and $\dfrac{SP}{SP^*}$ is a distributed lag of the relative index of real stock and share prices between Japan and other industrial countries.

The regression result indicates the importance of long-term real interest rate differential between Japan and the rest of the industrial world; the higher the Japanese real interest rate relative to other major countries, the smaller the net outflow of loans. The relative index of real stock and share prices has a statistically significant, negative influence on net outflows of loans, but this effect is not always robust and depends on specifications. For example, adding another explanatory variable, the real effective exchange rate, makes the distributed lag effect of $\dfrac{SP}{SP^*}$ statistically insignificant, thus lowering the explanatory power of the regression (see Table 5.10).

The estimation result of the net outflow of trade credits is as follows:

$$TRC = 1.55 - 9.31(LTR\text{-}LTR^*) - 0.29 \log E$$
$$(0.44) \quad (2.55) \qquad\qquad (0.09)$$

$$\bar{R}^2 = 0.57, \text{ Standard error} = 0.093, DW = 1.73$$

where TRC is the net outflow of trade credits as a percentage of GNP, $LTR\text{-}LTR^*$ is a distributed lag of the long-term real interest rate differential, and E is a distributed lag of the real effective exchange rate for Japan.

As in the equation for loans, this result also shows the importance of long-term real interest rate differential between Japan and abroad, though its effect is smaller than in the case of loans. The real effective exchange rate has a statistically significant, negative influence on net outflows of trade credits, but this effect is not always robust. Adding another explanatory variable, the relative real share price for Japan, makes the collective effect of E statistically insignificant (see Table 5.10).

To summarize, the regression results for the net outflows of loans and trade credits, expressed as a percentage of GNP, demonstrate that they are influenced strongly by the long-term real interest rate differential and possibly by other asset prices, such as real stock and share prices and real exchange rates. Since securities and direct investments are also influenced by asset prices, total long-term net capital outflows are expected to depend on the same explanatory variables.

Total long-term net capital outflows

The following is the summary of the regression result for the total long-term net capital outflows for the sample period, 1980.I–1990.III:

$$LTC = 12.54 - 72.51[(LTR\text{-}LTR^*)\text{-}(STR\text{-}STR^*)] - 29.71(LTR\text{-}LTR^*)$$
$$(23.72) \quad (28.94) \qquad\qquad\qquad\qquad\qquad (27.25)$$

$$+ 6.08 \log \frac{SP}{SP^*} - 2.57 \log E, \quad \rho = 0.48$$

$$(2.98) \qquad\qquad (5.24) \qquad\quad (0.14)$$

$$\bar{R}^2 = 0.62, \text{ Standard error} = 1.368, DW = 2.56$$

Here, LTC is the total net outflow of long-term capital as a percentage of GNP, $(LTR\text{-}LTR^*)\text{-}(STR\text{-}STR^*)$ is a measure of the term structure of the real interest rate differential between Japan and the major industrial countries, $LTR\text{-}LTR^*$ is a distributed lag of the long-term real interest rate differential, $\frac{SP}{SP^*}$ is the relative index of Japan's real stock and share prices, and E is a distributed lag of real effective exchange rate of the yen. ρ is the coefficient of first-order autoregression in the residuals. The regression result identifies the term structure of the real interest rate differential and the relative index of real stock and share prices as important determinants of the total net outflow of long-term capital. The term structure of the interest rate differential has a statistically significant, negative impact, and the relative index of real stock and share prices has a statistically significant, positive impact on total long-term net capital outflows. The long-term real interest rate differential and the real effective exchange rate exert negative influences, but their effects are statistically insignificant.

As is anticipated, the econometric result for the total net outflow is similar to that of the net outflow of securities investment. It does not capture the positive impact of the real exchange rate on direct investment and only partially captures the negative impact of the long-term real interest rate differential on loans and trade credits, presumably due to the small size of these net outflows. The empirical evidence, however, is consistent with the view that Japan's long-term net capital outflows have been influenced systematically by major asset prices in Japan and the rest of the industrial world.

Conclusion

This paper has presented data on Japan's NEAP and examined the causes of the rapid rise in net external assets in the 1980s. The conclusion is that Japan's NEAP expanded rapidly in the 1980s due to both factors of a long-term, structural nature and factors specific to the events in the 1980s. As discussed, the long-term, structural factors include (a) Japan's rapid productivity growth and the consequent strengthening of its international competitiveness and (b) high and stable household saving. The direct causes specific to the 1980s are: (c) Japan's liberalization of exchange and capital controls and (d) U.S. and Japanese macroeconomic conditions and the induced changes in their real domestic demand and in asset prices, such as the real interest rate, the real exchange rate, and real stock and share prices.

The analysis can be summarized as follows: When the U.S. economy entered a long expansion in 1983, its fiscal deficits persisted. The growth of real domestic demand together with the structural budget deficits raised the U.S. long-term real interest rate, which attracted capital from all over the world, including Japan. Japanese investors who had just been freed from exchange and capital controls found it profitable to purchase dollar-denominated securities for their global portfolio diversification. Long-term capital outflows in the form of foreign securities skyrocketed. This, however, led to an appreciation of the dollar and depreciation of the yen. Rising real domestic demand in the United States and yen depreciation stimulated Japanese net exports, particularly those of machinery and equipment. Japan had established its competitive industrial base to provide those manufactured products highly demanded in the United States and other industrial countries. As the United States increased net imports and ran large current account deficits, protectionist sentiments mounted and the strong dollar was no longer sustainable. The dollar started to decline in value in the spring of 1985, and this trend was reaffirmed at the Plaza G5 Agreement in September of the same year. The pace of dollar depreciation, however, became too fast and the yen appreciated too steeply. Fearing the possible deepening of the "endaka recession" (a recession induced by a steep appreciation of the yen, July 1985–November 1986), the Bank of Japan started to stimulate the economy by injecting liquidity in 1986. At the Louvre Accord of February 1987, the G7 countries decided to prevent further depreciation of the dollar and Japan agreed to adopt even more expansionary monetary policy. The-low-interest-rate policy continued well into 1989 even though (1) the economy had long recovered from the "endaka recession" and (2) U.S. current account deficits had already been shrinking and the confidence in the dollar had been restored. The official discount rate was kept at the historically low 2.5% level between February 1987 and May 1989. This was an important factor behind the great inflation of asset prices, such as those of stocks and shares and of land, which had to be dealt with later by an extremely tight monetary policy. The low interest rate and the subsequent rise in stock and share prices kept Japanese investment in foreign securities at high levels. As the Bank of Japan shifted its monetary policy to squeeze liquidity out of the economy, the Japanese interest rate started to rise and the stock and share prices started to fall. The monetary tightening was so severe that the stock and share prices virtually collapsed by the end of 1990, which eventually ended one of the longest expansions of the Japanese economy. The collapse of the stock market also reduced the net outflow of securities investment to a significant degree. The year 1991 witnessed net inflows of securities, loans, and trade credits and a surplus in the overall long-term capital account. While securities investment outflows were declining, direct investment that had been persistently rising since 1985 emerged as the most dominant form of long-term capital outflows.

Thus the macroeconomic developments in the United States and Japan and the consequent changes in real domestic demand and real asset prices, together with Japan's relaxation of exchange and capital controls, were directly responsible for the expansion of Japan's NEAP in the 1980s. At the same time it is important to reemphasize that the long-term, structural factors, such as continuous growth of labor productivity in manufacturing and high household saving, supported this process.

Finally, let us discuss briefly the international implication of Japan's ascendance to the status of a world-leading net creditor country. It is natural that Japan's influence and responsibility in international monetary and financial matters will inevitably rise. The real value of the yen will be under upward pressure as a trend, the role of the yen as an international currency will rise gradually, the function of Tokyo as an international financial center will be expanded over time, and Japan's influence as one of the core countries in a multiple currency system will increase. As a large creditor country with abundant financial resources, and as an important member of the industrialized world, Japan is expected to play an increasing role in international monetary and financial management. This includes, among other things, maintaining the stability of the international monetary system and providing smooth, stable flows of capital to the rest of the world.[20]

First, maintaining the stability of the international monetary system requires close coordination of macroeconomic policies among the industrialized countries, and Japan will be expected to play a bigger role than before. International policy coordination, however, invites the difficult problem of how to cope with possible conflicts between global and domestic objectives. As is discussed above, Japan pursued an overexpansionary monetary policy between 1986 and early 1989 partly to combat the "endaka recession," which was a domestic policy concern, and partly to avoid a free-fall of the dollar, which was one of the major global objectives at the time. This eventually led to the asset price inflation and the subsequent, sharp reversal of monetary policy. Although the ensuing tight monetary policy successfully eliminated asset price inflation, it caused a stock market collapse and ended one of the longest expansions in post–W.W. II Japan. Stability of domestic macroeconomic conditions, clearly a main objective of economic policy, was sacrificed. The increasing responsibility of Japan to coordinate its economic policy for the stability of the international monetary system sometimes poses the difficult problem of how to achieve both domestic macroeconomic stability and global objectives.

Second, Japan as a financial-resource-rich country is expected to secure smooth, stable flows of long-term capital and other financial resources for the growth and stability of the world economy. The experience in the

---

[20] Eichengreen (1989) provides interesting discussions on the responsibilities of a creditor nation in historical perspectives.

1980s gave the lesson that, in order to provide smooth flows of long-term capital to the rest of the world, it is vital to maintain a stable domestic macroeconomic environment. Japan's swing in monetary policy from excessive expansion to extreme tightening led to wild gyrations in asset prices and the consequent runup and rundown of the net outflow of long-term capital. In 1991 the pattern of capital flows was completely reversed; Japan borrowed long and lent short. Provision of stable long-term capital to the rest of the world was greatly hampered. The lesson to be learned is that Japan must ensure stable macroeconomic conditions in the domestic economy to provide smooth, stable flows of long-term capital to the rest of the world.

References

Bergsten, C. Fred, ed. (1991), *International Adjustment and Financing: The Lessons of 1985–1991*, Washington, D.C.: Institute for International Economics.

Corker, Robert (1989), "External Adjustment and the Strong Yen," *IMF Staff Papers*, 36 (Jun.), pp. 464–93.

Eichengreen, Barry (1989), "The Responsibilities of a Creditor Nation," in *The Advanced Industrial Societies in Disarray: What Are the Available Choices?*, *Annals of the Institute of Social Science*, Special Issue (Mar.), University of Tokyo, pp. 77–107.

Feldstein, Martin, and Charles Horioka (1980), "Domestic Saving and International Capital Flows," *Economic Journal*, 90 (Jun.), pp. 314–29.

Frankel, Jeffrey A. (1984), "The Yen-Dollar Agreement: Liberalizing Japanese Capital Markets," *Policy Analyses in International Economics*, No. 9 (Dec.), Washington, D.C.: Institute for International Economics.

Frankel, Jeffrey A. (1988b), "U.S. Borrowing from Japan," Discussion Paper Series 174D, (Nov.), John F. Kennedy School of Government, Harvard University.

Froot, Kenneth, and Jeremy C. Stein (1991), "Exchange Rates and Foreign Direct Investment: An Imperfect Capital Markets Approach," *Quarterly Journal of Economics*, CVI (Nov.) pp. 1191–1217.

Fujii, Mariko, and Kazuo Ueda (1986), "Japanese Capital Outflows: 1971 to 1985," paper presented at the NBER-MOF International Symposium on Current Theoretical and Policy Issues in the U.S. and Japanese Economy (Oct. 16–17), Tokyo.

Fukao, Mitsuhiro (1990), "Liberalization of Japan's Foreign Exchange Controls and Structural Changes in the Balance of Payments," *Bank of Japan Monetary and Economic Studies*, 8 (Sep.), pp. 101–65.

Kawai, Masahiro (1989), "Japan's Demand for Long-term External Financial Assets in the 1980's" *Asian Economic Journal*, 3 (Sep.), pp. 65–115.

Kawai, Masahiro (1991), "Japanese Investment in Foreign Securities in the 1980's," *Pacific Economic Papers*, 201 (Nov.), Australian National University.

Komiya, Ryutaro (1990), "Japan's Foreign Direct Investment," *in his The Japanese*

Economy: Trade Industry, and Government, Tokyo: University of Tokyo Press, pp. 111–56.

Komiya, Ryutaro, and Miyako Suda (1991), *Japan's Foreign Exchange Policy 1971–82*, translated and edited by Colin McKenzie, Sydney: Allen & Unwin.

Krugman, Paul (1988), "Sustainability and the Decline of the Dollar," *in* Ralph C. Bryant, Gerald Holtham, and Peter Hooper (eds.), *External Deficits and the Dollar: The Pit and the Pendulum*, Washington, D.C.: Brookings Institution, pp. 82–99.

Marris, Stephen (1989), "Deficits and the Dollar: The World Economy at Risk," *Policy Analyses in International Economics*, No. 14, updated edition (Aug.), Washington, D.C.: Institute for International Economics.

Shinkai, Yoichi (1988), "The Internationalization of Finance," *in* Takashi Inoguchi and Daniel I. Okimoto (eds.), *The Political Economy of Japan, Vol. 2: The Changing International Context*, Stanford: Stanford University Press.

Sinn, Stefan (1990), *Net External Asset Positions of 145 Countries: Estimation and Interpretation*, Kieler Studien 234, Institute fur Weltwirtschaft an der Universitat Kiel, J. C. B. Mohr (Paul Siebeck) Tubingen.

CHAPTER 6

Relative traded goods prices and imperfect competition in United States manufacturing industries

ROBERT E. CUMBY
JOHN HUIZINGA

The most striking features of the behavior of the real effective exchange rate of the U.S. dollar during the 1980s are the magnitude and persistence of its changes and the correlation of those changes with changes in the nominal effective exchange rate. An increasingly popular view, typified by Dornbusch (1987), is that imperfect competition among firms is an essential ingredient in understanding real exchange rate behavior.[1] Firms produce differentiated products and face wages that are assumed to be sticky in local currency terms. As a result, a depreciation of the home currency will raise foreign producers' marginal cost measured in home currency and will lead foreign firms to raise the price charged in the home market.

In this paper we paint with a broad brush. We examine features common to a number of models rather than testing the restrictions implied by a specific, tightly parameterized model. In doing so we hope to shed some light on whether the predictions of models with imperfectly competitive firms are broadly consistent with the data rather than take a position on a particular model. Since other explanations having nothing to do with imperfectly competitive firms are consistent with persistent real exchange rate changes, if one is to determine if imperfect competition is essential to an understanding of real exchange rate changes, one must look beyond the behavior of aggregate real exchange rates.[2] An important aspect of the models discussed by Dornbusch is that they yield predictions about the cross-sectional differences in relative price behavior when exchange

---

[1] Krugman (1987) and Giovannini (1988) also present models in which imperfect competition among firms determines real exchange rate behavior.

[2] Stockman (1988), for example, uses real shocks to explain real exchange rate behavior. Of course, nothing rules out the possibility that both real shocks and imperfect competition are important in understanding real exchange rate behavior. The models explored by Dornbusch are partial equilibrium with the exchange rate taken as exogenous. While he clearly has financial market disturbances in mind, nothing rules out real shocks being important. Klein (1988) examines the effect of exchange rate changes on traded goods prices in a general equilibrium macroeconomic model with imperfectly competitive firms.

rates change. In particular, the models generally predict that the extent to which relative prices within an industry change depends on the degree of competition (as measured by the ratio of price to marginal cost) and on the relative importance of foreign firms in the industry. This paper uses a data set comprised of U.S. manufacturing industries to examine the cross-sectional differences in relative price changes following exchange rate changes.

The plan of the paper is as follows. At first, we briefly describe the predictions of two of the models examined by Dornbusch (1987) and highlight the relationship between the exchange rate elasticity of relative prices and the markup of prices over marginal cost. Second, we present estimates of the exchange rate elasticity of relative prices in U.S. manufacturing industries. Then we turn to estimates of the markup of prices over marginal costs. These estimates are obtained following the suggestions of Hall (1986) but do not require his restrictive identifying assumption that there are no aggregate productivity shocks.[3] In the last section, we examine whether the variation across industries in the estimated exchange rate elasticity of relative prices varies with differences in the markup of prices over marginal costs in the way suggested by the models in the first section.

Models with differentiated products

Dornbusch (1987) offers a series of models in which domestic and foreign firms produce differentiated products and derives the elasticity of relative prices with respect to exogenous exchange rate changes in each of the models. In each model, firms face production costs that are sticky in nominal, local currency terms. More precisely, costs are exogenously given in the currency of the producer. In this section we will briefly discuss the implications of these models for the exchange rate elasticity of relative prices across industries.

The first model we consider is the "Dixit-Stiglitz" model in which each of the n_i domestic and n_i^* foreign firms in industry i faces a demand curve in the home market that depends on the price charged by the firm relative to the aggregate price in the industry and which has a constant elasticity, $\alpha_i/(\alpha_i - 1)$. If we let c_i be marginal cost of domestic firms in industry i measured in domestic currency, c_i^* be marginal cost of foreign firms in industry i measured in foreign currency, and p_i^d and p_i^m be the prices

---

[3] We require that lagged values of the labor capital ratio and the output capital ratio be uncorrelated with current productivity disturbances in each of the industries, while Hall requires that aggregate output growth is strictly exogenous.

charged by domestic and foreign firms in the domestic market, then

$$p_{it}^d = \alpha_i c_{it} \quad \text{and} \quad p_{it}^m = \alpha_i e_t c_{it}^{*4}$$

Two relative prices are of interest. First, consider the price of imported varieties relative to the price charged by domestic firms.

$$\frac{p_{it}^m}{p_{it}^d} = \frac{e_t c_{it}^*}{c_{it}}$$

Given local currency marginal costs, a depreciation of the home currency should cause the price charged by foreign firms to rise in proportion to the exchange rate and should leave the price charged by domestic firms unchanged. The elasticity of the relative price of foreign to domestic varieties will be one in all industries. Of course, if marginal cost depends on output, or if input costs are affected by the change in exchange rate, this elasticity will differ from one. Cross-sectional dispersion in this elasticity will depend on cross-sectional changes in marginal cost of domestic and foreign firms. It is difficult to measure these factors and therefore difficult to predict any particular pattern in the elasticity of this relative price across industries.[5]

Next consider the price of home country exports relative to the price of domestic varieties sold in the home market. Since home currency marginal cost will be unchanged by a change in exchange rates, the home currency price of exports relative to the price of domestic varieties sold at home will be unaffected by an exchange rate change. Thus the exchange rate elasticity of p_{it}^x/p_{it}^d is zero.

If the assumption that the elasticity of demand is constant in Dornbusch's version of the Dixit-Stiglitz model is relaxed, the relative price elasticities will no longer be zero and one. Rather than assuming that producers face an isoelastic demand curve, assume that the jth producers in industry i faced the linear demand curve $x_{ij} = a_i - b_i p_{ij}/P_i$, where P_i is the aggregate price in industry i. Assuming that marginal costs are given exogenously as c_{it} and c_{it}^*, profit maximizing producers will set prices,

$$p_{it}^d = .5\left(\frac{a_i P_{it}}{b_i + c_{it}}\right)$$

$$p_{it}^m = .5\left(\frac{a_i P_{it}}{b_i + e_t c_{it}^*}\right)$$

[4] If firms also sell in the foreign market where the elasticity of demand differs from $\alpha_i/(\alpha_i - 1)$, the prices charged by a given firm in the domestic market will differ from the price charged by the same firm in the foreign market (when expressed in a common currency). We must therefore rule out goods arbitrage between the two markets.

[5] Krugman (1987) finds the constant demand elasticity and constant marginal cost combination lacking as it predicts that import prices should change in proportion to a change in the exchange rate. This rules out "pricing to market" behavior.

The exchange rate elasticity of the relative price of imported varieties to domestic varieties is then

$$\frac{d\ln(p_{it}^m/p_{it}^d)}{d\ln(e_t)} = \frac{1}{2}\frac{1}{\alpha^*} + \frac{1}{2}\frac{a_i}{b_i}\eta\left(\frac{P_{it}}{p_{it}^m} - \frac{P_{it}}{p_{it}^d}\right)$$

where α^* is the markup of price over marginal cost for foreign firms in the home market and η is the exchange rate elasticity of the industry price. When domestic and foreign firms initially have marginal costs that are approximately equal, the elasticity simplifies to

$$\frac{d\ln(p_{it}^m/p_{it}^d)}{d\ln(e_t)} = \frac{1}{2}\frac{1}{\alpha^*}$$

The magnitude of the elasticity depends on the markup price over marginal cost, so that as the degree of competition in the market rises (the markup falls), the exchange rate elasticity rises.

Dornbusch (1987) also considers a simple version of a model of competition on a circle. Like the Dixit-Stiglitz model with linear demand, the circle model predicts that the price of imported varieties will move less than proportionately with a change in the nominal exchange rate. The two models yield similar predictions about the dependence of cross-industry differences in the exchange rate elasticity of the relative price of imported varieties on the degree of competition in the home market. The circle model also yields clear predictions about the exchange rate elasticity of the price of home country exports.

In the circle model, consumers have preferences for the attributes of goods that lead them to be spaced evenly along a unit circle. Domestic and foreign firms produce differentiated products with attributes that place them along the same unit circle. Consumers then choose to buy from one of the producers adjacent to them. That is, they choose between the firms producing the goods with the attributes that most closely correspond to their preferences. Consumers are assumed to purchase one unit and enjoy consumer's surplus that depends both on the price paid and on the distance between the consumer and the firm from which the good is purchased. Consumer surplus for the ith good is given by $h_i = v_i - \gamma_i \tau_i - p_i$, where τ is the distance between the consumer and the firm. When there is an equal number of domestic and foreign firms in alternating positions around the circle, the prices charged by domestic and foreign producers are[6]

$$p_{it}^d = \frac{\gamma_i}{n_i + n_i^*} + \frac{1}{k}(z\,c_{it} + (k-z)e_t c_{it}^*)$$

$$p_{it}^m = \frac{\gamma_i}{n_i + n_i^*} + \frac{1}{k}(z^* c_{it} + (k-z^*)e_t c_{it}^*)$$

[6] Producers are exogenously placed and evenly spaced along the circle.

where $k = 3, z = 2$, and $z^* = 1$. The price charged by domestic firms depends on the marginal cost of foreign producers. As a result, the price of domestic varieties will change when the nominal exchange rate changes. The exchange rate elasticity of the price of foreign relative to domestic varieties is

$$\frac{d\ln\{p_{it}^m/p_{it}^d\}}{d\ln(e_t)} = \frac{1}{k}\frac{1}{\alpha^*}\left(k - z^* - \frac{p_{it}^m}{p_{it}^d}\right)$$

where α^* is the ratio of the price of foreign varieties in the home market to the marginal cost of foreign production. The model predicts that the exchange rate elasticity of relative prices depends on the ratio of price to marginal cost.[7] Dornbusch (1987) also shows that if initially domestic and foreign marginal costs are approximately equal, the exchange rate elasticity of the relative price of foreign to domestic varieties can be written as

$$\frac{d\ln(p_{it}^m/p_{it}^d)}{d\ln(e_t)} = \frac{z^*}{k}\Psi$$

where $0 \leqslant \Psi \leqslant 1$ is an increasing function of the total number of firms in the market and an increasing function of the degree of substitutability of domestic and foreign varieties in the preferences of consumers. Since, in the circle model, the degree of competition in the market is determined by the number of firms and the degree of substitutability of the differentiated products, Ψ is an increasing function of the degree of competition in the market. The parameter z^*/k is a decreasing function of the percentage of foreign firms in the market.[8] Thus we find that, in the circle model, the exchange rate elasticity of the relative price of foreign to domestic varieties rises as the degree of competition increases and falls as the market share of foreign firms increases.[9]

The circle model also yields predictions concerning the behavior of export prices. Consider the price of home exports relative to the price of home production sold domestically. If the circle model describes the foreign market, and with domestic and foreign costs approximately equal,

$$\frac{d\ln(p_{it}^x/p_{it}^d)}{d\ln(e_t)} = 1 - \frac{k - z^*}{k}\Psi^* - \frac{k - z}{k}\Psi$$

where Ψ is as defined above and Ψ^* is the same increasing function of the degree of competition in the home country's export market. The

[7] The general structure of the solution does not depend on the assumption that domestic and foreign firms alternate along the circle. If, for example, we assume there are two adjacent domestic firms for each foreign firms, $k = 5$, $z = 4$, and $z^* = 2$.

[8] As the number of adjacent domestic firms per foreign firm increases, z^*/k rises toward $1/2$.

[9] Since domestic and foreign firms charge different prices, they will have sales that differ. Therefore the market share of foreign firms is not proportional to the percentage of foreign firms but should be an increasing function of the percentage of foreign firms.

elasticity falls as the degree of competition in the home and foreign markets increases. The elasticity takes on a value of zero when Ψ and Ψ^* are at their maximum value of one, $k = 3$, $z^* = 1$, and $z = 2$ (as is the case with one domestic firm per foreign firm in both the home and foreign markets). Thus a depreciation of the home currency should raise the (home currency) price of exports relative to the price of home production sold in the home market by an amount that declines as the degree of competition in the home and foreign markets rises. The reason for this is that when markets are competitive, unit cost (measured in home currency) will be unaffected by a depreciation, and thus the price of home production will remain unchanged.

Other models also predict that the extent to which relative prices change when there is a change in the nominal exchange rate depends on the degree of competition in the market. For example, in the two-period model of Froot and Klemperer (1988), a firm's second-period demand depends on its first-period market share. Following a first-period exchange rate change that is perceived to be temporary, a foreign firm selling in the home market will adjust its price less than proportionately in order to affect its first-period market share and therefore its second-period profits. The extent to which it adjusts its first-period price depends on the degree of competition in the market. The greater the degree of competition, the larger will be price changes in response to the exchange rate change. Their model predicts that the relative price of home exports will also change when the nominal exchange rate changes. As is the case in the circle model, the exchange rate elasticity of the relative price of home exports will be zero when the home and foreign markets are competitive. As the degree of competition decreases, the exchange rate elasticity will rise.

A number of models predict that the price of imported varieties relative to domestic varieties will change when the nominal exchange rate changes and that the exchange rate elasticity of this relative price depends positively on the degree of competition in the market (as measured by the markup of prices over marginal cost). Several of these models also predict that the price of domestic exports relative to the price of domestic production sold domestically will also change when the nominal exchange rate changes. The exchange rate elasticity of this relative price depends inversely on the degree of competition in the market. In the next sections we examine the extent to which these predictions are consistent with observed behavior of prices of U.S. imports, U.S. exports, and U.S. producer prices.

Exchange rates and relative prices

The United States Bureau of Labor Statistics compiles price indexes for imports and exports quarterly and reports these indexes for selected two-,

Table 6.1. *SIC industries.*

SIC no.	Description	First observation Exports	First observation Imports
20	Food and kindred products	1983:2	1980:4
22	Textile mill products		1982:3
23	Apparel and other textile products		1980:4
24	Lumber and wood products	1983:2	1980:4
25	Furniture and fixtures	1983:3	1980:4
26	Paper and allied products	1981:1	1980:4
28	Chemicals and allied products	1983:1	1983:3
29	Petroleum and coal products	1983:4	
30	Rubber and misc. plastic products		1980:4
31	Leather and leather products		1980:4
32	Stone, clay, and glass products		1980:4
33	Primary metal products	1982:1	1981:2
34	Fabricated metal products		1984:4
35	Industrial machinery and equipment	1980:4	1980:4
36	Electronic and other electrical equipment	1980:4	1984:3
39	Miscellaneous manufacturing industries		1982:3

three-, and four-digit SIC industries.[10] The primary shortcoming of this data set is that it covers only the 1980s. We have selected 15 two-digit SIC manufacturing industries with import price series that are long enough to include both the appreciation of the dollar between 1980 and the first quarter of 1985 and the subsequent depreciation of the dollar. The data on export prices are somewhat scarcer. We are able to make use of export prices for only ten two-digit industries. Table 6.1 summarizes the export and import price data used in the analysis. As can be seen from the table, not only are export price data available for fewer industries but the series generally covers a shorter time period as well. The analysis will therefore rely more heavily on the behavior of import prices relative to domestic prices.

While the models make separate predictions about the behavior of import prices, export prices, and domestic producer prices, we examine only the behavior of import prices relative to domestic producer prices and export prices relative to domestic producer prices. The reason for this choice is that several factors, in addition to the exchange rate, influence

[10] The data are indexes of transactions prices for the third month of each quarter. In addition to reporting indexes using the SIC classification, the Bureau of Labor Statistics also reports the data by SITC and by Bureau of Economic Analysis End-Use classification. We have chosen to work with the SIC-based data to facilitate comparison with domestic producer prices and industry characteristics that are available by SIC.

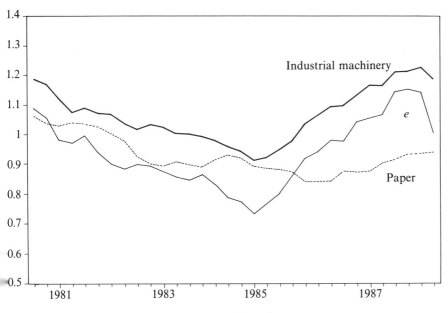

Fig. 6.1. Exchange rates and relative prices.

each of these prices, so that obtaining reliable estimates of the exchange rate elasticity of these prices requires a detailed specification of each of the markets. By considering relative prices we net out many of these factors and can focus on exchange rate shocks and obtain reliable estimates of the exchange rate elasticities of the relative prices.

Figure 6.1 illustrates the relative price behavior found in the data set. Three series are plotted. The first, labeled e, is the nominal effective exchange rate of the U.S. dollar.[11] The second, labeled "Paper," is the price of imports of paper products relative to domestic producer prices for paper products. The third, labeled "Industrial machinery," is the price of industrial machinery imports relative to domestic producer prices for industrial machinery. Both relative price series exhibit some correlation with the nominal exchange rate. A depreciation of the dollar is associated with an increase in both relative prices. It is apparent, however, that the extent of the correlation with nominal exchange rates is considerably

[11] This series is the reciprocal of the nominal effective exchange rate published in Morgan Guaranty's *World Financial Markets*. An increase in the series corresponds to a depreciation of the U.S. dollar.

greater for industrial machinery than for paper products.[12] Estimates of the exchange rate elasticity of the price of imports and exports relative to domestic producer prices should then exhibit considerable variation across industries.

Estimates of the exchange rate elasticity of import prices relative to domestic producer prices are found in Table 6.2. In all the models discussed in this section, the exchange rate is assumed to be exogenous. We therefore estimate the elasticity with an ordinary least squares regression of the log of the relative price on the log of the nominal effective exchange rate. While the models considered in this section are all static models, it is unlikely that there is only a once-and-for-all effect of exchange rate changes on relative prices. We therefore include a lagged dependent variable in the regressions and consider the "long run" elasticity $b_1/(1 - b_2)$ when examining the cross-sectional implications of the models discussed in this section. As can be seen from Table 6.2, the point estimates of the short-run elasticities are positive and less than one. In 12 of the 15 industries, the slope coefficients on the nominal exchange rate are statistically significantly different from zero. In all 15 cases they differ from one.

We can test the hypothesis that the long-run elasticity is significantly different from one by testing the hypothesis that the coefficients on the exchange rate and the lagged dependent variable sum to one. Since the coefficient on the lagged dependent variable is large in most cases, we reject the hypothesis that the long-run elasticity is one in only one-half of the cases at the 5% significance level. However, the point estimates of the long-run elasticities are generally not close to one and vary substantially across industries.[13] The hypothesis that the long-run elasticities differ across industries can be tested formally by estimating the regressions as a system. We have carried out such a test on the subset of industries that has data for the longest sample period and reject the hypothesis of equality quite strongly. To the extent that the elasticities vary across industries and to the extent that they differ from one, the estimates are not consistent with the predictions of the simple Dixit-Stiglitz model with constant marginal cost and constant elasticity of demand, but are consistent with the other models.

Since the models we consider make no predictions about the dynamic behavior of the relative price response to exchange rates, there is no *a*

---

[12] Both Dornbusch (1987) and Krugman (1987) present evidence similar to that found in Fig. 6.1. In this paper we examine relative price behavior in a broader set of industries than is the case in either of these two studies.

[13] The long-run elasticity will be significantly different from zero when the coefficient on the nominal exchange rate is significantly different from zero. As we noted above, 12 of the 15 elasticities are significantly different from zero.

Table 6.2. *Elasticity estimates: relative import prices*[a]

$$\ln(p_{it}^m/p_{it}^d) = b_0 + b_1 \ln(e_t) + b_2 \ln(p_{it-1}^m/p_{it-1}^d) + \varepsilon_t$$

SIC	b_1	b_2	$b_1/(1 - b_2)$	R^2
20	.048	.594	.118	.680
	(.038)	(.089)	[−4.21]	
22	.125	.832	.744	.832
	(.047)	(.091)	[−0.80]	
23	.035	.901	.343	.846
	(.034)	(.106)	[−0.72]	
24	.115	.431	.202	.591
	(.048)	(.173)	[−3.15]	
25	.237	.520	.494	.937
	(.042)	(.085)	[−4.39]	
26	.057	.880	.475	.927
	(.028)	(.049)	[−1.18]	
28	.073	.719	.260	.728
	(.025)	(.122)	[−1.74]	
30	.158	.535	.340	.943
	(.040)	(.112)	[−3.98]	
31	.038	.841	.239	.837
	(.028)	(.074)	[−1.60]	
32	.347	.570	.807	.941
	(.085)	(.129)	[−1.35]	
33	.107	.716	.377	.779
	(.038)	(.089)	[−2.00]	
34	.283	.528	.597	.985
	(.073)	(.138)	[−2.68]	
35	.484	.301	.694	.988
	(.036)	(.056)	[−8.24]	
36	.135	.558	.305	.704
	(.026)	(.113)	[−3.18]	
39	.185	.657	.539	.913
	(.037)	(.098)	[−2.03]	

[a] Ordinary least squares estimates using the maximum sample period for each industry as noted in Table 6.1. Standard errors are in parentheses. The t ratio for testing the hypothesis that the long-run multiplier is one ($b_1 + b_2 = 1$) is in brackets.

Table 6.3. *Elasticity estimates: relative import prices*[a]

$$\ln(p_{it}^m/p_{it}^d) = b_0 + b_1 \ln(p_{it-1}^m/p_{it-1}^d) + b_2 \ln(p_{it-2}^m/p_{it-2}^d)$$
$$+ b_3 \ln(e_t) + b_4 \ln(e_{t-1}) + \varepsilon_t$$

SIC no.	b_1	b_2	b_3	b_4	$(b_3+b_4)/(1-b_1-b_2)$	b_3+b_4	R^2
20	.65 (.21)	−.09 (.17)	.05 (.13)	−.00 (.14)	.10 [−3.16]	.043 [0.999]	.54
22	.77 (.22)	.07 (.20)	.25 (.07)	−.15 (.08)	.69 [−0.85]	.107 [2.061]	.98
23	1.08 (.20)	−.24 (.22)	.14 (.08)	−.10 (.08)	.24 [−1.22]	.038 [1.071]	.87
24	.43 (.21)	−.06 (.20)	.18 (.11)	−.06 (.11)	.20 [−2.75]	.123 [2.081]	.60
25	.66 (.20)	−.10 (.13)	.28 (.08)	−.07 (.11)	.47 [−2.98]	.205 [3.100]	.93
26	1.14 (.17)	−.32 (.15)	−.17 (.08)	.24 (.09)	.36 [−2.02]	.063 [2.287]	.94
28	.62 (.26)	.13 (.22)	.12 (.13)	−.05 (.15)	.30 [−0.85]	.066 [1.608]	.72
30	1.02 (.18)	−.32 (.13)	.20 (.04)	−.11 (.06)	.30 [−2.47]	.091 [1.963]	.96
31	.28 (.19)	.54 (.54)	−.01 (.08)	.05 (.09)	.21 [−1.85]	.038 [1.458]	.87
32	.98 (.16)	−.20 (.13)	.55 (.08)	−.37 (.11)	.79 [−0.84]	.176 [1.981]	.97
33	.43 (.27)	.17 (.21)	−.11 (.14)	.25 (.16)	.37 [−2.19]	.149 [3.253]	.77
34	.22 (.45)	.23 (.24)	.27 (.15)	.06 (.21)	.60 [−1.39]	1.108 [1.367]	.98
35	.31 (.18)	−.13 (.18)	.42 (.04)	.13 (.11)	.68 [−5.48]	.557 [5.835]	.99
36	−.06 (.29)	.37 (.18)	.08 (.09)	.13 (.12)	.32 [−3.07]	.217 [4.619]	.96
39	.48 (.20)	.20 (.16)	.13 (.10)	.07 (.14)	.63 [−1.20]	.202 [3.170]	.94

[a] Ordinary least squares estimates using the maximum sample period for each industry as noted in Table 6.1. Standard errors are in parentheses. The t ratios for testing $b_1 + b_2 + b_3 + b_4 = 1$ and $b_3 + b_4 = 0$ are in brackets.

Table 6.4. *Elasticity estimates: relative export prices*[a]

$$\ln(p_{it}^x/p_{it}^d) = b_0 + b_1 \ln(e_t) + b_2 \ln(p_{it-1}^x/p_{it-1}^d) + \varepsilon_t$$

SIC no.	b_1	b_2	$b_1/(1-b_2)$	R^2
20	.104	.850	.693	.695
	(.053)	(.145)	[−0.295]	
24	.212	.747	.838	.903
	(.110)	(.164)	[−0.463]	
25	.053	.773	.234	.952
	(.029)	(.125)	[−1.732]	
26	.118	.872	.922	.899
	(.044)	(.058)	[−0.144]	
28	.073	.894	.689	.862
	(.022)	(.104)	[−0.338]	
29	.370	.185	.454	.585
	(.154)	(.250)	[−2.668]	
33	.107	.706	.364	.769
	(.046)	(.114)	[−1.854]	
36	−.003	.843	.019	.926
	(.011)	(.046)	[−3.364]	

[a] Ordinary least squares estimates using the maximum sample period for each industry as noted in Table 6.1. Standard errors are in parentheses. The t ratio for testing the hypothesis that the long-run multiplier is one ($b_1 + b_2 = 1$) is in brackets.

priori reason to expect a first-order autoregressive response. As a result, we have estimated the elasticities using two lags of the dependent variable and one lag of the exchange rate as well. These results are found in Table 6.3. In three industries the second lag of the dependent variable is found to be significant at the 5% level, while in four industries the lagged exchange rate is significant. In nearly all industries, the estimate of the long-run elasticity is unaffected by adding the additional lags. The long-run elasticity will be significantly different from zero when the sum of the coefficients on the exchange rate is significant, which occurs in 10 of the 15 industries. The long-run elasticity will differ significantly from one when the sum of all coefficients except the constant differs significantly from one, which occurs in eight industries.

Table 6.4 contains estimates of the exchange rate elasticity of the price of home exports relative to domestic producer prices. The estimates are again obtained from ordinary least squares regressions with a lagged dependent variable. Seven of eight estimates are positive, and all of these are statistically significant (at least at the 10% level).[14] The estimates then indicate that domestic producers raise export prices relative to domestic prices when the home currency depreciates. This evidence of "pricing to market" by United States export industries is consistent with the evidence reported by Marston (1990a, 1990b), which finds that U.S. exporters tend to price to market somewhat less than do Japanese exporters. It is also consistent with the evidence reported by Schembri (1989) who finds a similar degree of pricing to market in a major Canadian export industry. The data are inconsistent with the prediction of the simple Dixit-Stiglitz model that there should be no change in the price of home exports relative to the price of domestic production when the nominal exchange rate changes. As is the case with the relative import price elasticities, there is considerable variation in the elasticity estimates across the industries examined. In the last section we ask if this variation can be explained by differences in varying degrees of competition across industries.

Estimates of price – marginal cost markups

The models considered in the preceding section point to the degree of competition in an industry as a key factor in determining the extent to which relative prices change in response to exchange rate changes. In this section we examine Hall's (1986) suggestion for estimating markups of price over marginal cost and present estimates of this ratio that do not rely on the assumption that aggregate GNP is strictly exogenous with respect to productivity shocks in the industries considered.

Hall (1986) begins by noting that if a firm experiences Hicks neutral technical progress at rate θ and is competitive in input markets, marginal cost can be written as

$$c = \frac{w \, \Delta N + r \, \Delta K}{\Delta Q - \theta Q}$$

where N and K are the labor and capital inputs of the firm, and w and r are the costs of labor and capital. If the technology of the firm exhibits constant returns to scale (so that $wN/cQ + rK/cQ = 1$), this expression for

---

[14] Industry 35 is excluded from the table since the estimated coefficient on the lagged dependent variable exceeds one. We also estimate the elasticities adding a second lag of the dependent variable and a lag of the exchange rate to each regression. Neither of the additional lagged variables is significant in any regression.

marginal cost can be manipulated to obtain

$$\frac{\Delta Q}{Q} - \frac{\Delta K}{K} = \alpha \frac{wN}{pQ}\left(\frac{\Delta N}{N} - \frac{\Delta K}{K}\right) + \theta$$

where α is again the ratio of price to marginal cost.

Since Q, K, w, N, and p are observable, $\lambda_t = w_t N_t / p_t Q_t$, $\Delta q_t = \Delta \ln(Q_t/K_t)$, and $\Delta n_t = \Delta \ln(N_t/K_t)$ can be computed.[15] If in addition α is assumed to be constant, an estimate of the markup of price over marginal cost can be obtained from the regression

$$\Delta q_t = \alpha \lambda_t \Delta n_t + \theta + u_t$$

where u_t is an unobserved shock to technological progress in period t.

Since the productivity shock will in general be correlated with the change in the labor to capital ratio, instrumental variables must be used to obtain consistent estimates of α. Hall (1986) assumes that the growth in aggregate GNP is exogenous with respect to the productivity shock in each industry and thus uses GNP growth as an instrument. This choice has the undesirable implication of ruling out productivity shocks that are correlated with changes in aggregate GNP such as would arise in real business cycle models and in models in which firms engage in labor hoarding. Fortunately, this assumption is unnecessary. Valid instruments need not be strictly exogenous, but may be merely predetermined. It is thus possible to use lagged industry-specific variables as instruments and thereby circumvent the assumption that there are no aggregate productivity shocks. This set of estimates may then be used to determine the extent to which Hall's estimates are robust with respect to his assumption of no aggregate productivity shocks.

If productivity shocks are serially correlated, lagged-industry specific variables may not be uncorrelated with the regression error. We therefore suggest the following procedure for obtaining consistent estimates of α. Suppose there is some lag k such that for $j \geqslant k$, u_t is uncorrelated with u_{t-j} (and with other variables dated $t - j$). Any variables X_{t-k} that are correlated with $\lambda_t \Delta n_t$ are then valid instruments and may be used to obtain consistent estimates of α. The problem with this procedure, of course, is that economic theory is unlikely to provide us with precise *a priori* information about the degree of serial correlation in productivity shocks. If we choose a large initial value of k, beyond which we may safely assume serial correlation dies away, we can obtain initial consistent estimates of

---

[15] The data are primarily from the National Income and Product Accounts. A detailed description of the data is contained in the data appendix.

Table 6.5. *Estimates of price – marginal cost markups*

SIC no.	Hall	ΔGNP	Lags of n, q, $\lambda\Delta n$, Δq	
20	3.09 (1.64)	1.437 (.942)	.908 (.758)	(1)
22	1.05 (.27)	.937 (.303)	1.134 (.458)	(1)
23	1.30 (.24)	1.209 (.216)	1.147 (.209)	(1)
24	1.00 (.21)	1.177 (.291)	1.395 (.319)	(1)
25	1.30 (.17)	1.213 (.134)	1.616 (.299)	(2)
26	2.68 (.33)	2.086 (.346)	2.910 (.380)	(1)
28	3.39 (.78)	2.144 (.500)	1.636 (.869)	(3)
29	2.08 (.83)	1.352 (.472)	0.736 (.290)	(1)
30	1.41 (.20)	1.301 (.178)	1.331 (.259)	(1)
31	1.59 (.33)	1.749 (.500)	1.851 (.195)	(3)
32	1.81 (.22)	1.426 (.136)	1.606 (.162)	(2)
33	2.06 (.15)	1.636 (.123)	1.910 (.165)	(1)
34	1.39 (.13)	1.230 (.077)	1.464 (.142)	(2)
35	1.39 (.10)	1.289 (.108)	1.271 (.286)	(2)
36	1.43 (.15)	1.249 (.108)	1.486 (.240)	(3)
38	1.29 (.15)	1.226 (.133)	1.134 (.097)	(2)
39	1.52 (.55)	2.067 (.671)	1.081 (.621)	(3)

α. We can then use the ℓ test proposed by Cumby and Huizinga (1992) to determine the maximum lag at which u_t is serially correlated. Details of the procedure we adopt are found below.

Table 6.5 contains three sets of estimates of the markup of price over marginal cost for 17 manufacturing industries in the United States. The first set of estimates are those reported by Hall. The second set of estimates are obtained when Hall's sample period is extended from 1978 to 1987.[16] The third set is obtained using $\lambda_{t-i}\Delta n_{t-i}$ and Δq_{t-i} as well as n_{t-i} and q_{t-i} as instruments. We assume that any serial correlation in productivity shocks has fallen to zero at a lag of 4 years. We begin by setting $i = 4$ and test the null hypothesis that the autocorrelation of the error is zero at a lag of 3 years, allowing serial correlation at lags up to 2 years. If we fail to reject that the third autocorrelation is zero, we reestimate with $i = 3$ and test the hypothesis that the second autocorrelation is zero, allowing for nonzero autocorrelation at a lag of 1 year. If we again fail to reject, we reestimate with $i = 2$ and then test the hypothesis that the first autocorrelation is zero. If we fail to reject once again, we reestimate with $i = 1$. The number of years the instruments are lagged is noted in parentheses next to the standard errors.

The point estimates from all three sets of estimates are broadly similar. The most striking differences between the sets of estimates is the increase in the standard errors of the estimates of α that occurs when the lagged instruments are used and the decline in the point estimates that occurs when the sample period is extended. Using this third set of estimates, we reject the null hypothesis that price exceeds marginal cost in only 7 of the 17 industries, while the hypothesis can be rejected in 10 industries using Hall's estimates. The similarities in the estimates of α suggest that Hall's choice of the contemporaneous change in aggregate GNP does not adversely affect his estimates.

Cross-sectional relationships

Do the differences in the exchange rate elasticities of relative prices reported in the preceding section correspond to differences in the degree of competition across industries reported in this section in the way predicted by the models examined in the earlier section on exchange rate and relative prices? In this section we examine the correlation across

[16] Hall ends his sample in 1978. National Income and Product Accounts do not report total hours for all employees after that date. In updating the estimation period, we compute annual hours worked by multiplying the number of employees by average weekly hours of production workers. Both series are obtained from U.S. Department of Labor, Bureau of Labor Statistics, *Employment and Earnings*.

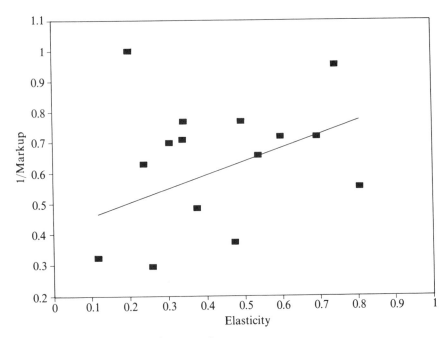

Fig. 6.2. Relative import prices.

industries in the exchange rate elasticities and the ratios of price to marginal cost.

Figure 6.2 plots the exchange rate elasticity of the price of imports relative to the price of domestic production along the horizontal axis and the reciprocal of Hall's estimates of the markup of price over marginal cost along the vertical axis. The models predict that as the degree of competition increases, the exchange rate elasticity should increase. We therefore expect a positive association between $1/\alpha$ and the elasticities. This positive association is clearly seen in the figure. Apart from the lumber industry, all the points in the scatter plot lie fairly close to a line with a positive slope.[17] The two industries chosen for Figure 6.1 illustrate the cross-sectional relationship between estimates of the markup and estimates of the exchange rate elasticity. Electrical machinery is estimated to be a relatively low-markup industry with a relatively high exchange rate elasticity. Paper products are estimated to be a high-markup industry with a relatively low exchange rate elasticity.

---

[17] The lines in Figs. 6.2 and 6.3 are drawn excluding the lumber industry.

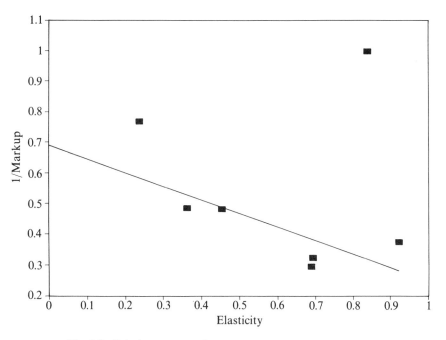

Fig. 6.3. Relative export prices.

Figure 6.3 plots the exchange rate elasticity of export prices relative to domestic producer prices along the horizontal axis and $1/\alpha$ along the vertical axis. There is a clearly discernable inverse relationship between the degree of competition and the elasticity. Elasticity estimates close to one are associated with large estimated markups of price over marginal cost. As the degree of competition in any industry rises (the estimate of α falls), the exchange rate elasticity estimates fall. Again, the lumber industry appears to be an outlier.

Is it possible to obtain formal tests of the cross-sectional association between the elasticity estimates and the price to marginal cost estimate? Unfortunately, both the elasticities and the markups of price over marginal cost are estimates obtained from regressions. As a result, regression estimates of the extent of cross-sectional association between the two values would not have statistical properties that will allow us to conduct a formal test. The fact that we have only estimates rather than the true values of the elasticities and the price-marginal cost markups also indicates that we should interpret the graphs with caution. It is certainly possible to fit lines with very different slopes using confidence regions around each point rather than the points themselves.

Concluding remarks

This paper has attempted to shed some light on the question of whether imperfect competition among firms is an essential part of understanding real exchange rate movements. Large and persistent movements in real exchange rates can be generated in models with competitive firms as well as in models with imperfectly competitive firms. On the other hand, models incorporating imperfect competition among firms predict dispersion across industries in the response of import prices and export prices relative to domestic producer prices. This dispersion across industries is linked in a number of models to differences in the degree of competition across industries.

The evidence examined in the paper clearly points to considerable variation across industries in the exchange rate elasticity of relative import and export prices. Do these differences correspond to differences in the degree of competition in the industries considered? In order to answer this question, we make use of Hall's (1986) estimates of the ratio of price to marginal cost in U.S. manufacturing industries. After checking the robustness of Hall's estimates to a removal of his assumption that there are no aggregate productivity shocks, we find that differences in price relative to marginal cost are generally associated with differences in the exchange rate elasticity of relative prices in the way suggested by the models considered in Dornbusch (1987).

References

Cumby, Robert E., and John Huizinga (1992), "Testing the Autocorrelation Structure of Disturbances in Ordinary Least Squares and Instrumental Variables Regressions," *Econometrica*, 60, 185–95.

Dornbusch, Rudiger (1987), "Exchange Rates and Prices," *American Economic Review*, 77, 93–106.

Froot, Kenneth A., and Paul Klemperer (1988), "Exchange Rate Pass-through When Market Share Matters," *American Economic Review*, 79, 637–54.

Giovannini, Alberto (1988), "Exchange Rates and Traded Goods Prices," *Journal of International Economics*, 24, 45–68.

Hall, Robert E. (1986), "The Relation Between Price and Marginal Cost in U.S. Industry," Stanford University, working paper.

Klein, Michael (1988), "Macroeconomic Aspects of Exchange Rate Pass-through," working paper, Clark University.

Krugman, Paul (1987), "Pricing to Market When Exchange Rates Change," *in* Sven W. Ardnt and J. David Richardson (eds.), *Real-Financial Linkages Among Open Economies*, Cambridge, MA: MIT Press, 49–70.

Marston, Richard C. (1990a), "Price Behavior in Japanese and U.S. Manufacturing," National Bureau of Economic Research Working Paper no. 3364.

Marston, Richard C. (1990b), "Pricing to Market in Japanese Manufacturing," *Journal of International Economics*, 29, 217–36.

Schembri, Lawrence (1989), "Export Prices and Exchange Rates: An Industry Approach," *in* Robert C. Feenstra (ed.), *Trade Policies for International Competitiveness*, Chicago: University of Chicago Press, 185–215.

Stockman, Alan (1988), "Real Exchange Rate Variability Under Pegged and Floating Nominal Exchange Rate Systems: An Equilibrium Theory," *in* Karl Brunner and Bennet T. McCallum (eds.), *Money, Cycles, and Exchange Rates: Essays in Honor of Allan H. Meltzer*, Carnegie-Rochester Conference Series on Public Policy 29, Amsterdam: North-Holland, 259–94.

Data Appendix

e Nominal effective exchange rate of the U.S. dollar. *Source*: Morgan Guaranty, *World Financial Markets*.

GNP Nominal Gross Domestic Product in billions of dollars (net of indirect business taxes). *Source*: Department of Commerce, National Income and Product Accounts.

K_i Capital Stock, Constant-cost net stock of fixed private capital, nonresidential and residential, by industry, in billions of 1982 dollars. *Source*: Department of Commerce, *Survey of Current Business*.

N_i Hours worked. Computed as the product of number of employees and average hours worked by production workers. Monthly hours worked are summed to obtain annual figure. *Source*: Bureau of Labor Statistics, *Employment and Earnings*.

p_i^d Domestic producer prices in the third month of the quarter, 1982 = 100. *Source*: Bureau of Labor Statistics, *Producer Price Indexes*.

p_i^m Import prices in the third month of the quarter, 1985 = 100. *Source*: Bureau of Labor Statistics.

p_i^x Export prices in the third month of the quarter, 1985 = 100. *Source*: Bureau of Labor Statistics.

Q_i Real GNP by industry, 1982 = 100. *Source*: Department of Commerce, National Income and Product Accounts.

w_i Total compensation per hour. Computed as total compensation divided by N_i. *Sources*: Compensation: Department of Commerce, National Income and Product Accounts. (N_i: see above.)

PART III

New financial products and the Japanese firm

CHAPTER 7

Synthetic Eurocurrency interest rate futures contracts: theory and evidence

ANNIE KOH
RICHARD M. LEVICH

Introduction

Over the last several decades, the process of financial innovation has been building and gaining momentum. Two important trends stand out.[1] The first is a proliferation of new products, many of which make possible funding strategies or investment strategies that circumscribe risks in ways that heretofore were not possible. A second trend is the decline in the importance of U.S. securities markets as a fraction of world market capitalization, and the decline in the role of the dollar as a *numeraire* in international financial markets.

An example of the first trend is the Eurodollar futures contract traded on the Chicago Mercantile Exchange. This contract began trading on December 9, 1981, and by 1984 its trading volume and open interest surpassed that of all other short-term interest rate hedging instruments. Today, the volume of trading in Eurodollar futures contracts typically surpasses 100,000 contracts daily ($100 billion of notional value). Recent research by Koh (1988) concludes that the Eurodollar futures contract is the most effective instrument for hedging interest rate risk in a variety of dollar-denominated securities.

To illustrate the second trend, as of December 1987, only 60% of the market for short-term Eurocurrency deposits were dollar denominated, and over the January–June 1988 period only 42% of the new issues of Eurobonds were dollar denominated.[2] Despite this second trend, markets for hedging interest rate risk for nondollar-denominated assets have been slow to develop.

---

[1] An extensive discussion of the major innovations in international financial markets, their causes and implications is presented in Levich (1988).

[2] Both the Eurocurrency deposit market and the Eurobond market began in the 1960s as wholly dollar-denominated markets. From the mid-1970s through the mid-1980s, roughly 70% to 80% of both markets were dollar denominated. Data are from Morgan Guaranty Trust Company, *World Financial Markets*, Aug. 17, 1988.

The purpose of this paper is to show that despite the absence of specific instruments for hedging nondollar interest rate risk, effective ways for managing this risk have existed for some time. First, we show that as a theoretical matter a synthetic nondollar interest rate futures contract can be created using available futures contracts – specifically, by using Eurodollar interest rate futures in conjunction with currency futures contracts. This technique thus permits us to construct interest rate futures contracts denominated in Euroyen, EuroDM, Euro£, and any other Eurodenomination that has an active currency futures market. Second, we offer empirical evidence that these synthetic, nondollar contracts have become increasingly effective at hedging nondollar interest rate risks. The results are most striking for Euro£ and Euro$C for which the hedging effectiveness exceeds 80% throughout our sample period. While the results for other currencies are somewhat less impressive, the synthetic Euroyen, EuroSwiss franc, and EuroDM interest rate futures produce hedging effectiveness measures averaging above 60% in the latter half of our sample period.

Our exposition of the synthetic interest rate futures contract should be familiar to those acquainted with the principles of covered interest arbitrage. In years past, the interest rate parity condition, $F = S(1 + r)/(1 + r^*)$, which links the foward exchange rate (F, in \$ per foreign currency unit) to the spot exchange rate and the yield on domestic currency funds $(1 + r)$ and foreign currency funds $(1 + r^*)$, has been invoked as an equilibrium condition required to eliminate risk-free arbitrage profits.[3]

More recently, however, the forward exchange market has been interpreted as a vehicle that transforms the currency dimension of a security while leaving the other characteristics of the security unchanged.[4] For example, a synthetic Japanese yen commercial paper security could be created by combining U.S. dollar commercial paper with yen-denominated spot and forward exchange contracts. Similarly, the cash flows of a long-term, Deutsche mark–denominated bond may be replicated by a dollar-denominated bond in conjunction with a collection of dollar-DM forward contracts, i.e., a currency swap. Such combinations of forward exchange contracts with existing securities would clearly be useful to overcome the lack of existence of a particular market or to overcome costly regulations and controls that may exist.

The threat of competition from synthetic contracts has not been enough to prevent the development of new interest rate futures contracts in markets

---

[3] For an extended discussion of the theory and empirical evidence on covered interest arbitrage, see Frenkel and Levich (1988).

[4] This principle of currency transformation of assets or liabilities using forward contracts is well known from the literature on foreign-exchange risk management. For more details on the role of forward contracts in financial innovation, see Levich (1988).

around the world. The recent introduction of Euroyen futures contracts in Tokyo and Singapore are examples of this. Even though true Eurocurrency interest rate futures may be available for some currencies, synthetic contracts offer a useful alternative. The reasons for this are: (1) the markets for some true Eurocurrency interest rate futures contracts may be illiquid, (2) the markets for true Eurocurrency interest rate futures have limited trading hours, and (3) markets for true Eurocurrency interest rate futures exist for only a small number of major currencies. In light of this, the synthetic approach may prove especially useful where product innovation is lagging, where regulation is costly, and where trading volume is too small to support an interest rate futures market in the desired currency.

In the second section, we develop the synthetic Eurocurrency interest rate futures contract based on the principle that forward contracts can be used to transform the currency of denomination of existing Eurodollar interest rate futures contracts. Empirical evidence on the hedging effectiveness of the synthetic contracts and comparisons of synthetic Euro£ contracts with actual British pound sterling interest rate futures contracts are presented in the third section. Conclusions and policy implications are offered in the final section.

Arbitrage pricing of synthetic Eurocurrency interest rate futures

In this section, we will demonstrate that a Eurocurrency interest rate futures contract for the interval (t_1, t_2) can be replicated by selling (buying) a Eurodollar interest rate futures contract for delivery on t_1 combined with the purchase (sale) of a foreign-currency futures contract for delivery on t_1 and the sale (purchase) of a foreign-currency futures contract for delivery on t_2. This combination is defined as a *synthetic Eurocurrency interest rate futures contract*. The price of the synthetic contract will depend on the prices of its constituents.

The synthetic pricing model

The replicating portfolio approach that we adopt is completely general and could be applied to construct synthetic Eurocurrency interest rate futures of any maturity. However, in order to simplify the exposition, we will assume that the maturity of the foreign-currency borrowing period exactly matches the maturity of the Eurodollar interest rate futures contact.

Assume that at time t_0, a corporate treasurer is making plans to borrow Euro–Foreign Currency (FC) at time t_1 to be repaid at time t_2. Interest

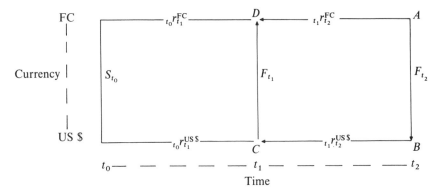

Fig. 7.1 Synthetic Eurocurrency interest rate pricing relationship.

rates are stochastic, so that at t_0, the FC interest rate at t_1 is uncertain. It is this risk that the treasurer is attempting to hedge.

In Fig. 7.1, we depict time along the horizontal dimension and currency along the vertical dimension. Spot and forward exchange rates measure the price of shifting between dollars and foreign currency, while interest rates measure the price of shifting cash flows across time. The equilibrium relationship between spot and forward exchange rates and interest rates on securities without intervening cash flows is well known from the interest rate parity theorem. In particular, the rate for a forward transaction on t_1 is given by

$$\frac{F_{t_1}}{S_{t_0}} = \frac{1 + {}_{t_0}r^{US\$}_{t_1}}{1 + {}_{t_0}r^{FC}_{t_1}} \tag{7.1}$$

and the rate for a forward transaction on t_2 is given by

$$\frac{F_{t_2}}{S_{t_0}} = \frac{1 + {}_{t_0}r^{US\$}_{t_2}}{1 + {}_{t_0}r^{FC}_{t_2}} \tag{7.2}$$

where

S_{t_0} = spot exchange rate expressed as US\$ per foreign currency (FC) at time t_0

F_{t_1} = forward exchange rate at t_0 for delivery at time t_1

F_{t_2} = forward exchange rate at t_0 for delivery at time t_2

${}_{t_0}r^{US\$}_{t_1}$ = US\$ interest rate for the period t_0 to t_1

${}_{t_0}r^{US\$}_{t_2}$ = US\$ interest rate for the period t_0 to t_2

${}_{t_0}r^{FC}_{t_1}$ = FC interest rate for the period t_0 to t_1

${}_{t_0}r^{FC}_{t_2}$ = FC interest rate for the period t_0 to t_2.

Noting that when Eq. (7.2) is written in terms of implied interest rates, we have

$$\frac{F_{t_2}}{S_{t_0}} = \frac{(1 + {}_{t_0}r_{t_1}^{US\$})(1 + {}_{t_1}r_{t_2}^{US\$})}{(1 + {}_{t_0}r_{t_1}^{FC})(1 + {}_{t_1}r_{t_2}^{FC})} \tag{7.3}$$

where

$_{t_1}r_{t_2}^{US\$}$ = implied forward Eurodollar interest rate at time t_0 for the period t_1 to t_2

$_{t_1}r_{t_2}^{FC}$ = implied forward EuroFC interest rate at time t_0 for the period t_1 to t_2

Equating S_{t_0} obtained from Eq. (7.1) and (7.3) results in the following relationship:

$$1 + {}_{t_1}r_{t_2}^{FC} = \frac{F_{t_1}}{F_{t_2}}[1 + {}_{t_1}r_{t_2}^{US\$}] \tag{7.4}$$

Notice that Eq. (7.4) is analogous to the traditional interest rate parity formula, except that the near-term cash flows pertain to a future time t_1 rather than to the present time t_0. Equation (7.4) suggests that the implied forward FC interest rate is closely linked to the implied forward dollar interest rate. Given a quotation on the implied forward dollar interest rate and a term structure of forward exchange rates, the implied forward FC interest rate is determined uniquely.

Quotations on the implied forward dollar interest rate ($_{t_1}r_{t_2}^{US\$}$) are available on a customized basis through banks in the so-called *Forward Rate Agreement* market. However, quotations on $_{t_1}r_{t_2}^{US\$}$ are more readily available based on Eurodollar interest rate futures prices. Under the assumption that futures prices (for foreign currency and interest rates) are identical with forward prices, Eq. (7.4) can be rewritten as

$$FP^{FC} = (FX_{t_1}/FX_{t_2})FP^{US\$} \tag{7.5}$$

where

FP^{FC} = price at t_0 for a .EuroFC interest rate futures contract spanning the period t_1, t_2

$FP^{US\$}$ = price at t_0 for a Euro\$ interest rate futures contract spanning the period t_1, t_2

FX_{t_1} = price at t_0 for foreign-currency futures contract for delivery at t_1

FX_{t_2} = price at t_0 for foreign-currency futures contract for delivery at t_2

In theory, the equivalence between forward contracts and futures contracts is open to question. Forward contracts entail cash flows only on maturity. Futures contracts on the other hand are marked-to-market daily, and intermediate cash flows may result from this daily cash settlement feature. It is well known [see Jarrow and Oldfield (1981), Cox, Ingersoll, and Ross (1981), and Richard and Sundaresan (1981)] that this institutional difference can generate differences between forward and futures prices if the prices on the underlying cash market (for foreign currency or interest rates) are stochastic.

As a practical matter, however, the cash flow risks of futures contracts do not make them strictly inferior since, to some extent, these risks are offset by the greater liquidity in futures markets. And while forward contracts require no initial margin and no intervening cash flows, forward contracts are relatively liquid, and access to the market is somewhat restricted, open only to agents with adequate credit standing to meet cash settlement at maturity only. Furthermore, the counterparty risk of forward contracts is variable depending on the bank counterparty. This risk may be significant relative to the risk of the clearinghouse, which is the counterparty for exchange-traded futures. The relationship between futures and forward contracts is therefore an empirical issue.

A study of the foreign-exchange market by Cornell and Reinganum (1981) found that mean differences between futures and forward prices were insignificantly different from zero, both in a statistical and economic sense. No similar study exists for the interest rate market, as each year there are only four data points of correspondence between implied forward interest rates and the matching interest rates obtained from futures prices.

In view of these findings, we will assume that forward prices and futures prices are on average identical. Equation (7.5) is our model for pricing the synthetic Eurocurrency interest rate futures contract. In the absence of transactions costs and default risk, our synthetic contract is a perfect substitute for the actual Eurocurrency interest rate futures. The sale of a Eurocurrency interest rate futures contract (line segment AD in Fig. 7.1) is replicated by combining the sale of a currency futures contract for date t_2 (segment AB) with the sale of a Eurodollar interest rate futures contract (segment BC) and the purchase of a currency futures contract for date t_1 (segment CD). In the examples that follow, we will assume that the interval (t_1, t_2) is 3 months. Our other key assumptions are (1) that interest rate parity holds at all times and (2) that futures prices and forward prices are equivalent.

A numerical synthetic hedge example

To illustrate the synthetic hedge strategy, consider the case of a West German manufacturing company that will be borrowing DM10 million

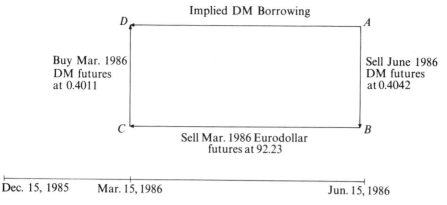

Fig. 7.2. Example of synthetic EuroDM hedge.

in the Eurocurrency market and is seeking to protect the rate it must pay. Let the current date be December 15, 1985; on March 15, 1986, the DM loan will be taken up and it will mature on June 15, 1986. The treasurer of our West German firm could obtain protection against unexpected EuroDM interest rate changes by obtaining a forward rate agreement to lock in the implied forward 3-month EuroDM rate. Assuming that the 6-month and 3-month EuroDM interest rates are currently at 4.75%, the implied forward rate is also 4.75%. This figure represents the cost of the direct approach (segment AD in Fig. 7.1).

Alternatively, the treasurer could implement our synthetic approach by selling March 86 Eurodollar futures (segment BC) and covering the exchange risk by buying the near-term, March 86 currency futures (segment CD) and selling the far-term, June 86 currency futures (segment AB).[5] The flow of funds is illustrated in Fig. 7.2.

We can assess the theoretical DM borrowing rate implied by these futures transactions by using Eq. (7.4) and Fig. 7.2.[6]

Observed market prices are

$$AB = 0.4042\$/DM = FX_{t_2}$$
$$BC = [1 + 0.0777(92/360)] = 1.019857 = (1 + {}_{t_1}r^{US\$}_{t_2})$$
$$CD = 0.4011\$/DM = FX_{t_1}$$

---

[5] The combination of buying and selling two futures contracts with different maturities is referred to as a calendar spread. As settlement gains and losses for the two currency futures contracts can be netted against each other, the cash flow risks associated with a calendar spread are typically less than for an individual contract.

[6] Market convention stipulates that short-term interest rates be calculated in simple interest terms, that is, multiplying the annualized interest rate by a factor of $n/360$, where n is the number of days for which the deposit is held or borrowed.

and so

$$(1 + \hat{r}^{DM}92/360) = (1 + {}_{t_1}r^{US\$}_{t_2})FX_{t_1}/FX_{t_2}$$
$$= 1.019857(.4011/.4042) = 1.0120350$$

Therefore, $\hat{r}^{DM} = 4.71\%$, which represents the effective DM borrowing rate over the interval March 15–June 15, 1986, constructed using our replicating approach.

In terms of the actual number of futures contracts to trade in, some rounding of the numbers are needed as future contracts are not traded in fractional amounts.

Jun86 Eurodollar futures:

$$\frac{DM10,000,000 \times 0.4011\$/DM \times 92/90}{\$1,000,000/contract} = 4.1(4 \text{ contracts})$$

Mar86 DM currency futures:

$$\frac{DM10,000,000}{DM125,000/contract} = 80 \text{ contracts}$$

Jun86 DM currency futures:

$$\frac{80 \text{ contracts} \times 0.4042\$/DM}{0.4011\$/DM} = 80.6 \text{ (81 contracts)}$$

These futures contracts will be closed out on March 15, 1986, when the borrower actually takes delivery of his DM10 million from the Eurocurrency market. Regardless of the 3-month EuroDM interest rate prevailing on March 15, 1986, the treasurer has effectively locked in the borrowing cost of 4.71%. This rate holds exactly because the borrowing period that runs from March 15, 1986, to June 15, 1986, also corresponds to the maturity of the Eurodollar deposit underlying the Eurodollar futures contract.

The role of basis risk

Our synthetic futures contract will provide a perfect hedge if there is perfect correlation between the price change in the futures contract and the price change in the anticipated cash transaction. Lack of perfect correlation implies a basis risk. Because of certain institutional features – that futures contracts are traded only for standardized sizes and mature on only a limited number of dates – some residual risk is likely to remain when using traded futures contracts to hedge planned cash flows. Our synthetic futures contract will be subject to the same kinds of residual risks when there is a mismatch between one of the features of the contract and the features of the underlying cash transactions.

In particular, we want to focus on the maturity of the implied forward interest rate. In our case, even if the maturity of the Eurocurrency contract is 3-months and matches the maturity of the Eurodollar contract, the synthetic contract will result in a perfect hedge only if there are no violations of interest rate parity.

Basis risk may also result when the synthetic hedge is lifted at a time t_z prior to the maturity of the futures contracts t_1. In this case, the correlation between changes in cash and futures prices need not be perfect. While the hedge need not actually be lifted, the situation would correspond to the case of a manger who undertook an anticipatory hedge as described above, but was required to report the market values of his positions every week prior to the maturity of his forward contracts. Weekly reporting might be designed for performance evaluation or regulatory purposes in the case of a bank trading operation that hedged its position *over a period* of time without intending either to take delivery or to liquidate its position *at a point* in time. Lack of perfect correlation on a week-to-week basis would indicate residual risk.

Empirical evidence on synthetic contracts

The adequacy of our proposed synthetic contract can be measured in two ways. First, we can compare the price of our synthetic with the price of an actual interest rate futures contract or an implied forward interest rate. These pricing discrepancies should be small, smaller than the cost of transactions to preclude arbitrage profit opportunities. In tests of an arbitrage boundary condition, care must be taken to obtain high-quality, time-synchronous data. Unfortunately, with synthetic prices determined by Chicago futures and Euro-interest rates based on London quotations, it may be difficult to obtain time-synchronized data. A second technique is to compute the hedging effectiveness of our synthetic contract. Comparing the hedging effectiveness with other hedging instruments offers an alternative measure of the adequacy of synthetic contracts.

Data description

Interactive Data Corporation (IDC) provided us with data on both Eurodollar and currency futures contracts as well as the 3-month and 6-month Eurocurrency offer rates. The currency futures settlement prices from IDC are given to three decimal places. We believe that having the exchange rates expressed in four decimal places is more appropriate and remedy this with data from the Chicago Mercantile Exchange (CME) *Annual Reports*, 1982–86.

Although we have daily data for Eurodollar futures starting from June 1982, we commence our hedging analysis from September 1982 to allow for seasoning of the contract. Wednesday's settlement prices are collected for the 9 months preceding the maturity date of each contract for the Eurodollar and currency futures. The prices within the settlement month itself are excluded, since contract volume declines rapidly as a contract approaches maturity. Only the near futures contract prices are used for hedging, as this contract attracts the highest liquidity and therefore represents the least costly and most efficient contract to use. Data points are excluded for those Wednesdays that are holidays.

Ideally, the prices of the cash and futures interest rates for our regression analysis should be measured at the same instant. Futures settlement prices are given at the close of trading on the International Monetary Market (IMM), 2:00 p.m. Chicago time, which is 3:00 p.m. New York time. The Eurocurrency cash deposit rates obtained from IDC are given by the London branch of the Chase Manhattan bank at the close of the London business day, 12:00 noon New York time. This gives rise to an approximate 3-hour gap. However, there is no reason why closing rates in Chicago should' be consistently higher or lower than those in London. This lack of time synchronization should not bias any of our coefficient estimates, although this could affect the R^2 measures.

The Eurocurrency deposit rates from IDC are indicative of the condition of the Eurocurrency deposit markets on the dates in question. These rates should not be considered as rates at which a trade actually takes place. Data on 3- and 6-month Eurocurrency offer rates[7] for the deposits, Euro£, EuroDM, EuroDM, EuroSFr are available since January 1982. However, for Euroyen and EuroCan$ deposits, the series from IDC started only from June 1, 1982. Therefore, the entire sample for the EuroCan$ and Euroyen synthetic hedges covers a shorter period from September 1982 to November 1986. We commence the hedging analysis from September 1982 in order to allow for the 3 months of data required for calculating the implied forward rates.

Finally, we also obtained data from IDC on the settlement prices of the London International Financial Futures Exchange (LIFFE) domestic sterling interest rate futures and the offer rates of the interbank domestic sterling deposits. These data series commenced from December 1982, but

---

[7] In addition to the 3-month rates, 6-month rates are needed in order to compute the implied forward interes rates for use in 13-week hedges.

we compare this contract's hedging performance with that of the synthetic Euro£ interest rate futures contract commencing March 1983 to allow once again for seasoning.

Synthetic prices – empirical results

In the absence of transactions costs, our model predicts that the synthetic Eurocurrency interest rate futures price should be identical to the implied Eurucurrency forward interest rate computed from the term structure of interest rates. Given our data, there are four dates per year when 3-month synthetic and implied forward rates may be compared. Descriptive statistics on the price differences for five currencies are summarized in Table 7.1. On average, these deviations appear small, ranging from between 0.1% and 0.3%. However, some individual observations are much larger, which because of the lack of time synchronization in the data is expected. As we will argue later (see Table 7.8), deviations as small as 6 basis points may be sufficient to induce arbitrage between our synthetic contract and an alternative futures contract.

Deviations between the synthetic Euro£ futures and the LIFFE domestic sterling futures computed using weekly data are also reported in Table 7.1. Again, the average deviation is small, although 11% of the observations exceed 50 basis points in absolute value. These deviations do not represent a pure arbitrage possibility as the underlying instrument of the synthetic and the LIFFE contract are not identical.

Perhaps a more important measurement is the correlation between the price of the synthetic and the alternative instrument. The correlation is uniformly high, exceeding 0.95 in four cases. This suggests that the synthetic contract should provide hedging protection nearly equivalent

Table. 7.1. *Descriptive statistics relating synthetic Eurocurrency interest rate futures and alternative instruments*

Alternative instrument	Mean deviation, %	Mean absolute, %	Minimum deviation, %	Maximum deviation, %	Correlation	No. of observations
Implied forward						
Pound	.305	.305	.047	1.033	.974	19
DM	.008	.193	−.553	.435	.976	19
SF	.093	.294	−.874	1.137	.893	19
Yen	.194	.320	−.533	2.133	.806	18
Can$	.185	.261	−.319	.703	.994	18
LIFFE	−.026	.259	−1.629	1.247	.953	194

to the next best alternative. The synthetic contract, however, has the advantage that it is based upon futures contracts that trade in highly liquid markets.

Methodology for measuring hedging effectiveness

In this paper, we use the anticipatory hedge model to examine the hedging performance of synthetic Eurocurrency interest rate futures contracts.[8] Without loss of generality, we assume that the foreign interest rate hedging problem involves an anticipated cash borrowing of 3-month foreign-currency (FC) funds in the Eurocurrency market at an interest rate linked to the London Interbank Offered Rate (LIBOR). We assume that the hedger's objective is to minimize the fluctuations in realized borrowing costs denominated in the foreign currency relative to their anticipated values.

Our research design involves two stages. First, we measure the hedging effectiveness of our synthetic contract for hedging interest rate risk for five currencies: EuroDM, EuroSFr, Euroyen, EuroCan$ and Euro£. Second, we compare the hedging performance of our synthetic contract with an actual interest rate futures contract – the London International Financial Futures Exchange (LIFFE) 3-month *domestic* interest rate futures contract – for hedging both domestic sterling and Euro£ interest rate risk.

In order to measure hedging effectiveness, we estimate the following regression model:

$$r^{FC}_{t+k} - E(r^{FC}_{t+k}|\phi_t) = \alpha + \beta(f^{FC}_{t+k} - f^{FC}_t) + \mu_t \qquad (7.6)$$

where

r^{FC}_{t+k} = the yield on our synthetic foreign-currency interest rate futures contract

$E(r^{FC}_{t+k}|\phi_t)$ = the expected foreign-currency interest rate in the cash market at time $t + k$, conditional on the information ϕ available at time t when the hedge is established and $k = 1, 2, 4,$ or 13 weeks and represents the holding period for the hedge.

The coefficient β measures the hedge ratio, defined as the percentage of futures contracts to sell per unit of anticipated borrowing. A hedge ratio of unity implies that the naive hedge, matching futures contracts on a

---

[8] The anticipatory hedge model is adapted from Peck (1975) and modified for use on financial futures by Franckle and Senchack (1982) and Overdahl and Starleaf (1986).

one-for-one basis with planned cash positions, is the optimal hedge. The estimated R^2 of Eq. (7.6) measures the percentage reduction in risk, assuming that the optimal hedge ratio has been applied. A perfect hedge with no residual risk corresponds to the case with $R^2 = 1.00$.

To implement Eq. (7.3), we use Wednesday settlement prices for Eurodollar and currency futures to calculate a series of synthetic Eurocurrency interest rate futures yields (in annualized terms) based on an underlying 3-month Eurocurrency deposit. This calculation is based on Eq. (7.5) modified as follows:

$$f_t^{FC} = \{[(\text{Near FC/Far FC})(1 + (f_t^\$/100)1/4)] - 1\} \times 400 \qquad (7.5')$$

where $f_t^\$$ is obtained by taking the difference of the Eurodollar futures settlement prices from 100. The Near and Far FC prices are the settlement prices of the two currency futures contracts that constitute the calender spread expressed in terms of $ per FC.

We calculated the synthetic yields for each of the currencies, £, DM, SFr, yen, and Can$ from June 1982 to August 1986. For the June 1982 series, we use the September 1982 Eurodollar futures and the September 1982 (Near) and December 1982 (Far) currency futures contracts. The contracts are switched when we enter into the delivery month. In the above example, come September 1, 1982, the relevant Eurodollar futures contract is the December 1982 contract, and the currency futures are the December 1982 and March 1983 ones. There are a number of missing observations, as some of the Far exchange contracts required for the calendar spread do not trade until the contracts are about 8 months from maturity. These missing observations are excluded from the regression.

Eurocurrency rates are available only for 1, 2, 3, 6, and 12 months and do not permit us to measure the implied 3-month forward rates for most intervals. Consequently for the short-period hedges – $k = 1, 2$, and 4 weeks – the spot Eurocurrency offer rates r_t^{FC} are used as proxies for $E(r_{t+k}^{FC}|\phi_t)$. However, the implied 3-month forward rate derived from the 6- and 3-month Eurocurrency cash rates can be used to serve as the corresponding proxy for $E(r_{t+k}^{FC}|\phi_t)$ in the 13-week hedges.

The empirical work in this paper is conducted within a standard regression framework. The major econometric difficulty in our application is one that is now familiar from the work of Hansen and Hodrick (1980) and others; we have weekly observations but holding periods that go beyond a week (that is, 2-weeks, 4-weeks, and 13-weeks). The method proposed in Cumby, Huizinga, and Obstfeld (1983) has the ability to estimate the covariance matrix of the coefficients consistently when the errors are serially correlated, conditionally heteroscedastic, or both. Therefore, we adopt the CHO program based on this methodology to correct for the autocorrelation problem in Eq. (7.6) that results from weekly overlapping observations.[9]

Hedging effectiveness of synthetic contracts – empirical results

Before presenting our results, it is useful to consider what an appropriate benchmark would be for gauging the success of our synthetic contract. In this respect, Black (1986) has argued that the success of a new futures contract depends heavily on its ability to provide superior hedging capabilities relative to alternative vehicles. The results of using Eurodollar futures contracts alone as a cross-hedge for nondollar Eurocurrency interest rate risk have been reported by Koh (1988). For the five Eurocurrencies analyzed here, hedging effectiveness as measured by R^2 was most often under 10%, with the exception of the Canadian dollar, where the R^2 for the 13-week holding period reached 70%. The latter result is somewhat surprising but illustrates the close corelation between U.S. and Canadian dollar interest rates.

Another benchmark might be the hedging effectiveness of the Eurodollar interest rate futures contract itself to hedge Eurodollar interest rate risk. These results are presented in Table 7.2 for our total sample period. The results indicate a level of hedging effectiveness that rises steadily as the holding period increases from 1 to 13 weeks. At the 13-week period, the optimal hedge ratio is not significantly different from unity, and the R^2 is near 90%. Our finding that the Eurodollar futures contract is not a perfect hedge at the 13-week horizon may in part reflect the lack of time synchronization in the data and the cash flow risk associated with interim futures price changes, factors that will also affect our analysis of the synthetic contracts. This is an important empirical result in that the Eurodollar futures contract is the best individual contract available for hedging Eurodollar interest rate risk, yet in this context it still falls short of providing a perfect hedge.

Our results on the synthetic futures contracts are presented in Table 7.3. In each case, the sample period is divided into two subperiods (I and II) of approximately equal size. Because the foreign-exchange value of the dollar went through a turbulent period, peaking in February 1985, we also make a second subdivision with observations from October 1982– February 1985 as subperiod I′, and March 1985–November 1986 classified as subperiod II′.[10] Only the 13-week hedge results are reported in this

---

[9] CHO refers to the "two-step, two-stage least squares" computer program, version 2.1, written by Robert Cumby and John Huizinga, based on the methodology given in Cumby, Huizinga, and Obstfeld (1983).

[10] The second subdivision begins from Oct. 1982 to allow for the effects of the Federal Reserve Board's change in targeting monetary policy.

Table 7.2. *Eurodollar direct hedge results*

(a) *Entire sample (Jun. 9, 1982–Nov. 26, 1986)*			
Holding period	N	$\hat{\beta}$ (Standard error)	R^2
1 week	234	.7953 (0.03634)*#	.6761
2 weeks	234	.8161 (0.03833)*#	.7340
4 weeks	234	.8342 (0.04217)*#	.7764
13 weeks	234	1.0351 (0.03479)*	.8999
(b) *Subperiod I (Jun. 9, 1982–Aug. 29, 1984)*			
Holding period	N	$\hat{\beta}$ (Standard error)	R^2
1 week	117	.8436 (0.04956)*#	.7192
2 weeks	117	.8680 (0.05305)*#	.7677
4 weeks	117	.8663 (0.09058)*#	.7810
13 weeks	117	1.0608 (0.04327)*	.9212
(c) *Subperiod II (Sep. 5, 1984–Nov. 26, 1986)*			
Holding period	N	$\hat{\beta}$ (Standard error)	R^2
1 week	117	.6329 (0.05422)*#	.5356
2 weeks	117	.6593 (0.05369)*#	.6438
4 weeks	117	.7262 (0.06102)*#	.7012
13 weeks	117	1.0231 (0.05795)*	.8671

* Significantly different from zero at 5% level.
\# Significantly different from one at 5% level.

paper since the 1-week, 2-week, and 4-week holding period results reflect similar improvements in hedging performance in the second subperiod.[11]

Further insights into our results may be revealed by noting that the hedge ratio is equivalent to the covariance between futures and cash price changes scaled by the variance in futures prices, while hedging effectiveness (R^2) is equal to the square of the covariance between futures and cash price changes divided by the variance of each factor. Table 7.4 provides an overall picture of how covariance and variance measures of daily changes in cash and futures prices have changed over the sample period. Note that the synthetic futures rates for all currencies are more volatile than the cash rates.

For the synthetic Euro£ hedge, hedging effectiveness as measured by R^2 reached 84% for the 13-week holding period. This figure is only slightly smaller than the 90% figures reported for the Eurodollar contract in Table 7.2. For the 13-week holding period, the optimal hedge ratio is not significantly different from unity. Comparing subperiods I and II, we find

[11] The results for the 1-, 2-, and 4-week periods were reported in an earlier version of this paper, released as working paper #3003, National Bureau of Economic Research, Aug, 1989.

Table 7.3. *Synthetic hedge results*, 13-week holding period

(a) *Entire period*[1]	N	$\hat{\beta}$ (Std. error)	R^2
Euro£	222	.9708 (.03998)*	.8391
EuroCanadian$	212	.9670 (.03600)*	.8752
EuroDM	204	.4873 (.03638)*#	.5629
EuroSFr	213	.6632 (.08635)*#	.3471
EuroYen	195	.4595 (.05631)*#	.3794

(b) *Subperiod I*[2]			
Currencies	N	$\hat{\beta}$ (Std. error)	R^2
Euro£	114	.8975 (.05393)*	.8303
EuroCanadian$	107	.9507 (.04297)*	.8971
EuroDM	95	.4286 (.05438)*#	.4833
EuroSFr	105	.6481 (.14770)*#	.2500
Euroyen	91	.1688 (.05319)*#	.1424

(c) *Subperiod II*[3]			
Currencies	N	$\hat{\beta}$ (Std. error)	R^2
Euro£	108	1.0196 (.06198)*	.8254
EuroCanadian$	105	1.0102 (.06731)*	.8345
EuroDM	107	.7098 (.04348)*#	.8061
EuroSFr	108	.5636 (.08172)*#	.4501
Euroyen	104	.7632 (.09535)*#	.6081

(d) *Subperiod I'*[4]			
Currencies	N	$\hat{\beta}$(Std. error)	R^2
Euro£	120	.8395 (.04975)*#	.8153
EuroCanadian$	120	.9645 (.03656)*	.9078
EuroDM	107	1.1297 (.05438)*	.5430
EuroSFr	112	.4541 (.11601)*#	.3026
Euroyen	104	.9273 (.09750)*	.1308

(e) *Subperiod II'*[5]			
Currencies	N	$\hat{\beta}$(Std. error)	R^2
Euro£	85	.8193 (.05688)*#	.8312
EuroCanadian$	86	.8166 (.06084)*#	.8169
EuroDM	84	1.2279 (.13564)*	.5587
EuroSFr	84	.8657 (.09923)*	.5343
Euroyen	85	.7955 (.07530)*#	.6850

[1] Entire period for sterling, DM, and Sfr is from Jun. 9, 1982, to Nov. 26, 1986. For Can$ and yen, entire period is from Sep. 1, 1982 to Nov. 26, 1986.
[2] Subperiod I for sterling, DM, and Sfr is from Jun. 9, 1982, to Aug. 29, 1984. For Can$ and yen, subperiod I is from Sep. 1, 1982, to Oct. 10, 1984.
[3] Subperiod II for sterling, DM, and Sfr is from Sep. 5, 1984, to Nov. 26, 1986. For Can$ and yen, subperiod II is from Nov. 17, 1984, to Nov. 26, 1986.
[4] Subperiod I' for all currencies is from Oct. 6, 1982, to Feb. 27, 1984.
[5] Subperiod II' for all currencies is from Mar. 6, 1985 to Nov. 26, 1986.
* Significantly differently from zero at 5% level.
# Significantly different from one at 5% level.

Table 7.4. *Covariance and variance measures for daily changes in cash and synthetic futures rates*

(a) *Euro£ (Jan. 1982–Dec. 1986)*

Year	$\text{Cov}(\Delta s_t, \Delta c_t)$	Corr coeff	$\text{Var}(\Delta c_t)$	$\text{Var}(\Delta f_t)$
Whole sample	.0120	.2760	.0250	.0750
1982	.0075	.1960	.0180	.0810
1983	.0027	.0750	.0100	.1250
1984	.0120	.3320	.0280	.0470
1985	.0280	.4390	.0490	.0850
1986	.0079	.3210	.0170	.0350

(b) *EuroCanadian dollar (Jun. 1982–Dec. 1986)*

Year	$\text{Cov}(\Delta s_t, \Delta c_t)$	Corr coeff	$\text{Var}(\Delta c_t)$	$\text{Var}(\Delta f_t)$
Whole sample	.0049	.1510	.0300	.0360
1982	.0160	.1850	.0660	.1080
1983	.0002	.0100	.0150	.0210
1984	.0023	.0720	.0480	.0210
1985	.0034	.1690	.0130	.0310
1986	.0061	.2850	.0200	.0230

(c) *EuroDM (Jan. 1982–Dec. 1986)*

Year	$\text{Cov}(\Delta s_t, \Delta c_t)$	Corr coeff	$\text{Var}(\Delta c_t)$	$\text{Var}(\Delta f_t)$
Whole sample	.0011	.0620	.0058	.0550
1982	.0043	.1150	.0094	.1520
1983	−.0007	−.0290	.0083	.0700
1984	−.0003	−.0310	.0053	.0240
1985	.0013	.1660	.0035	.0180
1986	.0004	.0940	.0021	.0078

(d) *EuroSFr (Jan. 1982–Dec. 1986)*

Year	$\text{Cov}(\Delta s_t, \Delta c_t)$	Corr coeff	$\text{Var}(\Delta c_t)$	$\text{Var}(\Delta f_t)$
Whole sample	.0029	.0830	.0210	.0600
1982	.0094	.1180	.0440	.1430
1983	.0016	.0490	.0250	.0450
1984	.0020	.0910	.0120	.0390
1985	.0004	.0170	.0100	.0470
1986	.0002	.0170	.0110	.0200

(e) *Euroyen (Jun. 1982–Dec. 1986)*

Year	$\text{Cov}(\Delta s_t, \Delta c_t)$	Corr coeff	$\text{Var}(\Delta c_t)$	$\text{Var}(\Delta f_t)$
Whole sample	.0014	.0790	.0060	.0510
1982	.0048	.1280	.0085	.1660
1983	−.0011	−.0650	.0051	.0580
1984	.0009	.0750	.0047	.0330
1985	.0023	.1480	.0077	.0310
1986	.0013	.1980	.0049	.0091

that hedging effectiveness is higher in subperiod I, although the hedge ratio is higher in subperiod II. However, under our second subdivision, the results tend to show higher hedging effectiveness but lower hedge ratios in subperiod II' as compared to I'. From Table 7.4, we see that the variance of Euro£ interest rates increased in 1985. Therefore, despite the higher covariance between cash and futures prices, hedging effectiveness changed only slightly.

Turning to the EuroCan$ deposit in Table 7.3 we observe an R^2 of .88 for the 13-week holding period. This figure is very near the hedging effectiveness of the Eurodollar contract in hedging dollar risk. For the 13-week period, the optimal hedge ratio is not significantly different from unity. Viewing the parameters in terms of subperiods I and II indicate that the R^2 is slightly higher in subperiod I than in subperiod II. However, in terms of the second subdivision based on the relative strength of the dollar, the 13-week hedge ratio in subperiod I' is not significantly different from one. Hedging effectiveness is again slightly lower in subperiod II' as compared to subperiod I'. While the covariance between changes in EuroCan$ cash and synthetic EuroCan$ futures rates increased over 1985 and 1986, the volatilities of both cash and futures rates have increased.

For the entire sample period, it appears that the hedging effectiveness of the synthetic hedge for the EuroDM hedge is not as impressive as that of the Eurosterling and EuroCan$. However, examining the results by subperiods allows us to have a better understanding of the potential hedging effectiveness of the EuroDM synthetic hedge. We observe that subperiod I is characterized by much higher residual risk for the synthetic DM hedge than is the case in subperiod II. For example, the 13-week R^2 of .81 in subperiod II is almost double that of .48 registered in subperiod I. This takes place despite the greater volatility of US$/DM exchange rates in 1985 and 1986 (annualized volatilities of 15% and 13%) compared to the average volatility of 10% from 1982–84. From Table 7.4, we see that the variance for changes in EuroDM cash and synthetic futures rates declined progressively over the years. Both cash and futures interest rates' volatilities peaked in 1983, with cash rates' volatility getting lower faster while futures rates' volatility decline at a slower rate given the higher volatilities of the US$/DM exchange rate in 1985 and 1986. The improvement in hedging effectiveness for the 13-week hedge in subperiod II is due to the fact that the volatility of the synthetic futures rates register a large drop going from 1983 to 1984.

When we examine the hedge ratios under the second subdivision, both subperiods' hedge ratios are not very far from the naive hedge given the decline in EuroDM futures volatility. On the whole, hedging effectiveness improves under the second subdivision and interestingly, the R^2 measures are not sensitive to foreign-exchange trends, giving about the same values regardless of whether the U.S. dollar is appreciating or depreciating. The covariance between changes in EuroDM cash and futures rates declines in 1983 and 1984, with the highest covariance reported for 1985. This suggests that the greater coordination between U.S. and German interest rate policies during the latter half of the sample period resulted in a closer relationship between EuroDM cash and synthetic EuroDM futures rates. This also contributes to the higher hedge ratios reported in subperiod II'.

While the results reported in Table 7.3 on the EuroSFr hedge over the entire sample period may represent an improvement over that of cross-hedging with Eurodollar futures, the R^2's do not appear too impressive. But the picture is again different when viewed across subperiods. Under the first subdivision, subperiod II's R^2 measure for the 13-week hedge of .45 is almost double that of subperiod I's. The US$/SFr exchange rate was the most volatile among exchange rates, and this certainly affected the volatility of the synthetic EuroSFr interest rate futures. In fact, changes in both EuroSFr cash and futures rates had higher variances in the first half of the sample period than the later half. This helps to explain the improvement in hedging effectiveness during subperiod II.

When the subdivision is based on the relative strength of the US$, the R^2 of the 13-week hedge again showed an improvement with R^2 at .53 in subperiod II' compared to a R^2 of .30 in subperiod I'. Also, the hedge ratio derived from this hedge is not significantly different from one. The relatively high basis risks in the EuroSFr hedges as compared to that of the other currencies can be explained in terms of the much lower cash to futures market linkage as well as the higher volatility of the futures rates. While volatility has declined over the past few years, the covariance has not changed. The covariance between the daily changes in EuroSFr cash rates and the synthetic EuroSFr rates was in fact higher in the early part of the sample period and declined over 1985 and 1986, but the R^2's still improve due to lower volatilities of both cash and futures rates.

Levich (1982) found that in tests of interest rate parity for 3-month EuroSFr deposits, more than 20% of the observations appear to lie outside the stated no-arbitrage boundaries of .25%. Of course, if traders have transactions costs in excess of .25%, then the bounds are too low. However, it would appear that the deviations from interest parity are higher during periods of higher volatility in both Swiss franc interest rates and exchange rates. Therefore, the better hedging performance of the synthetic EuroSFr futures over the last 2 years of our sample period may also be attributed to more efficient pricing of the synthetic contract in accordance with interest rate parity.

Finally, we present the results of the synthetic Euroyen hedges. Clearly, over the whole sample period, the synthetic hedges do better than using Eurodollar futures alone to hedge the fluctuations in Euroyen borrowing costs. While the R^2 for the 13-week hedge is only .38 for the whole sample period, the results in terms of subperiods are more encouraging. From Table 7.3, we observe that for 13-week hedges, the R^2 of .61 in subperiod II is significantly higher than the corresponding figure of .14 in subperiod I. A number of important changes in regulations governing the Japanese financial market were instituted immediately before and during subperiod II.[12] All these changes were in the direction of relaxing controls over the participation by foreign banks and nonresidents in the Euroyen market. It could be argued that these moves allowed for greater liquidity in the Euroyen deposit market and contributed to the higher hedging effectiveness measures of the synthetic Euroyen hedges. The hedge ratio is also higher in subperiod II, attesting to the increased covariance of cash and futures rates in the Euroyen markets. The higher R^2 and hedge ratio were also reinforced by the decreasing volatility of the synthetic Euroyen futures rates.

When hedging effectiveness is examined under the second subdivision, the 13-week R^2 of .69 is an improvement of about $4\frac{1}{2}$ times in comparison to subperiod I'. Under the second subdivision, the 13-week hedge ratio of .93 in subperiod I' is not significantly different from one. However, the 13-week hedge ratio of .80 in subperiod II' represents a less costly hedge (less futures needed to be sold), and, in addition, results in higher hedging effectiveness. Therefore, the synthetic Euroyen hedge has been increasingly effective after 1985.

Stability of regression parameters: To examine the stability of the slope and intercept coefficients over the two subdivisions for all the synthetic hedges, we perform a dummy variable test as in the following equation:

$$r_{t+k}^{FC} - E(r_{t+k}^{FC}|\phi_t)$$
$$= \alpha + \beta_1(f_{t+k}^{FC} - f_t^{FC}) + \beta_2 D_1 + \beta_3[D_1(f_{t+k}^{FC} - f_t^{FC})] + \mu_t \qquad (7.6)$$

$$\text{where } D_1 = 1 \text{ for subperiod I}$$
$$= 0 \text{ for subperiod II.}$$

The relevant standard errors and Wald statistic that tests $\hat{\beta}_2 = \hat{\beta}_3 = 0$ are given in Table 7.5.[13] The results confirm our observations made earlier. All of the Wald statistics across all currencies and hedge horizons reject the equality of the joint hypothesis $\hat{\beta}_2 = \hat{\beta}_3 = 0$.

---

[12] See Occasional Paper 43, *International Capital Markets – Developments and Prospects*, International Monetary Fund, Washington, D.C., Feb. 1986.

[13] The Wald statistic is distributed as an F statistic.

Table 7.5. *Tests of the stability of intercept and slope coefficients in synthetic hedges, 13-week holding period*

Currencies	α_0	$\hat{\beta}_1$	$\hat{\beta}_2$	$\hat{\beta}_3$	Wald stat	R^2
Euro£	.2096 (.07831)*	1.0196 (.06045)*	−.1297 (.11727)	−.1221 (.08418)	2.990#	.8432
EuroCan$	−.2034 (.08306)	1.0102 (.06499)*	−.0031 (.11781)	−.0594 (.07811)	.676	.8761
EuroDM	−.1990 (.05946)*	.7098 (.08333)*	−.0743 (.08849)	−.2813 (.09247)*	9.329#	.5938
EuroSFr	−.0176 (.11812)	.5636 (.14041)*	−.2300 (.18631)	.0845 (.18101)	2.755#	.3669
Euroyen	−.0274 (.05187)	.7632 (.06959)*	−.0033 (.08345)	−.5944 (.09722)*	41.460#	.5432

Note: Standard errors in parentheses.
* Significantly different from zero at 5% level.
# Significant for rejection of joint equality of $\hat{\beta}_2$ and $\hat{\beta}_3$ to zero.

In the case of the Eurosterling and EuroCan$ synthetic hedges, the R^2's arrived at allowing for changes in parameters are only 1 to 2 percentage points higher than the R^2's obtained in Table 7.3. The $\hat{\beta}_2$'s and $\hat{\beta}_3$'s are not individually significantly different from zero although the Wald statistics show that they are jointly significant.

On the other hand, for EuroDM, EuroSFr, and Euroyen synthetic futures, parameter shifts play a more important role. First, for the EuroDM deposit, the R^2 improves by approximately 3 percentage points when parameter shifts are allowed. Furthermore, the slope coefficient change is significant, implying that the relationship between changes in the EuroDM cash rates and the synthetic futures rates differs over the two subperiods. We know that the volatilities of both US$/DM exchange rate futures and Eurodollar futures increased in subperiod II as compared to that in subperiod I. Therefore, we can safely conclude that the higher slope coefficient for a subperiod II hedge is a result of an increase in the covariance measure that surpasses the variance increases.

In the case of the EuroSFr deposit, the R^2 measure is only slightly better than the one shown in Table 7.3. It appears that market imperfections are present that prevent the EuroSFr interest rates from being closely related to the synthetic EuroSFr futures yields.

Finally, as expected, incorporating shifts in the intercept and slope parameters results in significantly higher R^2's for the synthetic Euroyen hedge. Hedging effectiveness improves by 19 percentage points. Furthermore, the slope coefficient $(\hat{\beta}_3)$ is significantly higher in subperiod II. It could be argued that the relaxation of controls over activities in the Euroyen market resulted in a closer alignment of the synthetic Euroyen futures rates to the Euroyen cash rates.

Comparison of synthetic Euro£ futures with LIFFE domestic £ futures

The underlying instrument of the LIFFE domestic sterling interest rate futures is the 3-month sterling deposit in the London interbank market. Our synthetic Eurosterling futures contract is designed to hedge the 3-month Eurosterling deposit. In this section, we analyze the hedging performance of the two contracts in terms of hedging both domestic sterling deposit and Eurosterling deposit offer rates. These results are given in Table 7.6. We start the hedging analysis for identical periods from March 1983 to November 1986 in order to allow the LIFFE contract a seasoning period. In this case, the R^2 measures are directly comparable across contracts as the dependent variables are the same.

Taking the domestic sterling deposits as the cash instrument shows that the LIFFE contract narrowly outperforms the synthetic contract. The difference in R^2 is only 4% for the 13-week hedge over the whole sample period. The higher R^2's in favor of the LIFFE domestic sterling interest rate futures contract are to be expected since the synthetic contract represents a cross-hedge in comparison. When the cash instrument is the Eurosterling deposit, the LIFFE contract also performs better consistently. However, this time, the difference in hedging effectiveness averages only about 3% in favor of the LIFFE domestic sterling interest rate futures. To measure the significance of these results, we use an F test suggested by Black (1986):

$$F = \frac{\text{Residual risk of synthetic sterling futures}}{\text{Residual risk of LIFFE sterling futures}}$$

$$= (1 - R^2)_{\text{Syn}}/(1 - R^2)_{\text{LIFFE}}$$

The F statistics in Table 7.7 show that only for one case (the 4-week hedge) is it possible to reject the null hypothesis H_0: $(1 - R^2)_{\text{Syn}} = (1 - R^2)_{\text{LIFFE}}$ at the 5% significance level.[14] With this exception, the results confirm that the hedging effectiveness of the LIFFE contract and the synthetic contract are not statistically different. The decision to use the

---

[14] The critical value of F (184, 184) at the 97.5% confidence level for a two-tailed test is 1.336.

Table 7.6. *Comparison of synthetic Eurosterling futures with LIFFE domestic sterling futures, 13-week holding period*

		Cash market Domestic sterling	Eurosterling
	LIFFE	$R^2 = .8383$ $\hat{\beta} = 1.0036$	$R^2 = .8317$ $\hat{\beta} = 1.0155$
Futures contract	Synthetic Eurosterling	$R^2 = .7975$ $\hat{\beta} = 1.0249$	$R^2 = .8060$ $\hat{\beta} = 1.0484$

For 13-week hedges, entire period Mar. 1983–Nov. 1986 ($N = 185$)

		Cash market Domestic sterling	Eurosterling
	LIFFE	$R^2 = .6984$ $\hat{\beta} = 1.0151$	$R^2 = .6188$ $\hat{\beta} = .9355$
Futures contract	Synthetic Eurosterling	$R^2 = .6194$ $\hat{\beta} = .9415$	$R^2 = .6132$ $\hat{\beta} = .9389$

For 13-week hedges, subperiod I: Mar. 1983–Jan. 1985 ($N = 92$)

		Cash market Domestic sterling	Eurosterling
	LIFFE	$R^2 = .8589$ $\hat{\beta} = .9875$	$R^2 = .8709$ $\hat{\beta} = 1.0112$
Futures contract	Synthetic Eurosterling	$R^2 = .8259$ $\hat{\beta} = 1.0159$	$R^2 = .8395$ $\hat{\beta} = 1.0419$

For 13-week hedges, subperiod II: Jan 1985–Nov. 1986 ($N = 93$)

Table 7.7. *Comparison of synthetic Eurosterling futures with LIFFE domestic sterling futures—F statistics (for entire period Mar. 1983 – Nov. 1986)*

		Cash market Domestic sterling	Eurosterling
	1 week	1.2254	1.2294
Holding periods	2 weeks	1.1736	1.0849
	4 weeks	1.4299*	1.0241
	13 weeks	1.2523	1.1527

* Significant for rejection of the null hypothesis at 5% level.

LIFFE Euro£ contract or the synthetic contract would depend on other economic factors, in particular contract prices and transaction costs. The synthetic contract involves Eurodollar and currency futures contracts that trade in deeper and more liquid markets that may be subject to less mispricing in comparison to the LIFFE contract. However, transaction costs will be greater for the synthetic contract, perhaps by about $137 per synthetic contract (See Table 7.8). At $25 per basis point in contract price, $137 represents 5.48 basis points. Holding hedging effectiveness fixed, a synthetic contract would need to be priced 5.48 basis points more favorably to be competitive with the LIFFE contract.

The subperiod hedging performance of the LIFFE domestic sterling interest rate futures contract and that of the synthetic Euro£ interest rate futures are also interesting. For the LIFFE contract, R^2's in subperiod II are generally higher than the ones in subperiod I. For the 13-week hedge on domestic sterling cash deposit, R^2 increases from .70 to .86; when the underlying cash instrument is the Euro£ deposit, R^2 increases from .62 to .87.

Likewise for the synthetic Eurosterling interest rate futures, hedging performance improves in the second half of the sample period. When the underlying deposit is the domestic sterling deposit, the synthetic cross-hedge R^2 for the 13-week holding period increases from .62 in subperiod I to .83 in subperiod II. For the Euro£ cash deposit, R^2 also improves from .61 to .84, moving from subperiod I to subperiod II.

All these results speak well of the hedging performance of the synthetic Euro£ interest rate futures. However, the market is the best judge of a futures contract's success. We suspect that the LIFFE domestic sterling futures contract manages to succeed because it meets the direct hedging function on domestic sterling deposits and the cross-hedging function on Eurosterling deposits more cost effectively than the next best alternative, the synthetic Eurosterling contract.[15]

Conclusions and policy implications

Our purpose in this paper was to show that, despite the absence of specific instruments for hedging nondollar interest rate risk, an effective way for managing this risk has been feasible, using readily available futures contracts. We have demonstrated that, in theory, it is possible to replicate a Eurocurrency interest rate futures contract using Eurodollar interest rate futures in conjunction with currency futures. In principle, our

---

[15] LIFFE reported the following figures for their domestic sterling contract. In early 1986, volume averaged approximately 50,000 contracts per month (2500 per day) and in Jan. 1989, this had grown to 400,000 contracts per month (20,000 per day).

proposed synthetic contract perfectly mimics the cash flows of a true, Eurocurrency interest rate futures contract. In practice, the limited availability of Eurodollar futures at all maturity dates, the fixed size of available contracts, and deviations from Interest Rate Parity in the currency futures market may make our synthetic contract an imperfect substitute for a true Eurocurrency interest rate futures. However, given that the deviations from Interest Rate Parity are likely to be extremely small, our synthetic contract should hold considerable promise for corporations with large positions denominated in Eurocurrency interest rates, and for which the terms on these positions float continuously vis-à-vis the Eurocurrency LIBOR rate.

The empirical evidence presented in this paper shows that with the greater integration and liberalization of financial markets, there is increasing potential for higher hedging effectiveness in the synthetic futures contracts. For the latter half of our sample period, the 13-week R^2 measures for the synthetic Euro£ futures and that of the EuroCanadian dollar futures are both as high as .83. The respective hedge ratios of 1.02 and 1.01 are both not significantly different from the naive hedge. For the synthetic EuroDM, the 13-week hedging effectiveness measure reported that 81% of the cash market risk is eliminated, although the presence of higher basis risk resulted in a hedge ratio of .71, which is significantly less than one. The synthetic Euroyen futures performance is also exceptional with a 13-week R^2 measuring .61 and a commensurate hedge ratio of .76, once again suggesting that underhedging is optimal. The least effective results are for the EuroSFr synthetic hedge. For the 13-week hedge, only 45% of the cash market risk is reduced by hedging with a hedge ratio of .56 reflecting the higher amount of basis risk present.

We also compared the hedging performance of the synthetic Eurosterling futures with that of the LIFFE domestic sterling futures contract. The differences in 13-week R^2's are extremely small. Both contracts eliminated over 80% of the risk present in a portfolio of futures and cash deposits, whether the cash deposit rate is that of a domestic sterling deposit or a Euro£ deposit.

In recent months, several Eurocurrency interest rate futures contracts have been introduced on exchanges around the world: a EuroFrench franc contract in Paris (MATIF, September 1988), a EuroDM contract in London (LIFFE, April 1989), a Euroyen contract in Tokyo (TIFFE, June 1989), a similar EuroYen contract in Singapore (SIMEX, October 1989), and a EuroDM contract in Singapore (SIMEX, September 1990). In July 1989, the Chicago Mercantile Exchange introduced the DIFF contract, the price of which depends on the interest differential between the 3-month Eurodollar and a 3-month Eurocurrency rate. Another synthetic Eurocurrency interest rate futures could be constructed by combining a Eurodollar interest rate futures with a DIFF contract.

Notwithstanding these recent developments, the research reported here suggests several important implications for the future of international financial markets and for the development of corporate financial policies. First, as far as government policymakers are concerned, our synthetic Eurocurrency interest rate futures contract represents yet another example of how financial innovation allows agents to circumvent market controls or redress a market failure. The slow development of true, nondollar interest rate futures markets has very likely encouraged agents to consider the types of synthetic arrangements we have described. Artificial impediments to the development of nondollar interest rate futures markets may have simply altered the locus of trading and the specifics of the contracting, without actually halting the hedging or speculation on nondollar interest rate movements.

Statistics from the Chicago Mercantile Exchange reveal that in the 1981–85 period, more than 25% of the open interest in Eurodollar futures was attributed to non-U.S.-based commercial banks.[16] It is not possible to know exactly why these transactions occurred. They may reflect attempts to manage risks associated with dollar or Eurodollar positions held by foreigners. But they also may reflect an attempt to manage nondollar interest rate risks in the manner in which we have suggested.[17]

Second, from the standpoint of corporations or portfolio managers, our theoretical pricing model clearly shows how synthetic contracts can be constructed even for currencies without an actual Euro-interest rate futures contract. Managers with interest rate exposure in Australian dollars, Belgian francs, Italian lire, ECU, and so forth may find synthetics a useful risk management too¹.

Third, the synthetic approach raises possibilities for commercial and investment banks. Banks could construct synthetic contracts to hedge their own nondollar interest rate risk or offer synthetic contracts for sale to clients. Banks could also attempt to earn arbitrage profits by monitoring price differences between existing interest rate futures contracts (or implied forward interest rates) and synthetic prices. It appears as though at least a 5 to 6 basis point spread would be necessary to induce arbitrage.

Fourth, the rapid development of new financial products and financial marketplaces raises the issue of whether a true Eurocurrency and foreign-currency interest rate futures contract will soon be developed. As

---

[16] Calculated from data in the Bank for International Settlements (1986) report, p. 146.
[17] Rombach and Walsh (1988) describe an example using the cash Eurocurrency market and foreign-exchange forward contracts to hedge foreign-currency interest rate risk.

Black (1986) has argued, for a futures contract to be successful, it must fill a gap – it must provide a new or more cost-effective mechanism for hedging risks that previously was not satisfied. For the new contracts at LIFFE, MATIF, TIFFE, and SIMEX to succeed, they must compete with synthetics of two types, the one described in this paper and another built around the CME's DIFF contract. Our analysis demonstrates that the former synthetic contracts offer an effective means (and in some cases, very highly so) for hedging Eurocurrency interest rate risk. Furthermore, the individual components of our synthetic contract are well known for trading in deep and liquid markets that encourage accurate pricing. The lack of true futures contracts for nondollar Eurocurrency interest rates in this situation may not represent a market failure and may not represent a profitable, new contract for an exchange to develop.

An analogy can be drawn to the market for "cross-rates" in the foreign-exchange market. With N currencies in the world, there are $(N^2 - N)/2$ bilateral exchange rates. (With $N = 150$ countries, the total is 11,175 bilateral exchange rates.) In practice these markets are served by the $N - 1$ individual exchange rates of each currency vis-à-vis the U.S. dollar.[18] A transaction between, for example, the Swedish kroner (SK) and the Mexican peso (MP) is done indirectly, using SK/$ and $/MP quotations and exchanges. The U.S. dollar here serves the role of a vehicle currency; the two transactions involve lower liquidity risks and transaction costs than a single exchange in the SK/MP market. The absence of a separate SK/MP foreign-exchange market is not a market failure but an optimal response to the cost of establishing and maintaining the SK/MP market relative to the synthetic, indirect approach.

In a similar fashion, Eurodollar and currency futures contracts may play a role as "vehicle instruments," allowing agents to construct synthetic Eurocurrency interest rate futures at low cost. The demand for a true Eurocurrency interest rate futures market would depend on a comparison with the pricing, transaction costs, and hedging effectiveness of synthetic contracts. In this paper, we have focused on one of those attributes, hedging effectiveness. Our results suggest that on this basis the synthetic contract may often be a highly effective substitute for actual interest rate futures contracts.

Contract pricing and transactions costs are also important determinants of the success or failure of a new product. From our analysis (in Table 7.8) it is clear that the CME's DIFF contract is equivalent to a jumbo calendar spread – a portfolio of many near-term and far-term forward exchange contracts. However, even though the DIFF contract is redun-

[18] The DM/pound sterling cross-rate is one exception.

Table 7.8. *Comparison of transactions costs between actual LIFFE sterling futures contract and synthetic Eurosterling futures contract*

Synthetic contract for £500,000		
1 CME Eurodollar futures		$11.00
(contract size is $1,000,000)		
8 CME $/pound near-term currency futures		72.00
8 CME $/pound far-term currency futures		72.00
(contract size is £62,500)		
	Total	155.00
Actual LIFFE sterling futures contract		
1 LIFFE contract (size is £500,000)		18.00
	Difference $	137.00

Note: At $25 per tick, $137 equal 5.48 ticks. If a LIFEE sterling contract were priced at 87.50 (12.50%), a synthetic contract would have to be priced at 87.44 (on the buy side) or 87.56 (on the sell side) to make the synthetic contract competitive in terms of price. Calculations assume exchange rate of $2.00/£.
Source: Transaction costs supplied by large New York futures trading firm.

dant, it may offer substantial savings in terms of transaction costs. A clearer picture of the role of synthetic interest rate futures will emerge once our analysis is extended to include pricing and transaction cost considerations.

References

Bank for International Settlements, *Recent Innovations in International Banking,* Basle: BIS, 1986.

Bank for International Settlements, *59th Annual Report,* Basle: BIS, 1989.

Black, D. G. (1986), *Success and Failure of Futures Contracts: Theory and Empirical Evidence,* New York University Salomon Center, Monograph Series in Finance and Economics, Monograph 1986–1.

Cornell, B., and M. Reinganum (1981), "Forward and Futures Price: Evidence from the Foreign Exchange Markets," *Journal of Finance,* 36, No. 5 (Dec.), pp. 1035–45.

Cox, J. L., Ingersoll, J. E., and S. A. Ross (1981). "The Relation Between Forward Prices and Futures Prices," *Journal of Financial Economics,* 9, pp. 321–46.

Cumby, R. E., J. Huizinga, and M. Obstfeld (1983), "Two-Step Two-Stage Least Squares Estimation in Models with Rational Expectations," *Journal of Econometrics,* 21, pp. 333–55.

Figlewski, S. (1986), *Hedging with Financial Futures for Institutional Investors: From Theory to Practice,* Cambridge, Mass.: Ballinger.

Franckle, C. T., and A. J. Senchack Jr. (1982), "Economic Considerations in the Use of Interest Rate Futures," *Journal of Futures Markets,* 2, no. 1, pp. 107–16.

Frenkel, J. A., and R. M. Levich (1988), "Spot and Forward Contracts," in J. Eatwell, M. Millgate, and P. Newman (eds.), *The New Palgrave: A Dictionary of Economic Thought and Doctrine*, London: Macmillan, 4, pp. 442–44.

Hansen, L., and R. Hodrick (1980), "Risk Averse Speculation in the Forward Foreign Exchange Market," *in* J. Frenkel (ed.), *Exchange Rates and International Macroeconomics*, Chicago: University of Chicago Press.

Jarrow, R. A., and G. S. Oldfeld (1981), "Forward Contracts and Futures Contracts," *Journal of Financial Economics*, 9, pp. 373–82.

Koh, Annie (1988), *A Study of the Effectiveness of Hedging Dollar and Non-Dollar Borrowing Costs with Eurodollar and Currency Futures Contracts*, Unpublished Ph.D. dissertation, New York University, April.

Levich, R. M. (1982), "The Efficiency of Markets for Foreign Exchange: A Review and Extension," *in* R. Kolb and G. Gay (eds.), *International Finance: Concepts and Issues*, Richmond, Va.: Robert F. Dame, Inc.

Levich, R. M. (1988), "Financial Innovations in International Financial Markets," *in* M. Feldstein (ed.), *The United States and the World Economy*, Chicago: University of Chicago Press.

Morgan Guaranty Trust Company, *World Financial Markets*, Aug. 17, 1988.

Overdahl, J. A., and D. R. Starleaf (1986), "The Hedging Performance of the CD Futures Markets," *Journal of Futures Markets*, 6, no. 1, pp. 71–81.

Peck, A. E. (1975), "Hedging and Income Stability: Concepts, Implications and An Example," Journal paper 5858, Purdue University Agricultural Experiment Station.

Richard, S. F., and M. Sundaresan (1981), "A Continuous Time Equilibrium Model of Commodity Prices in a Multigood Economy," *Journal of Financial Economics*, 9, pp. 347–71.

Rombach, Edward and Carl Walsh, (1981), "Synthesising Non-Dollar Interest Rate Futures," *Risk*, 1, no. 9, Aug.–Sep.

CHAPTER 8

The volatility of the Japanese stock indices: evidence from the cash and futures markets

MENACHEM BRENNER
MARTI SUBRAHMANYAM
JUN UNO

Introduction

Recently, there has been considerable interest among both academics and practitioners in the study of the volatility of prices of financial assets. Part of the reason for this interest is the widespread perception that the volatility of financial markets has increased over the past 2 decades and especially so in the last 3 years.

Several explanations have been offered for the purported increase in volatility of financial markets, in general, and stock markets, in particular, during this period. First, it is argued that since the first oil price shock of 1973, there has been greater economic uncertainty in many industrialized countries. In turn, this uncertainty may have been transmitted to the prices of financial assets. Second, financial markets in many countries have been deregulated in the past few years, making them more competitive and responsive to the arrival of new information. The deregulation of financial markets has taken many forms, ranging from the removal of barriers to entry for new market participants to the relaxation of restraints on trading. It is argued by some that this deregulation has allowed prices to fluctuate more freely and has contributed to an increase in volatility.

A third factor that is often cited as being responsible for the increase in volatility and its transmission from one market to another is the strengthening of the linkages between markets in different countries. Examples of such linkages are trading networks, multiple listing of stocks, and more efficient mechanisms for relaying information. The transmission of price shocks from one market to the other was seen quite clearly during the October 1987 crash, and also subsequently, whenever there were large fluctuations in prices in any of the major financial markets of the world.[1]

Fourth, there has been an explosion in terms of the number and variety of derivative securities that are traded in financial markets around the

---

[1] See Hamao, Masulis, and Ng (1990) for an empirical analysis of the transmission of price shocks from one market to the other.

176

world. Products such as futures and options contracts on stocks, bonds, foreign exchange, and most important commodities are now traded in many countries. Some market observers have blamed these derivative products for the increase in volatility. Hence, the issue of trading in such products has received much attention in academic research as well as in the many studies commissioned in the aftermath of the October 1987 crash.

A fifth issue that is closely related to the introduction of derivative products is the rapid change in trading technology that has taken place in recent years. Various forms of computerized order routing systems, automatic trading systems, and information systems are being used today that were unknown even a few years ago. The combination of liquid markets for derivative products and computerized trading technologies has made it possible for market participants today to implement complex trading strategies, such as portfolio insurance and program trading, in a matter of seconds, that would have been infeasible in earlier years.

It is important to verify whether volatility has, in fact, increased over the past 2 decades, and particularly, in the last 5 years or so. Furthermore, distinguishing between the various hypotheses explaining the increase has many ramifications. Policymaking regarding financial regulation of markets and the introduction of new financial products will depend on the validity of one or more of the alternative explanations. For example, the impact of trading in derivative products on the volatility of the underlying asset has obvious implications for regulatory policy relating to new financial products. At a more microeconomic level, a better understanding of the behavior of volatility and its causal factors would be useful in designing trading systems. Such an understanding is also important in the valuation and hedging of derivative products such as options, warrants, and convertible securities, since the volatility of the underlying asset is a crucial variable in these cases.

In the present study, we examine the evidence in the context of the Japanese stock market and provide some stylized facts regarding the behavior of volatility in this market. In particular, we analyze the behavior of the volatility of the two main Japanese stock market indices and the futures contracts based on these indices. We test hypotheses regarding the behavior of volatility and autocorrelation of price changes before and after the introduction of the futures contracts. We also present evidence regarding the volatility of the futures contracts compared with the respective underlying spot indices.

Prior research

Most of the previous studies of volatility have been carried out in the context of U.S. financial markets and, in particular, U.S. stock markets.

Broadly speaking, these studies examine three related questions. First, what was the pattern of volatility of financial markets in the past? Second, was there a secular change in the volatility of these markets, particularly in the post-1973 period? Third, what was the impact on volatility of the introduction of derivative instruments such as futures and options contracts?

Anderson (1985) investigates the behavior of volatility of selected commodity futures contracts and finds that the volatility is not constant. The principal predictable factor in explaining the fluctuations in volatility. is seasonality. French, Schwert, and Stambaugh (1987) examine the relationship between stock returns and volatility. They find that the expected market risk premium is positively related to the predictable component of the volatility of the return on the Standard and Poor's 500 (S&P500) stock index. More recently, Schwert (1989) analyzes the behavior of the monthly volatility of the S&P500 stock index and finds that the fluctuations in volatility cannot be accounted for by macroeconomic variables such as inflation and money growth.

Edwards (1988) examines the data on U.S. stock market indices and short-term riskless debt instruments during the period from 1973 to 1987. He concludes that the volatility of the stock market, as measured by that of two commonly used indices, the Standard and Poor's 500 Index (S&P500) and the Value Line Stock Index, either remained the same or declined during the period 1982–86 as compared with the period 1973–79. A similar secular decline in volatility was recorded in the case of the volatility of short-term interest rates as measured by those on Treasury Bills and Eurodollar deposits. However, in both cases, the peak volatility occurred during the period 1979–82, which Edwards ascribes to shifts in monetary policy that took place in October 1979 and October 1982.

The impact of introduction of derivative assets on the volatility of the underlying assets has been studied by several authors in the recent past. There are several aspects of the general question that have been examined. The first is a comparison of the volatility of the underlying asset markets before and after the introduction of derivative instruments.[2] With the exception of one study [Harris (1989)] that documents a slight increase in volatility, these studies conclude that there was a decline in volatility after the introduction of futures trading. For example, Edwards (1988) concludes that, with the possible exception of the period 1979–82, when

---

[2] Figlewski (1981), Edwards (1988), and Harris (1989) follow this approach. Harris conducts a more detailed examination by making a cross-sectional comparison of the volatility of stocks that are part of the index with that of stocks that are not part of the index. The difference in volatility may then be attributed to the effect of trading derivative products on the index.

there were shifts in the monetary regime, volatility declined in both the stock and short-term debt markets after the introduction of futures trading.

A second approach used in studying the impact of trading in derivative assets is a cross-sectional comparison of the behavior of stocks on which derivative assets are traded for those without them. This approach, used mainly in the context of options has led many researchers to conclude that the introduction of options trading generally dampens the volatility of the underlying stock.[3]

A third aspect of the behavior of volatility studied by Kawaller, Koch, and Koch (1987) and Ng (1988) concerns the intra-day behavior of futures and spot prices. The specific issue here is regarding whether the futures market aids the price discovery process. This is studied by examining the lead and lag relationships between cash and futures prices based on the S&P500 stock index. The general conclusion here is that the futures markets usually lead the underlying cash market by several minutes, while the opposite rarely happens. This conclusion is consistent with the ease and lower cost of trading in the futures markets as well as the time taken for new information to be reflected in the prices of all the underlying stocks in the index.

A particular issue that has received a lot of attention in both academic and practitioner circles is the relationship between cash and future markets on the expiration day of the futures contracts and, in particular, on "triple witching days," when stock index futures, options on the stock index, and options on individual stocks expire. The evidence suggests that stock price volatility is indeed higher on these days than on other days. Furthermore, much of the increase in volatility seems to happen during the last hour of trading.[4] This increase in volatility has been attributed to substantial order imbalances in the cash market and the inability of specialists in the underlying stocks to provide sufficient liquidity to the market.

The institutional setting of the Japanese stock and stock index futures markets

The Japanese financial markets have witnessed rapid changes in the past 5 years. These changes have been particularly noticeable in the stock market where the value of outstanding securities and trading volume have grown so rapidly that the Tokyo Stock Exchange (TSE) is one of the two

---

[3] See, for example, Conrad (1989), Damodaran and Lim (1988), Detemple and Jorion (1988), Harris (1989), Nabar and Park (1988), Rao and Ma (1987), and Skinner (1988). With the exception of Harris, who studies the impact of trading futures contracts, the other studies examine the impact of options listing and trading.

[4] See Edwards (1988), Kawaller, Koch, and Koch (1987), and Stoll and Whaley (1986).

premier stock markets in the world. This rapid growth has been accompanied by the opening of various markets for derivative products based on Japanese stock market indices.

The first derivative product based on Japanese stocks to be traded on an exchange is a stock index futures contract based on the Nikkei Stock Average (NSA) listed on the Singapore International Monetary Exchange (SIMEX) in September 1986. A few months later, the first stock index derivative product to be traded in Japan itself, the Osaka Stock Futures 50 (OSF50), was introduced on the Osaka Securities Exchange (OSE) in June 1987. In September 1988, two new stock index futures contracts were introduced: another NSA contract traded on the OSE, and one based on the Tokyo Stock Price Index (TOPIX) traded on the TSE.[5] More recently, trading was introduced on options based on the NSA and TOPIX stock indices. The NSA options started trading on the OSE in June 1989, while the TOPIX options were listed in October 1989.[6]

With the exception of the OSF50 contract, which is no longer actively traded, all the Japanese stock index futures contracts and options have good trading volume and open interest. In late 1989, trading volume on the NSA (OSE) contract averaged about 25,000 contracts per day, while that of the NSA (SIMEX) contract, which has half the face value of the NSA(OSE) contract, averaged about 4000 contracts per day. The TOPIX contract, whose face value is about 80% of that of the NSA(OSE), had an average daily trading volume of about 15,000 contracts. The total face value of the daily trading volume in the three stock index futures contracts exceeded the value of shares traded on the Japanese stock markets on a typical trading day.

In this study, we analyze the behavior of the volatility of the two major Japanese stock indices, the NSA and TOPIX, and the stock index futures contracts based on them. In the case of the NSA index, there are two futures contracts, one traded on the SIMEX and the other on the OSE.

The NSA index is an arithmetic price average based on the prices of 225 stocks traded on the First Section of the TSE. The index is computed by adding the prices of all 225 stocks and dividing by a divisor that changes over time as a result of stock splits, rights issues, and so on. The TOPIX index is a value-weighted index of the prices of *all* the common stocks listed on the First Section of the TSE (in 1989, the number was about 1150).

The NSA(SIMEX) futures contract is traded continuously throughout the trading day from 9 A.M. to 3.15 P.M. Tokyo time (8 A.M. to 2.15 P.M.,

---

[5] For a description of these contracts and their specifications, see Brenner, Subrahmanyam, and Uno (1990).

[6] Options on a narrower stock index, the Nagoya 25 index, were also listed for trading in October 1989.

Singapore time). In contrast, the underlying stocks in the index do not trade on the TSE and the OSE between 11 A.M. and 1 P.M. Tokyo time (10 A.M. to 12 noon Singapore time). In 1989, the other NSA contract listed on the OSE, as well as the TOPIX contract listed on the TSE, trade between 9 A.M. and 11.15 A.M. and again between 1 P.M. and 3.15 P.M. Tokyo time. The basic features of the NSA(OSE) and the TOPIX contracts are quite similar.[7]

For all three Japanese stock index futures contracts, the settlement price on each trading day was determined 1: minutes after the close of trading in the underlying stocks, as in the case of stock index futures contracts in other markets, such as those in the United States. However, there is a difference between the trading systems used in the markets for the three contracts. Unlike the NSA(SIMEX) contract, which is traded using the open outcry system, as in the case of the Chicago futures exchanges, the NSA(OSE) and TOPIX contracts are traded in computer-assisted auctions.

Analysis of volatility

The volatility of the spot and futures prices are measured by the respective standard deviations of the log-price relatives of daily closing prices. Specifically,

$$R_{S,t} = \ln \frac{S_t}{S_{t-1}} \tag{8.1a}$$

and

$$R_{F,t} = \ln \frac{F_t}{F_{t-1}} \tag{8.1b}$$

where:

S_t is the closing price on day t of the stock index
F_t is the settlement price on day t of the futures contract
$R_{S,t}$ is the log-price relative on day t of the stock index
$R_{F,t}$ is the log-price relative on day t of the futures contract.

The volatility in a given month is defined to be the sample standard deviation of the log-price relatives based on daily data of the spot or futures contract in the month.[8,9]

---

[7] See Brenner, Subrahmanyam, and Uno (1990) for details.
[8] In computing the volatilities of returns for each month, French, Schwert, and Stambaugh (1987) make an adjustment for one lagged cross-covariance and do not make any adjustment for the mean return. Schwert (1989) finds that the estimates of the sample

The price of a forward contract can be related to the price of the underlying spot asset, the cash flows on the asset such as dividends, the riskless rate of interest, and the time to maturity of the contract. Ignoring the effect of marking-to-the-market, which is reasonable when (overnight) interest rates are nonstochastic, the price of a forward contract is equal to the price of a similar futures contract. Hence, in general, in frictionless markets, the volatility of the futures contract differs from that of the underlying spot asset, due to the volatility of cash payments on the underlying asset, the riskless rate of interest, and the correlation of these variables with the returns on the spot index. In previous studies, we have documented evidence regarding the relatively small variability of the dividends on stocks in Japan, as well as the short-term riskless rate of interest (the Gensaki rate).[10] Hence, in the absence of frictions such as transactions costs or restrictions on trading, the volatility of price changes for the futures contract should be the same as that for the spot asset. In the next section, we shall discuss the evidence on the validity of this hypothesis as well as related empirical results.

Empirical results

In order to assess the impact on volatility of the introduction of stock index futures contracts, we divide our sample into three subperiods. The first subperiod of our sample runs from January 1984 to August 1986, before exchange-traded derivative products based on Japanese stock indices were introduced. We confine our attention to only the period since January 1984, in view of the fundamental changes in the structure of Japanese financial markets that occurred in the 1980s, which may have altered the behavior of stock prices during the decade. The second subperiod is the period between the date when the first futures contract based on a Japanese stock index, the NSA(SIMEX), was introduced, and

---

standard deviation are similar to this statistic and, furthermore, are guaranteed to be always positive.

[9] The estimates of volatility, as measured by the standard deviation of the daily log price relatives, are reported here on a daily basis rather than the conventional annualized basis. The reason for this is that the number of trading days in the year for the Japanese stock and stock index futures markets changed during the period under study. Until June 1983, the third Saturday of each month was a holiday. The market was open for the morning session (9 A.M. to 11 A.M.) on the other Saturdays. In July 1983, the second Saturday of the month became the holiday for the financial markets, and the markets were open in the morning on other Saturdays. From August 1986 to January 1989, both the second and third Saturdays were holidays, with the market being open on the other Saturdays for the morning session. Since February 1989, the markets have been closed on all Saturdays.

[10] See Brenner, Subrahmanyam, and Uno [(1989A), (1989B), and (1990)].

the opening of the NSA(OSE) and TOPIX futures markets in Japan itself, i.e., from September 1986 to August 1988. The third subperiod covers the time since the introduction of the NSA(OSE) and the TOPIX futures contracts in September 1988. Our data set runs until November 1989, close to the expiration date of the December 1989 futures contracts, the contracts that expired toward the end of our sample period.

A few caveats are in order in interpreting the data from the three subperiods. First, there were several changes in the structure of the Japanese financial markets that occurred during the period under study, of which one was the introduction of futures contracts. Although the opening of stock index futures markets was a major development, one has to be careful in ascribing the effects witnessed in the three subperiods entirely to futures trading. Several other regulatory changes were occurring at the same time as the opening of new futures markets, such as the reduction of transaction costs in the cash markets and the admission of new members to the Japanese stock exchanges. Second, the data from the second subperiod have to be interpreted with caution since the NSA(SIMEX) contract did not have a major impact on the Japanese markets. The volume of trading in this contract during this period was fairly modest (less than 2000 contracts per day, on average), and arbitrage activity between the cash and futures markets was at a low level. Hence, the futures market was unlikely to have had an impact on the market for the underlying stocks. Third, the data from the period immediately after the October 1987 crash have been excluded for purposes of statistical testing, since this period was characterized by unusual market behavior.

Table 8.1 provides the summary statistics of the daily log price relatives of the spot and futures markets during the three subperiods defined above. It is clear from the table that there were substantial differences between the volatilities of the price changes of the markets in the three subperiods. The volatilities of the spot indices increased from the first to the second subperiod: from 0.66% to 1.00% on a daily basis (roughly corresponding to 10.43%) to 15.81% on an annual basis), in the case of the NSA index, and from 0.66% to 1.08% (corresponding to 10.43% to 17.08% on an annual basis), in the case of the TOPIX index.[11] These increases are both significant at the 1% level, based on an F test comparing the respective variances.

We observe a decline in volatility from the second subperiod (September

---

[11] The annualized numbers are based on 250 trading days in the year. Since the number of actual trading days in the year changed during the period under study due to the inclusion of fewer trading Saturdays, these numbers have to be interpreted only as rough indications. All the statistical tests described below are based on the volatility estimates on a daily basis.

Table. 8.1. *Summary statistics of the daily log price relatives in percent (Mean, Std., Dev., Max., Min., Rho's, No. of Obs.) for Japanese stock indices and the near-term stock index futures contracts between Jan. 1984 and Nov. 1989*

	NSA	NSA Futures		TOPIX	
Period	SPOT	(SIMEX)	(OSE)	SPOT	Futures
Jan. 1984–Aug. 1986					
Mean	0.08	—	—	0.10	—
Stdv.	0.66	—	—	0.66	—
Max.	2.47	—	—	2.59	—
Min.	−2.79	—	—	−3.73	—
Roh1	0.18*	—	—	0.27*	—
Roh2	−0.01	—	—	−0.03	—
Roh3	−0.05	—	—	−0.05	—
Rho4	0.06	—	—	0.08	—
Rho5	−0.02	—	—	−0.01	—
No. of Obs.	764	—	—	764	—
Sep. 1986–Aug. 1988 (excluding 10/20/87–11/30/87)[a]					
Mean	0.10	0.08	—	0.10	—
Stdv.	1.00	1.13	—	1.08	—
Max.	5.48	5.15	—	6.36	—
Min.	−4.58	−4.80	—	−3.74	—
Roh1	0.17* 0.08	0.09 0.07	—	0.22* 0.16*	—
Roh2	−0.03 0.03	0.05 0.05	—	−0.02 −0.01	—
Roh3	−0.06 −0.17*	−0.02 −0.25*	—	−0.05 −0.07	—
Rho4	−0.03 −0.17*	−0.10 −0.21*	—	−0.01 −0.07	—
Rho5	0.03 −0.01	−0.02 0.01	—	0.04 −0.11	—
No. of Obs.	485	475	—	485	—
Sep. 1988–Nov. 1989					
Mean	0.10	0.10	0.08	0.09	0.08
Stdv.	0.58	0.52	0.49	0.58	0.58
Max.	2.49	2.34	1.88	2.43	1.85
Min.	−1.86	−1.68	−1.54	−1.74	−1.61
Roh1	0.00	0.02	0.07	0.11*	0.07
Roh2	0.02	0.00	0.02	0.06	0.03
Roh3	0.06	−0.02	−0.02	0.10	0.03
Rho4	−0.03	0.04	0.03	−0.06	−0.01
Rho5	−0.02	−0.07	−0.05	−0.12*	−0.07
No. of Obs.	307	302	300	307	300

Note: * Significant at the 1% level.
[a] During the second subperiod, Sep. 1986–Aug. 1998, the days' unusual market behavior, in the aftermath of the Oct. 1987 crash, are excluded. Therefore, the autocorrelation coefficients are presented for the period before Oct. 20, 1987, and the period after Dec. 1, 1987, in the two columns below the NSA SPOT, NSA (SIMEX), and TOPIX SPOT, respectively.

1986 to August 1988) to the third subperiod (September 1988 to November 1989) for both spot indices. In the case of the NSA index, the volatility on a daily basis declined from 1% to 0.58% (roughly 15.81% to 9.17% on an annualized basis), while it went from 1.08% to 0.58% on a daily basis for the TOPIX index (17.08% to 9.17% on an annualized basis). Again, these declines are statistically significant at the 1% level, based on an F test of the variances.

The next comparison that can be made on the basis of the statistics in Table 8.1 is for the equality of variances of the futures versus the corresponding spot log price relatives. In order to test for the equality of the variances, one has to be careful to adjust for the correlation between the two series of log-price relatives, since it is to be expected that the price changes in the cash and futures markets will be highly correlated. In the second subperiod when only the NSA(SIMEX) futures contract was traded, the estimate of the coefficient of correlation between the daily price changes in the NSA spot and NSA(SIMEX) series was 0.8330. In the third subperiod, the coefficients of correlation between the log-price relatives of the futures contract and the underlying spot in the case of the NSA(SIMEX), NSA(OSE), and the TOPIX were 0.8521, 0.8483, and 0.6482, respectively.

The Pitman test statistics for equality of variances of two dependent variables for the log-price relatives of the three futures contracts and the underlying spot indices were as follows.[12] -0.205, -0.305, and 0.0, for the period September 1988–November 1989, for the SIMEX futures (vs. NSA), the OSAKA futures (vs. NSA), and the TOPIX futures (vs. TOPIX), respectively. For the period September 1986–August 1988, the test statistic for SIMEX futures (vs. NSA) was 0.217. Given the relatively large sample sizes, these statistics are all significant at the 1% level, except in the case of TOPIX. In the second subperiod, the volatility of the futures contract is higher than that of the spot in the case of the NSA(SIMEX). This is similar to the experience in the U.S. markets. However, it is interesting to note that in the third subperiod, the volatilities of both the NSA(SIMEX) and NSA(OSE) contracts are *lower* than the underlying NSA index. For the TOPIX index, the volatilities of the spot and futures contracts are insignificantly different from one another.

A question that is related to the changes in volatility is the issue of efficiency of the market as measured by the coefficients of autocorrelation in Table 8.1. In the first subperiod, only the first-order autocorrelation coefficients are significantly different from zero at the 1% level, 0.18 for the NSA index and 0.27 for the TOPIX index. In the second subperiod, there is a gap in the data due to the exclusion of the data from the period

[12] See Snedecor and Cochran (1967) for details.

just after the October 1987 crash. In the period before Oct. 20, 1987, the first-order autocorrelation coefficients are again significant at the 1% level, 0.17 for the NSA and 0.22 for the TOPIX index, respectively. After Dec. 1, 1987, the first-order autocorrelation coefficient declined to 0.09 where it was no longer significant for the NSA index. At 0.11, it was still marginally significant in the case of the TOPIX index. With the exception of the NSA index in the postcrash part of the second subperiod, where the second- and third-order autocorrelation coefficients are significant, the higher-order autocorrelation coefficients are not statistically significant. This evidence is somewhat similar to that in the case of U.S. markets where the first-order autocorrelation coefficients have been found to be significant.[13] However, the striking feature of the autocorrelations in the case of the Japanese indices is that in the period since active trading in stock index futures contracts began (the third subperiod), the autocorrelations for lags from 1 to 5 are not significantly different from zero at the 1% level.[14]

The coefficients of autocorrelation for the futures contracts are, by and large, not significant (again, with the exception of the second- and third-order coefficients for the NSA(SIMEX) in the postcrash part of the second subperiod). In the third subperiod, after the introduction of futures trading in Japan, all the point estimates of the autocorrelation coefficients decline. These findings are broadly similar to the evidence from the U.S. markets, where the daily price changes of futures contracts exhibit no autocorrelation.[15]

We turn now to an examination of the volatility of daily price changes for each month in our sample period for the stock indices and the futures contracts. A glance at Figs. 8.1 and 8.2 and the NSA SPOT and TOPIX SPOT columns in Table 8.2 shows that there were large fluctuations in the daily volatility from one month to another. Even after excluding the data for the months of October and November 1987, which may have been affected by unusual market conditions in the aftermath of the stock market crash, the volatility of daily log price changes ranged from 0.3% to 1.67%.[16] This 5.5-to-1 range of fluctuations in the volatility for the month is much greater than the range of roughly 2.5-to-1 observed in the U.S. stock market during the same period.[17] The other striking feature

---

[13] See, for example, MacKinlay and Ramaswamy (1988) and Conrad and Kaul (1989) for details.

[14] The first-order autocorrelation coefficient for the TOPIX index just falls short of significance at the 1% level.

[15] See MacKinlay and Ramaswamy (1988).

[16] The daily volatility was as high as 1.79% for the month of October 1987.

[17] See Schwert (1989).

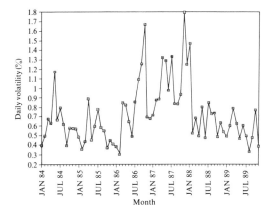

Fig. 8.1. Volatility of the natural logarithm of daily price-relative of the NSA index plotted by month from Jan. 1984 to Nov. 1989.

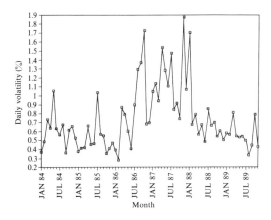

Fig. 8.2. Volatility of the natural logarithm of daily price-relative of the TOPIX index plotted by month from Jan. 1984 to Nov. 1989.

of the charts of volatility by month is the marked decline in the level and range of fluctuations after October 1988.

Figures 8.3, 8.4, and 8.5 show the historical trends in the estimates of daily volatility for each month in the sample period, for the futures contracts compared with the corresponding spot index. Figure 8.3, which refers to the NSA(SIMEX) futures contract compared with the NSA spot index, shows that the volatility of the futures contract was invariably higher than that of the spot index in the second subperiod, i.e., before the introduction of stock index futures contracts in Japan in September 1988.

Table 8.2. *Summary statistics of estimates of the volatility of the daily log price relatives, in percent (Mean, Std., Dev., Max., Min., Rho's, No. of Obs.) for Japanese stock indices and the near-term stock index futures contracts for each month between Jan. 1984 and Nov. 1989*

	NSA	NSA Futures		TOPIX	
Period	SPOT	(SIMEX)	(OSE)	SPOT	Futures
Jan. 1984–Aug. 1986					
Mean	0.60	—	—	0.59	—
Stdv.	0.21	—	—	0.23	—
Max.	1.18	—	—	1.29	—
Min.	0.30	—	—	0.28	—
No. of Obs.	32	—	—	32	—
Sep. 1986–Aug. 1988 (excluding 10/20/87–11/30/87)					
Mean	0.94	1.04	—	1.01	—
Stdv.	0.34	0.40	—	0.37	—
Max.	1.67	1.71	—	1.73	—
Min.	0.47	0.48	—	0.48	—
No. of Obs.	22	22	—	22	—
Sep. 1988–Nov. 1989					
Mean	0.56	0.56	0.48	0.56	0.57
Stdv.	0.14	0.13	0.09	0.13	0.10
Max.	0.79	0.81	0.60	0.81	0.69
Min.	0.33	0.33	0.33	0.33	0.37
No. of Obs.	15	15	15	15	15

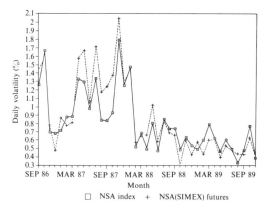

Fig. 8.3. Volatility of the natural logarithm of daily price relative of the NSA index and the NSA (SIMEX) futures contract plotted by month from Sep. 1986 to Nov. 1989.

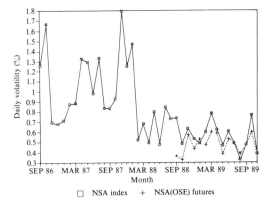

□ NSA index   + NSA(OSE) futures

Fig. 8.4. Volatility of the natural logarithm of daily price-relative of the NSA index and the NSA(OSE) futures contract plotted by month from Sep. 1986 to Nov. 1989.

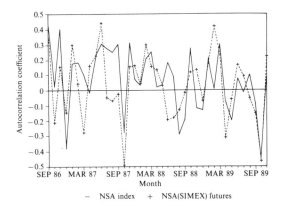

− NSA index   + NSA(SIMEX) futures

Fig. 8.5. Volatility of the natural logarithm of daily price-relatives of the TOPIX index and the TOPIX futures contract plotted by month from Sep. 1986 to Nov. 1989.

In contrast, after September 1988, the volatility of the futures contract was mostly lower than that of the underlying index. A similar pattern is noticed for the third subperiod for the NSA(OSE) and TOPIX futures contracts, in relation to their underlying spot indices, since their inception in September 1988, as shown in Figs. 8.4 and 8.5, respectively. These findings are in contrast to the evidence in the U.S. markets, where the volatility of the futures market has been found to be invariably higher than that of the underlying cash markets.[18]

The above discussion can be confirmed by an explicit statistical test using the estimates of the volatility of daily log price relatives by month. We first examine the secular changes in the volatility of the two spot indices. For the NSA index, the mean daily volatility changed substantially over time. From 0.60% in the first subperiod, it went up to 0.94% in the second subperiod, and declined to 0.56% in the third subperiod. Using a t test for the difference in the means, we find that the changes in the mean volatility are statistically significant at the 1% level – the t statistics are 4.17 and 4.69 for the differences between the first and second periods and the second and third periods, respectively. In the case of the TOPIX index, the daily volatility increased from 0.59% in the first subperiod to 1.01% in the second subperiod, and then fell to 0.56% in the most recent subperiod. These changes are also significant at the 1% level (the respective t statistics are 4.73 and 5.25, respectively). It is interesting to note that the estimates of volatility by month fluctuated less (as measured by the standard deviations) in the most recent subperiod compared with the previous ones. These results are consistent with those from Table 8.1 discussed earlier.[19]

Table 8.2 also provides evidence regarding the relative magnitudes of the volatility of the futures contracts versus the corresponding spot indices. These results also show that in the third subperiod, the mean volatility of the futures contracts is either insignificantly different from that of the respective spot index [0.57% versus 0.56%, with a t statistic of the difference of 0.20 for the TOPIX futures vs the TOPIX spot, and 0.56% vs. 0.56%, with a t statistic for the difference of -0.17 for the NSA(SIMEX) futures vs. the NSA spot], or lower [as in the case of the NSA(OSE) futures vs. the NSA spot, where the mean volatility of the futures contract is lower at 0.48% than the mean volatility of the spot, which is 0.56%, with a significant t statistic of the difference of -2.97]. In the second subperiod, the mean volatility of the NSA(SIMEX) futures contract was 1.04%, which was insignificantly different from the mean volatility of the NSA spot at 0.94% at the 1% level of significance (t statistic, 2.10)

Table 8.3 presents the summary statistics of the estimates of the first three coefficients of autocorrelation by month. The first-order autocorrelation coefficients for the three futures contracts and the respective under-

[18] See MacKinlay and Ramaswamy (1988) and Edwards (1988).
[19] It should be noted that the means of the estimates of volatility by month in Table 8.2 are lower than the estimates of volatility over each subperiod in Table 8.1. The difference is accounted for by the sample variance of the mean log price relative in the subperiod.

Table 8.3. *Summary statistics (Mean, Std., Dev., Max., Min., No. of Obs.)*
of the estimates of the coefficients of autocorrelation of the daily log price
relatives for Japanese stock indices and the near-term stock index futures
contracts for each month between Jan. 1984 and Nov. 1989

Period	NSA SPOT	NSA Futures (SIMEX)	(OSE)	TOPIX SPOT	Futures
Jan. 1984–Aug. 1986					
Roh1: Mean	0.108*	—	—	0.212*	—
Stdv.	0.203	—	—	0.196	—
Roh2: Mean	−0.028	—	—	−0.053	—
Stdv.	0.179	—	—	0.233	—
Roh3: Mean	−0.116	—	—	−0.106	—
Stdv.	0.165	—	—	0.162	—
No. of Obs.	32	—	—	32	—
Sep, 1986–Aug. 1988 excluding Oct. and Nov. 1987)					
Roh1: Mean	0.132*	0.055	—	0.183*	—
Stdv.	0.197	0.200	—	0.193	—
Roh2: Mean	−0.052	−0.008	—	−0.034	—
Stdv.	0.173	0.158	—	0.209	—
Roh3: Mean	−0.095	−0.100	—	−0.083	—
Stdv.	0.196	0.169	—	0.196	—
No. of Obs.	22	22	—	22	—
Sep. 1988–Nov. 1989					
Rho1: Mean	−0.010*	0.030	0.035	0.116	0.011
Stdv.	0.206	0.226	0.203	0.192	0.215
Roh2: Mean	−0.004	0.028	−0.035	0.017	−0.040
Stdv.	0.219	0.204	0.247	0.240	0.182
Roh3: Mean	0.032	−0.071	−0.030	0.031	0.016
Stdv.	0.141	0.137	0.116	0.129	0.136
No. of Obs.	15	15	15	15	15

lying index are plotted in Fig. 8.6 through 8.8. As mentioned in our
discussion of Table 8.1, the Japanese stock indices exhibit positive
first-order autocorrelation, like their U.S. counterparts before September
1988. The means of the first-order autocorrelation coefficients are 0.108
($t = 3.01$) and 0.212 ($t = 6.12$) for the NSA and TOPIX indices, respectively
for the January 1984–August 1986 subperiod, and 0.132 ($t = 2.85$) and
0.183 ($t = 3.95$) for the Septemer 1986–August 1988 subperiod. These are
all significantly different from zero at the 1% level.[20] However, for the
September 1988–November 1989 subperiod, the means of the first three

[20] The means of the second- and third-order autocorrelation coefficients are all insignificantly different from zero.

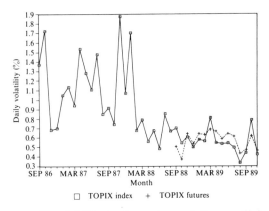

Fig. 8.6 First-order autocorrelation coefficient of the NSA index and the NSA (SIMEX) futures contract plotted by month from Sept. 1986 to Nov. 1989.

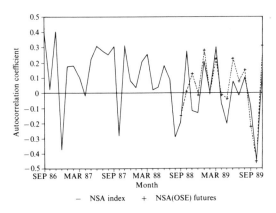

Fig. 8.7. First-order autocorrelation coefficient of the NSA index and the NSA(OSE) futures contract plotted by month from Sep. 1986 to Nov. 1989.

autocorrelation coefficients are indistinguishable from zero for both indices. In the case of the futures contracts, the means of the first three autocorrelation coefficients are all insignificantly different from zero for the third subperiod. In the second subperiod for the NSA(SIMEX) contract, except the third-order autocorrelation coefficient, which turns out to be significant, the means of the autocorrelation coefficients are insignificant.

Table 8.4 provides statistics of the volatility of the price changes over 1, 2, 3, and 6 days, using nonoverlapping data over the three subperiods.

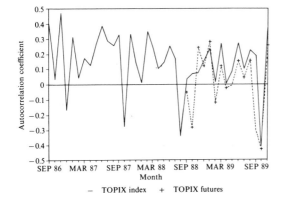

Fig. 8.8. First-order autocorrelation coefficient of the TOPIX index and the TOPIX futures contract plotted by month from Sep. 1986 to Nov. 1989.

Table 8.4. *Estimates of volatility of log price relatives over 1-, 2-, 3-, and 6-day holding periods for Japanese stock indices and the near-term stock index futures contracts between Jan. 1984 and Nov. 1989*

Period	NSA SPOT	NSA Futures (SIMEX)	(OSE)	TOPIX SPOT	Futures
Jan. 1984–Aug. 1986					
1-day	0.66	—	—	0.66	—
2-day	0.99	—	—	1.05	—
3-day	1.23	—	—	1.32	—
6-day	1.78	—	—	1.85	—
Sep. 1986–Aug. 1988 (excluding 10/20/87–11/30/87)					
1-day	1.00	1.11	—	1.08	—
2-day	1.49	1.60	—	1.65	—
3-day	1.88	2.16	—	2.11	—
6-day	2.14	2.89	—	2.51	—
Sep. 1988–Nov. 1989					
1-day	0.56	0.52	0.49	0.56	0.57
2-day	0.89	0.79	0.72	0.93	0.84
3-day	1.15	0.94	0.81	1.24	0.96
6-day	1.59	1.41	1.14	1.68	1.36

These numbers, which are not annualized, give us an indirect measure of the effects of autocorrelation as well as shifts in the mean returns. In the absence of autocorrelation and mean reversion, one would expect the standard deviations over different holding periods to increase roughly by the square root of time. In other words, one would expect that the volatility of the 2-day return would be 1.41 times the volatility of the 1-day return, the volatility of the 3-day return would be 1.73 times the volatility of the 1-day return, and so on. Even without formal hypothesis testing, it is clear from the table that this relationship does not hold. Given the large number of observations, one would reject the hypothesis that the ratio of variances will be equal to the ratio of the holding periods. We leave a more detailed investigation of the effects of autocorrelation and mean reversion to subsequent research.

Summary and conclusions

This paper examines the volatility and autocorrelation structure of daily price changes in the two major Japanese stock price indices, the NSA and the TOPIX, and the stock index futures contracts based on them. The evidence presented here is useful in establishing certain stylized facts and is a first step in gaining a better understanding of the impact of futures trading on the underlying cash markets in the Japanese context. The data here are also useful in performing a comparative analysis of the behavior of the two major stock markets in the world, those in the United States and Japan.

The volatility of the Japanese stock market as reflected by the standard deviation of daily price changes of the NSA and TOPIX indices has declined since the period before futures trading. However, there was an increase in the interim period between September 1986 and August 1988. The other interesting aspect of volatility is that the range of fluctuations in the volatility from one month to the next has diminished over the period under study. Another noteworthy fact about the volatility of the Japanese stock and stock index futures markets is that in the past 15 or so months of active stock index futures trading, the evidence suggests that the volatility of the futures contracts was the same or even *lower* than that of the corresponding cash markets. This is in striking contrast to the stylized facts that have emerged from studies of U.S. markets.

The evidence on the autocorrelation of daily price changes in the Japanese stock markets is equally interesting. In the earlier part of our sample, the first-order autocorrelation coefficients of daily price changes for the two stock indices were significantly positive, as in the case of the U.S. stock indices. However, in the more recent period, the narrower NSA index exhibits virtually no autocorrelation for the first five lags in its series of daily price changes. The broader TOPIX index still has some first-order autocorrelation in daily price changes. As in the case of the U.S. market, there is virtually no autocorrelation in the series of price changes for all three stock index futures contracts.

What explains the observed pattern of behavior of volatility and autocorrelation of changes of the cash and futures prices? While one must be cautious in attributing the decline in volatility and the elimination of autocorrelation entirely to the opening of futures markets, the evidence here suggests that futures markets at least do not exacerbate the volatility of the underlying cash markets, as many critics have alleged. This is true, one might add, despite the recent increase in the volume of program trading activities in the Japanese financial markets, and the concern expressed in many circles about its impact on volatility of the cash markets, particularly on expiration days, Indeed, the price discovery mechanism of futures trading seems to have had a positive impact on market efficiency as reflected in the decline in autocorrelations of daily price changes.

References

Amihud, Y., and H. Mendelson (1989), "Index and Index-Futures Return," Working Paper, Salomon Brothers Center for the Study of Financial Institutions, New York University.

Anderson, R. W. (1985), "Some Determinants of the Volatility of Futures Prices," *Journal of Futures Markets*, 5, 331–48.

Brenner, M., M. G. Subrahmanyam, and J. Uno (1989A), "The Behavior of Prices in the Nikkei Spot and Futures Market," *Journal of Financial Economics*, 23, 363–83.

Brenner, M., M. G. Subrahmanyam, and J. Uno (1989B), "Stock Index Futures Arbitrage in the Japanese Markets," *Japan and the World Economy*, 1, 303–30.

Brenner, M., M. G. Subrahmanyam, and J. Uno (1990), "Atbitrage Opportunities in Japanese Stock and Futures Markets," *Financial Analysts Journal*, 46, 14–24.

Conrad, J. (1989), "The Price Effect of Option Introduction," *Journal of Finance*, 44, 487–498

Conrad, J., and G. Kaul (1989), "Mean Reversion in Short-Horizon Expected Returns," *Review of Financial Studies*, 2, 225–40.

Damodaran, A., and J. Lim (1988), "The Effects of Option Listing on the Underlying Stocks' Return Processes: A Study," Working Paper, Salomon Brothers Center for the Study of Financial Institutions, New York University.

Detemple, J., and P. Jorion (1988), "Option Listing and Stock Returns," Working Paper, Columbia University.

Edwards, F. R. (1988), "Futures Trading and Market Volatility: Stock Index and Interest Rate Futures," *Journal of Futures Markets*, 8, 421–39.

Figlewski, S. (1981), "Futures Trading and Volatility in the GNMA Market," *Journal of Finance*, 36, 445–56.

French, K. R., G. W. Schwert, and R. F. Stambaugh, (1987), "Expected Stock Returns and Volatility," *Journal of Financial Economics*, 19, 3–29.

Grossman, S. J. (1988), "An Analysis of the Implications for Stock and Futures Price Volatility of Program Trading and Dynamic Hedging Strategies," *Journal of Business*, 61, 278–98.

Hamao, Y., R. Masulis, and V. Ng (1990), "Correlations in Price Changes and Volatility across International Markets," *Review of Financial Studies*, 3, 281–313.

Harris, L. (1989), "S&P 500 Cash Price Volatilities," *Journal of Finance*, 44, 11 5575.

Kawaller, I. G., P. D. Koch, and T. W. Koch (1987), "The Temporal Price Relation between S&P 500 Futures and the S&P 500 Index," *Journal of Finance*, 42, 1309–29.

MacKinlay, A. C., and K. Ramaswamy (1988), "Index-Futures Arbitrage and the Behavior of Stock Index Futures Prices," *Review of Financial Studies*, 1, 137–58.

Nabar, P. G., and S. Y. Park (1988), "Options Trading and Stock Price Volatility," Working Paper, Southern Methodist University.

Ng, N. (1987), "Detecting Spot Price Forecasts in Futures Prices Using Causality Tests," *Review of Futures Markets*, 6, 250–67.

Rao, R. P., and C. K. Ma (1987), "The Effect of Call Option-Listing Announcement on Shareholder Wealth," *Journal of Business Research*, 15, 449–65.

Schwert, G. W. (1989), "Why Does Stock Market Volatility Change Over Time?" *Journal of Finance*, 44, 1115–54.

Skinner, D. J. (1988), "Options Markets and Stock Return Volatility," Working Paper, University of Rochester.

Snedecor, G. W., and W. G. Cochran (1967), *Statistical Methods*, 6th ed., The Iowa State University Press, Ames, Iowa.

Stoll, H. R., and R. Whaley (1986), *Expiration Day Effects of Index Options and Futures*, Monograph Series in Finance and Economics, Salomon Brothers Center for the Study of Financial Institutions, New York University.

CHAPTER 9

Capital markets and the banking sector: efficiency of Japanese banks in reducing agency costs

AKIYOSHI HORIUCHI
RYOKO OKAZAKI

Introduction

The capital market, comprising stocks and other securities markets, is supposed to play the following two roles: (1) provide investors and other agents with opportunities of risk sharing and (2) discipline corporate managers to practice efficient management. As exemplified by the tremendous increase in trading volume in the stock exchange since the mid-1980s in Japan, the capital market has developed the capability to fulfill the first role. But this is just a recent phenomenon. Until the beginning of the 1980s, the secondary markets had been, if anything, stagnant. The primary markets were much less important, although, as Chart 1 shows, the increase in the relative importance of equity financing was remarkable in Japan's financial system in the latter half of the 1980s. The amount of funds raised by Japanese companies in securities markets had stayed at very low levels during the 1960s and 1970s.

What about the second role, i.e., the role of disciplining corporate managers? It has been a stated principle that the board of directors and the system of auditing accounts are important in disciplining corporate managers, because they are assumed to fill an informational gap between shareholders and managers. In reality, however, they are not so effective as this principle suggests. Individual investors could exert some influence on managers by actively trading shares. But they do not seem to have much incentive to closely monitor specific companies' management because monitoring is costly, and because they hold a well-diversified portfolio of stocks to lower the degree of risk.[1]

Managers who have expertise in business management are considered more reliable as auditors of individual corporations than are investors in general. These expert managers can accurately assess whether there is any

---

[1] Many authors emphasize this difficulty. See, for example, Jensen and Meckling (1976) and Fama (1980).

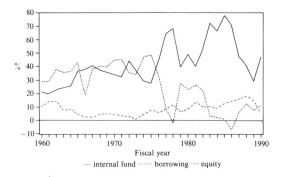

Fiscal year

— internal fund ····· borrowing ··· equity

Note: $I_t 0$ is obtained from the following equation: $Z(I_t 0, K_t) = F_t{}^*$.

discrepancy between the potential and the actual performance of a specific company. If a discrepancy is discerned, they may attempt to take over the firm. Taking over and rearranging the management of a firm will raise its market value, bringing forth capital gains for those who succeed in such takeovers. A takeover, especially a hostile one, implies competition for the rights to manage corporate resources. Thus, the possibility of being taken over should discipline incumbent managers to manage efficiently, resulting in maximization of their firms' values.

But Japanese are only reminded of the role of takeovers when they observe the surge of hostile takeovers in the United States. In Japan, hostile takeovers are almost nonexistent, even though the number of mergers and acquisitions (M&A) has been increasing since around 1980. Since 1986 the annual number of Japanese companies' M&A whose targets are Japanese firms has been more than 200.[2] For example, the number of M&As was 220 in 1988. A rough classification of the M&A is as follows: (1) takeovers of firms in trouble, which implies a program to rescue those firms; (2) mutual shareholdings in order to strengthen cooperative relationships; (3) friendly mergers; and (4) buying up shares of Japanese and foreign joint enterprises by the Japanese partner. At any rate, all of them are clearly not hostile takeovers. The attempt of Minebea, the world's largest miniature bearing maker, to take over Sankyo Seiki, which produces electronic parts and music boxes, was a rare case of a hostile takeover. It was started in 1984 and ended in failure in 1988.[3]

---

[2] See Ubukata (1988). This is not unique to the Japanese capital market. For example, in France and Germany there have until very recently been no reported cases of hostile acquisitions" [Frank and Mayer (1990: p. 198)].

[3] Isaacs and Ejiri (1990: pp. 109–10) concisely explain how Minebea failed in taking over Sankyo Seiki.

Reorganization through takeover, however, may not work so efficiently in disciplining corporate managers as many people expect. As Grossman and Hart (1980) claim, there is a free-rider problem about the process of takeovers, in the sense that some stockholders (or bondholders) would decline a tender offer but hope a sufficient number of their fellow shareholders will accept it and make the bid successful.[4] Some scholars emphasize instead the danger of destructive impacts associated with hostile takeovers. According to their argument, the hostile takeover tends to destroy specific (quite often invisible or intangible) capital assets accumulated in the target firm.[5] Therefore, they want methods more suitable for disciplining corporate managers than a hostile takeover.

Of course, the banking sector can be to some extent a substitute for the capital market. Particularly, the banking sector seems to have played an important role in postwar Japan as a medium both for providing wide opportunities of risk sharing and for disciplining corporate management. Some people go so far as to say that the "miraculous" achievement of the Japanese economy was essentially based on the financial structure in which banks played dominant roles as financial intermediaries.

The purpose of this paper is to review some arguments about the working of the banking sector in the Japanese economy and to provide an empirical test concerning its efficiency. Specifically, in the following section, we give an overview of various arguments concerning the efficiency of the bank, in particular the main-bank relationship, in reducing agency costs associated with external fund raising by companies. In the third section, we test an important hypothesis: The main-bank relationship – defined as a lasting financial transaction between a bank and a specific firm – is useful in reducing agency costs of external funds. Although others before us have made comparable empirical analyses, a number of issues remain to be investigated. In this paper, we particularly consider problems of how to quantify the main-bank relationship and how important is shareholding by the main bank in reducing the agency costs. Finally in the fourth section, we summarize tentative results of our investigation and some remaining issues.

The banking sector in Japan's corporate finance

In place of the securities market, the banking system can provide opportunities for risk sharing and for disciplining corporate management. Many scholars argue that the Japanese banking system has successfully

---

[4] See also Barnea, Haugen, and Senbet (1985: pp. 69–71).
[5] See Shleifer and Summers (1988) and Frank and Mayer (1990).

played such a note for the capital market. In this paper we present short overviews of the different arguments.

Economies of scales in banking: As is well known, due to economies of scale in financial intermediation, banks can provide investors with highly safe stores of values in the form of bank deposits. At the same time, Japanese banks provide a sort of (or *de facto*) syndicated loans to specific companies, thereby avoiding extreme concentration of their loans on a small number of big borrowers. We can suppose that the main bank of a company is an effective coordinator of the syndicated loan to the company. It is a conspicuous feature of Japanese banking that an individual firm borrows from many banks at the same time. This feature reflects a scheme of risk sharing between banks that the main bank informally mediates.[6]

Banks have also been important producers of information concerning borrowing companies. They examine investment projects proposed by companies; reports are sometimes based on inside information. Banks can monitor the management of borrowing companies because of the banks' long-term relationships with borrowers. The main bank is throught of as an accumulation of information on individual companies, and this characteristic results in a long-term relationship between the main bank and the individual firm. This monitoring mechanism is a noteworthy benefit of the main-bank relationship, which effectively prevents opportunistic behavior by manager.[7]

Personnel connections with firms: Executive boards of many firms include members sent from their main banks. These personnel connections are regarded as useful, allowing the main bank to examine the quality of managerial resources of borrowers and to monitor their management. Moreover, when a firm faces financial distress, the main bank can distinguish between a temporary "liquidity crisis" and a "solvency crisis," and give financial support to the troubled firm in a "liquidity crisis" thereby preventing unnecessary directions of bankruptcy. The main bank can do this also because it has accumulated information about borrowers as a result of its long-term relationship with individual borrowing firms.[8]

---

[6] Horiuchi, Kato, and Packer (1991) developed a model to explain the main-bank's coordinating role in a sort of syndicated loan. See also Sheard (1991).

[7] As for the role of main-bank relationships in Japan, see Sheard (1985) and Horiuchi, Packer, and Fukuda (1988). Greenbaum, Kanatas, and Venezia (1989) and Sharpe (1990) investigate how the specific nature of information on borrowers will bring forth a long-term relationship between banks and firms.

[8] See Sheard (1985) and Hoshi, Kashyap, and Scharfstein (1990).

Importance of equity positions taken by banks: Some people emphasize the importance of Japan's banks as shareholders of big companies. It is well known that banks, especially big city banks, have been the most important players in the framework of "mutual shareholdings" in Japan.[9] Particularly, the main bank is more often than not one of the largest shareholders of a borrowing company. By taking large portions of the debt and equity of the same firm, Japanese banks can restrain managers from transferring wealth from debt-holders to both themselves and shareholders. This is the financial unification that some scholars believe effectively mitigates the agency problem associated with external fund raising by the firm.[10]

Under the system of mutual shareholding, banks seem to play very delicate roles. On the one hand, the mutual shareholding has been developed as a tool for incumbent managers to ward off hostile takeovers by outsiders. We have observed many cases in which banks accommodate the needs of incumbent corporate managers whose firms are threatened by hostile takeovers by increasing the banks' equity positions in those firms to support the managers. In this sense, banks involved in the system of mutual shareholding may contribute to weakening the capital market discipline enforced on corporate management and to strengthening the discretionary power of managers.[11] Therefore, there exists the danger that incumbent managers may waste corporate resources by inefficient management of numerous perks.

However, the fact that corporate managers can remain immune from disciplinary pressure from the capital market does not necessarily mean that they can enjoy the perks in the way described by Jensen and Meckling

[9] The Antitrust Law forbids banks to hold more than 5% of shares issued by each corporation. But a small percentage of shareholding will sufficiently make a bank one of the biggest shareholders of big public corporations in Japan.

[10] Barnea, Haugen, and Senbet (1985: pp. 63–65) explain the effectiveness of financial unification in mitigating the agency problems. See also an interesting empirical study by Prowse (1990), who argues that the agency problem is mitigated to a great degree in Japan by this financial unification.

[11] After the "*zaibatsu*-resolution" immediately after World War II, some big companies that had belonged to the *zaibatsu* groups in prewar times wanted to preserve their intimate relationship with each other through mutual shareholding. Therefore, mutual shareholding in itself is not a recent phenomenon in the Japanese capital market. But it became prevalent after the mid-1960s because of corporations' policies of the "stabilizing shareholding (*kabunushi antei-ka kousaku*)" stimulated by the liberalization of capital movements started around 1965. Most Japanese were concerned about the danger that capital liberalization would give foreign investors a big chance to dominate Japanese business by acquiring stocks in the capital market. Japanese managers in those days were eager to strengthen barriers against the intrusion of foreign capital into Japan's corporate sector, which was expected to occur in the process of the liberalization of capital movements.

(1976). As explained above, banks are supposed to monitor managerial behavior closely from the viewpoint of both major lenders and major shareholders. In this sense, we think that agency problems related to corporate governance are resolved in Japan not by the capital market mechanism but by the working of the banking sector. Some economists consider that involvement of banks in corporate activities through their taking equity positions in other firms is much more efficient as a measure of corporate control than the capital market discipline that comes from hostile takeovers. This is probably tame because hostile takeovers undermine contractual relations between investors, managers, and employees and consequently prevent such firm-specific investments as expenditures in R&D projects that would increase the firm's productivity in the long run.[12]

In reality, it has not yet been settled whether the mutual shareholding involving banks is an efficient means of disciplining corporate management or a form of conspiracy among incumbent managers to defend their positions and enjoy their perks. The remarkable achievement by the Japanese corporate sector during the "high-growth era" of the 1960s and 1970s seems to indicate the efficiency of this system. On the other hand, the experience of the late 1980s, when many firms were engaged in speculative investment in stocks and other financial assets (called *zai-tech* in Japanese) and eventually incurred heavy capital losses because of sharp decreases in stock prices since 1990, seems to suggest that corporate managers indulged in such wasteful activities as the "free cash flow" hypothesis argued by Jensen (1986).

Need for empirical investigation: We have briefly described some hypotheses about the role of the banking sector in solving the agency problem in corporate finance. Many anecdotes support and refute those hypotheses. A full-scale analysis of the hypothesis has just been started by Hoshi, Kashyap, and Scharfstein (1991), Prowse (1990) and others. Unfortunately, we cannot dwell on all of them in this paper. In the third section, we concentrate on the problem of how main-bank relationships reduce agency costs associated with external finance in Japan. It is widely acknowledged that the Japanese banking sector is characterized by the main-bank relationship. Our arguments in this section can thus be closely related to the working of the main-bank relationship. Empirical analysis of some

---

[12] See Shleifer and Summers (1988) and Frank and Mayer (1990). According to Jensen (1989), the golden age of the active investor was destroyed in the United States by government edict of the Glass-Steagall Act of 1934, which prevented banks from taking equity positions in other companies. He claims that hostile takeovers were a response to those regulatory restrictions on corporate control.

features of the main-bank relationship in the third section will shed some light on those arguments.

Empirical analysis of corporate investment and the main-bank relationship

In this section we focus our investigation on the effectiveness of the main-bank relationship in reducing agency costs associated with external fund-raising. A number of empirical researchers have found a positive relationship between the availability of either internal funds or the amount of liquid assets and investment expenditures by the firm.[13] We could interpret these results as being a consequence of differences in the cost of capital for various methods of fund-raising. Use of internal funds are cheapest for firms because the funds are immune from agency costs that account from external fund-raising such as borrowing. Thus, the firm tends to finance its investment expenditure first of all by the use of internal funds. Therefore, the availability of internal funds is one of the most important determinants of investment by the firm. More specifically, the availability of internal funds reduces the cost of capital and, other things being equal, induces the firm to increase investment expenditure.[14]

But as has been explained in the previous section, in the context of Japan's financial system, it is widely believed that the lasting relationships between the main banks and their borrowers are effective in reducing the agency costs of debt. If this is true, internal funds are less important in determining corporate investment in Japan, or, if there is variation in the degree of strength of main-bank relationships, those firms having a strong relationship with their main banks can be freer from constraints of internal-funds use than those with weak main-bank relationships.

The main-bank relationship and investment expenditure

The basis of the following analysis is the hypothesis proposed by Fazzari, Hubbard, and Petersen (1988), and Hoshi, Kashyap, and Scharfstein (1991), namely that the cost of capital for individual firms decreases as the amount of internal funds increases, and that the internal fund is less

---

[13] For example, see Meyer and Kuh (1957), Fazzari, Hubbard, and Petersen (1988), Gertler and Hubbard (1988), and Hubbard and Kashyap (1989) for empirical study of United States data, and see Hayashi and Inoue (1990) and Asako, Kuninori, and Murase (1991) for the Japanese data.

[14] See the seminal works by Jensen and Meckling (1976) and Myers (1977) concerning the agency costs in corporate finance.

important as the relationship between the firm and its main bank becomes stronger.

Particularly, Hoshi, Kashyap, and Scharfstein (1991) have investigated Japanese firms' investment by making use of the "Tobin's Q" theory of corporate investment with a view to testing the hypothesis concerning the roles of the main bank we have discussed above. They divide the sample of firms into two sets: one consists of "affiliated" firms belonging to the *keiretsu* groups; another is a set of "independent" firms not affiliated to the *keiretsu*. Their statistical investigation shows that the amount of internal funds influences more strongly the investment behavior of independent firms than that of affiliated firms. On the assumption that affiliated firms have stronger relationships with their main banks than do the independent firms, we can interpret their results as implying that the main-bank relationships contribute to reduction of agency costs, thus making internal funds less important in the investment function of the affiliated firms.

Although their investigation is relevant and their conclusion seems to be convincing, we should be careful not to regard the main-bank relationship in the same light as the *keiretsu* group. The main-bank relationship is more universal than the *keiretsu* group in the sense that most Japanese firms have their own main bank regardless of whether or not they belong to any *keiretsu* groups. On the one hand, there may be some independent firms that have very strong relationships with their main banks. On the other hand, the relationships between some affiliated firms and their main banks are not so intimate as is generally believed. We need to differentiate the main-bank relationship from the *keiretsu* grouping.

It has been conventional to assume that the strength of the main-bank relationship and a firm can be measured by the relative share of the main-bank's loan in the total amount of borrowing by the specific firm.[15] But it is not necessarily clear why there is a definite relationship between the main-bank's essential role of information production and the relative importance of its loan. At present we have not yet established a theory to make clear what variables are appropriate to quantify the effectiveness of the main-bank relationship.[16]

---

[15] For example, Hoshi, Kashyap, and Scharfstein (1990) propose this measure in their empirical study about the role of the main bank during the period of financial distress of borrowing firms.

[16] Leland and Pyle (1977) and Campbell and Kracaw (1980) emphasize that it is rational for the financial intermediary in charge of producing information on a specific firm to commit some amount of funds to the firm. According to their argument, the relative share of the main-bank loan to the total borrowing by the firm is an effective signal of the quality of the firm to other investors.

In some arguments explained in the previous section, banks are supposed to get specific information and control managers' behavior through both shareholding and personnel connections with firms. Therefore, we should pay attention to these factors to evaluate activities of the main bank. Although it remains to be settled how to measure the effectiveness (or strength) of the main-bank relationship, we try to quantify that relationship not only in terms of the relative importance of main-banks' loan or but also in terms of main-banks' shareholding and/or personnel connections.

A simple model of corporate investment

Before proceeding to an estimation, we must derive an investment function with agency costs that provides a basis for the following empirical investigation. Particularly, we discuss how agency costs influence the cost of capital for investing firms.

The value of the firm under agency costs: In the following we derive the relationship between investment expenditure and the availability of internal funds under the assumption of agency costs of debt. To simplify our discussion, we consider the case in which the firm is in a stationary state and will decide its investment expenditure once and for all. The essence of our argument is not changed by introducing more sophisticated dynamic elements.[17]

When perfect arbitrage is possible in financial markets, the stockholders of a firm must bear entirely the agency costs. We assume that the agency costs of debt will rise as the debt increases:

$$A_t = A(B_t); \quad A_B > 0, \quad A_{BB} > 0 \tag{9.1}$$

where A_t is agency costs during the period t, and B_t is the stock of debt at the beginning of period t. The current net revenue X_t of the firm is dependent on the capital stock K_t at the beginning of period t; i.e., $X_t = X(K_t)$. We assume that the marginal efficiency of capital is positive but decreasing; i.e., $X_k(K_t) > 0$, $X_{kk}(K_t) \leq 0$. By assuming the constant interest rate r on the borrowing, we can present the profit after interest payments at period t as follows:

$$X_t - A_t - rB_t = X(K_t) - A(B_t) - rB_t$$

If the firm does not invest at period t, its financial and real structure are preserved at the levels achieved before period t. In this case the total

---

[17] For example, see Chirinko (1987) for a dynamic analysis of the firm's investment.

market value of the firm's stock S_{0t} is presented by Eq. (9.2), where u_{0t} is the cost of capital for the firm without investment expenditure.

$$S_{0t} = [X(K_t) - A(B_t)] + \frac{[X(K_t) - A(B_t)]}{(1 + u_{0t})}$$

$$+ \frac{[X(K_t) - A(B_t)]}{(1 + u_{0t})^2} + \cdots - B_t$$

$$= \frac{[X(K_t) - A(B_t)](1 + u_{0t})}{u_{0t}} - B_t \tag{9.2}$$

Consider the case in which the firm decides investment expenditure Z_t financed by both internal fund F_t and additional borrowing V_t. The internal fund F_t is defined as the amount of profit after dividend D_t paid out to shareholders. Thus,

$$Z_t = F_t + V_t \tag{9.3}$$

$$F_t = X(K_t) - A(B_t) - rB_t - D_t \tag{9.4}$$

where the internal fund F_t and dividend D_t cannot be negative; i.e.,

$$F_t, D_t \geqq 0 \tag{9.5}$$

The dividend policy of the firm is a very intricate problem. The level of dividend may be a signal for presenting the firm's value under asymmetric information.[18] But in the following discussion we assume for simplicity that the dividend does not play any meaningful role, and therefore the optimum level of dividend is zero.

The increment of capital stock I_t ($= K_{t+1} - K_t$) realized by the investment expenditure Z_t is dependent on the adjustment costs C_t of investment. In other words, the increment of capital stock is presented by deducting adjustment costs from investment expenditure: i.e.,

$$Z_t = I_t + C_t \tag{9.6}$$

Following the formulation by Uzawa (1969), we assume that adjustment costs can be presented by the following function:

$$C_t = C(I_t, K_t); C(0, K_t) = 0, \quad C_I \geqq 0$$
$$C_I(0, K_t) = 0, \quad C_{II} > 0, \quad C_{IK} < 0 \tag{9.7}$$

From Eqs. (9.6) and (9.7), we can derive a function for investment

---

[18] See Easterbrock (1984) and the related literature.

expenditure as follows:

$$Z_t = Z(I_t, K_t); \quad Z(0, K_t) = 0, Z_t > 0$$
$$Z_I(0, K_t) = 1, \quad Z_{II} > 0, \quad Z_{IK} < 0 \tag{9.8}$$

The investment at period t increases the capital stock at the beginning of period $t + 1$ from K_t to K_{t+1}. In period $t + 1$ the profit after interest payments will be

$$X(K_{t+1}) - A(B_t + V_t) - r(B_t + V_t)$$

But after period t, the firm is assumed to stay at stationary state. In this case, the stock value of firm S_{1t} at the beginning of period t can be presented by Eq. (9.9), where u_t is the cost of capital when the firm decides the investment expenditure.

$$S_{1t} = [X(K_t) - A(B_t) - F_t] + \frac{[X(K_{t+1}) - A(B_t + V_t)]}{(1 + u_t)}$$
$$+ \frac{[X(K_{t+1}) - A(B_t + V_t)]}{(1 + u_t)^2} + \cdots - (B_t + V_t)$$
$$= [X(K_t) - A(B_t) - F_t] + \frac{[X(K_{t+1}) - A(B_t + V_t)]}{u_t} - (B_t + V_t) \tag{9.9}$$

Optimum conditions for investment and borrowing: Investment Z_t in the period t is expected to give net gain $S_{1t} - S_{0t}$ to the present stockholders. By making use of the foregoing equations, we can present the net gain to stockholders as follows;

$$S_{1t} - S_{0t} = \frac{X(K_{t+1}) - A(B_t + V_t)}{u_t} - \frac{X(K_t) - A(B_t)}{u_{0t}} - (F_t + V_t) \tag{9.10}$$

Managers of the firm are assumed to decide the levels of investment expenditure Z_t (or capital increment I_t) and additional debt V_t so as to maximize the net gain in Eq. (9.10) subject to constraints in Eqs. (9.3) to (9.5).

The first-order conditions for the optimum decision are summarized by Eqs. (9.11.1), (9.11.2), and (9.11.3):

$$q_t^* = Z_t(I_t^*, K_t) \tag{9.11.1}$$
$$Z(I_t^*, K_t) = F_t^* + V_t^* \tag{9.11.2}$$
$$D_t^* = 0 \tag{9.11.3}$$

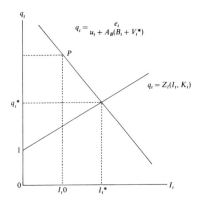

Fig. 9.1. Investment I_t and q_t.

where

$$q_t^* = \frac{X_k(K_t + I_t^*)}{u_t + A_B(B_t + V_t^*)} \qquad (9.12.1)$$

$$F_t^* = X(K_t) - A(B_t) - rB_t \qquad (9.12.2)$$

Asterisks indicate the optimum levels for respective variables. F_t^* in Eq. (9.12.2) is the amount of internal funds predetermined in period t, and q_t^* in Eq. (9.12.1) is the marginal Tobin's Q that takes agency costs of debt into consideration.[19]

Equation (9.11.1) presents a relationship between the increment of capital I_t and the marginal Tobin's Q. This relationship is depicted by the positively sloped Z curve in Fig. 9.1. This curve is positively sloped because we assume that the marginal adjustment cost is increasing $[Z_{II}(I_t, K_t) > 0]$. We can also derive another relationship between investment and the marginal Tobin's Q from Eq. (9.12.1). An increase in I_t decreases the marginal efficiency of capital $X_k(K_t + I_t)$ because of the assumption of decreasing marginal efficiency of capital $[X_{kk}(K_t) \le 0]$. On the other hand, the increase in I_t needs an increase in the investment expenditure Z_t. Since the amount of internal funds F_t^* is predetermined in period t, the increase in investment expenditure leads to the increase in debt outstanding at the beginning of period $t + 1$, which incurs additional agency costs. We assume for simplicity that the marginal efficiency of capital X_k depends on only the capital stock K_t. Thus, an increase in I_t will reduce q_t, i.e., the marginal

[19] If there is no agency cost accompanied with debt, $A_B(B_t + V_t) = 0$, the marginal Tobin's Q is $q_t^* = X_k/u_t$, which would be represented by the horizontal q curve in Fig. 9.1. In this case, the optimum level of investment I_t^* does not depend on both outstanding debt B_t and internal funds F_t^*.

Tobin's Q. The q curve in Fig. 9.1 indicates the relationship between the increment of capital I_t and q_t. When the investment expenditure Z_t is equal to the internal funds F_t^*, the stock of borrowing does not increase (i.e., $V_t = 0$) and, therefore, the marginal Tobin's Q is $X_k/[u_t + A_B(B_t)]$. Point P on the q curve presents the increment of capital stock I_t and q_t when the investment expenditure is entirely financed by the internal funds.

The intersection of the q curve and Z curve in Fig. 9.1 gives the optimum levels of I_t and q_t. We can intuitively understand how both optimum investment I_t and q_τ (marginal Tobin's Q) would be influenced by changes in exogenous variables by observing Fig. 9.1:

1. An increase in the marginal efficiency of capital X_k (for simplicity, we assume it to be a constant e_t hereafter) shifts the q curve upwards and increases the optimum levels of both investment I_t and q_t. Similarly, a rise in cost of capital u_t and an increase in outstanding debt B_t, respectively, shift the q curve downwards, leading to a decrease in investment.

2. The increase in the amount of internal funds F_τ^* shifts the q curve to the right by a smaller distance than the increment in F_t^*.[20] Therefore, it increases the investment I_t, but less than the increment in F_t^*.

3. The increase in capital stock K_t shifts the Z curve downwards and q curve upward, respectively. The optimum level of investment I_t obviously increases as K_t increases.

We can summarize these results in the investment function of Eq. (9.13.1) and the function of marginal Tobin's Q, in Eq. (9.13.2), corresponding to the optimum investment. To avoid complicated notation, we delete the asterisk indicating the optimum levels of respective variables.

$$I_t = f(K_t, B_t, F_t, u_t, e_t); \quad f_k > 0, f_B < 0, f_F > 0, f_u < 0, f_e > 0$$
$$(9.13.1)$$

$$q_t = g(K_t, B_t, F_t, u_t, e_t); \quad g_k > 0, g_B < 0, g_F > 0, g_u < 0, g_e > 0^{[21]}$$
$$(9.13.2)$$

The influence of the main-bank relationship: From the previous discussion, we conclude that an increase in debt raises the agency cost $[A_B(B_\tau + V_t) > 0]$, suppressing investment expenditure by individual firms. The larger amount of internal funds available to the firm will lessen the need for additional borrowing to finance capital expansion, so that these funds will, *ceteris paribus*, lead to larger investment expenditures. In this sense, the availability of the internal funds restrains the firm's investment.

---

[20] The increment dF_t^* of the internal funds shifts the q curve rightwards by $(1/Z)dF_t$, which is smaller than dF_t because Z_l is larger than unity by the assumption Eq. (9.8).

[21] An increase in debt stock B_t increases I_t since we assume that the marginal agency cost associated with debt is increasing (i.e., $A_{BB} > 0$).

However, if the intimate relationship between the main bank and its borrowing firm diminishes the agency cost of debt, how does it change the influence of the internal fund on the firm's investment? To answer this question, we modify the function of agency costs $A(B_t)$ to explicitly consider the main bank's role of reducing agency costs. Specifically, we assume the agency costs of debt to be represented by the following function

$$A_t = mA(B_t) \qquad (9.14)$$

where m is a parameter to measure the impact of the main-bank relationship. We assume that m becomes smaller as the relationship between the main bank and the firm become more intimate.

It is intuitively obvious that the q curve in Fig. 9.1 slopes more gently as parameter m becomes smaller, because the more intimate main-bank relationship is supposed to lessen the extent to which an increase in investment incurs additional agency costs. Thus, the same rightward shift of the q curve caused by an increase in F_t will increase investment I_t less in the case of a smaller m (i.e., in the case of the more intimate main-bank relationship) than in the case of a large m (i.e., in the case of the less intimate main-bank relationship).

Thus, the main-bank relationship will reduce the influence of internal funds on the firm's investment expenditure. Although we neglect it for simplicity, the main-bank relationship also influences the response of investment to changes in other exogenous variables. Similarly, the response of marginal Q to changes in the internal-fund availability will be less significant as m becomes larger. In the following empirical investigation, however, we focus on the influence of the main-bank relationship on an individual firm's capital investment.

Empirical analysis of the main-bank variables

In this section, we empirically investigate the relationship between investment by individual firms and their internal funds, and the influence of the main-bank variables on the relationship. The sample of the empirical analysis is a group of 38 companies belonging to the electric equipment industry. We confine our analysis to those 38 companies mainly because we have easy access to necessary data of those companies during the period of 1972–88 (fiscal year). We give a detailed explanation about the data in our Appendix.

The estimation of the basic investment function: The purpose of our analysis is to learn how the main-bank variables influence investment expenditure based on estimation of the investment function Eq. (9.13.1). We transform

Table. 9.1. *The result of a basic estimation*

a_0	−1.0631	(−2.32)
a_1	0.6021	(4.27)
a_2	−0.0492	(−1.37)
a_3	0.4292	(3.69)
a_4	−0.0740	(−2.09)
a_5	0.0129	(0.42)
R^2	0.62	
DW	1.80	

Note: The parentheses present t values.

Eq. (9.13.1) into the following log-linear function;

$$\log I_t = a_0 + a_1 \log K_t + a_2 \log B_t + a_3 \log F_t + a_4 u_t + a_5 e_t + v_t \tag{9.15}$$

where u_t and e_t are proxies for the cost of capital and the marginal efficiency of capital, respectively, and v_t is a term of disturbance. We approximate the cost of capital u_t by the weighted average of the call rate and the discount bill rate, and the marginal efficiency of capital by the rate of increase in operating profits.

Under the assumption that the debt is associated with the agency cost, the coefficients of Eq. (9.15) are expected to satisfy the following inequalities:

$$a_1 > 0, \quad a_2 < 0, a_3 > 0, \quad a_4 < 0, \quad a_5 > 0 \tag{9.16}$$

Table 9.1 presents the result of estimating the investment function, Eq. (9.15), based on panel data of the 38 companies. We utilized the PANEL command of the RATS by assuming a random effects model.[22] All coefficients satisfy theoretically expected conditions presented by Eq. (9.16), although a_5 is not significant at all. Particularly, the internal fund has a significantly positive coefficient a_3, suggesting the importance of agency costs of debt. This is consistent with the result Hoshi et al. (1991) obtained in their empirical study based on more comprehensive data.

Main-bank variables: It is conventional to assume that the fraction of all bank borrowing that comes from the firm's main bank represents the

---

[22] The same method of estimation is used in Table 9.3. See Hsiao (1986) for the random effect model.

Table 9.2. *Characteristics of main-bank variables (the average, the standard deviation, and the coefficient of correlation: 1972–88)*

	M_L	M_s	N_0
Average	19.9	4.0	4.1
Standard deviation	12.1	2.5	3.6
Coefficient of M_L	1.000	0.026	0.118
correlation M_s	0.026	1.000	0.455
M_0	0.118	0.455	1.000

Source: Toyokeizai-shimposha, *Kigyo Keiretsu Soran.*

strength of the relationship between the firm and its main bank.[23] We call this fraction "the ratio of the main-bank loan." But, as has already been explained, it is ambiguous whether the ratio of the main-bank loan truly indicates strength of the main-bank relationship. In addition to the ratio of the main-bank loan, we introduce the fraction of the firm's outstanding shares held by the main bank ("the ratio of main-bank share holding") and the fraction of all members of the firm's executive board that comes from the main bank ("the ratio of main-bank officers") to measure strength of the main-bank relationship. The ratio of main-bank shareholding is particularly important because, as has been explained in the previous section, some scholars have emphasized the importance of shareholding by banks as a measure of reducing the agency cost. Table 9.2 summarizes statistical characteristics of those main-bank variables: the ratio of the main-bank loan M_L, the ratio of main-bank shareholding M_s, and the ratio of main-bank officials M_0 calculated for each of the sampled firms. According to the table, these variables do not highly correlate with each other except for M_s and M_0.

Impact of the main-bank variables: We estimate the investment function with agency costs discussed in this section. If any one of the main-bank variables M_L, M_s, M_0 is a relevant proxy of the strength of the main-bank relationship, and if the main-bank relationship is effective in reducing the firm's agency costs of borrowing, we expect that the amount of internal funds will be less important for the firm that has larger main-bank variables. Specifically we test the following investment function, which is

[23] See, for example, Hoshi, Kashyap, and Scharfstein (1990).

Table 9.3. *Estimation of the investment function*

$$\log I_t = a_0 + a_1 \log K_t + a_2 \log B_t + (a_3 + a_{31}M_{Lt} + a_{32}M_{st}$$
$$+ a_{33}M_{0t})\log F_t + a_4 u_t + a_5 e_t + v_t$$

a_1	0.5465	(3.39)	+
a_2	−0.0581	(−1.54)	−
a_3	0.4955	(3.62)	+
a_{31}	−0.0008	(−1.53)	−
a_{32}	0.0008	(0.26)	−
a_{33}	0.0016	(0.64)	−
a_4	−0.0727	(−2.04)	−
a_5	0.0065	(0.22)	+
R^2	0.63		
DW	1.81		

a modified version of the basic investment function Eq. (9.15):

$$\log I_t = a_0 + a_1 \log K_t + a_2 \log B_t + (a_3 + a_{31}M_{Lt} + a_{32}M_{st}$$
$$+ a_{33}M_{0t})\log F_t + a_4 u_t + a_5 e_t + v_t \qquad (9.17)$$

We are interested in whether the coefficient a_3 for the internal funds F_t is positive, and whether we can find any significantly negative coefficient among a_{31}, a_{32}, and a_{33} in the estimated investment function Eq. (6.17).

Table 9.3 presents the estimated result of the investment function Eq. (9.17) based on the same panel data as those utilized in estimating Eq. (9.15). the result of estimation supports the hypothesis that the amount of internal funds F_t positively influences the firm's investment $(a_3 > 0)$. This is what the estimation of Eq. (9.15) has already confirmed.

Table 9.3 also suggests that the main-bank relationship measured by the ratio of main-bank loan M_L is effective in reducing the restrictive influence of internal funds, because the coefficient a_{31} of M_L is negative at 10% significance level. The other main variables M_s and M_0 are not so effective as the theory expects, because their coefficients a_{32} and a_{33} are positive, though they are statistically insignificant. We may say that both of M_s and M_0 are meaningless in reducing the agency costs of debt.[24]

---

[24] Hoshi, Kashyap, and Scharfstein (1990) adopt and method similar to that of this paper to investigate investment behavior of financially distressed firms. They conclude that those firms belonging to the *keiretsu* groups can maintain higher levels of investment than those independent from the *keiretsu*, that the main-bank relationship measured by the relative importance of the main-bank loan (the ratio of the main-bank loan in this paper) appears to help financially distressed firms maintain the level of investment outlay. They conclude also that the firm's relative share of stocks held by the main bank does not statistically influence the firms' investment. Their conclusions seem to be consistent with our empirical results, summarized in Table 9.3.

From the result presented in Table 9.3, we conclude that the main-bank relationship measured by the relative importance of the main-bank loan M_L contributes to mitigating the constraint of availability of internal funds on the firm's investment. On the other hand, both the shareholding by the main bank and the number of officials sent from the main bank are not significant in reducing the internal-funds constraint. Particularly, it is noteworthy that the equity positions taken by main banks are not so powerful in mitigating agency problems as some people have thought. This may not be surprising, because the equity position would scarcely provide more meaningful information about borrowing firms than what has already accumulated through the long-term loan transaction with the firm.[25] At any rate, this result suggests that we need to reconsider carefully the hypothesis that the equity position taken by banks is an efficient measure to resolve the agency problems of external fund-raising.

We should pay some attention to the magnitude of the contribution by the main-bank variables to reduce the agency cost. The absolute value of the coefficient of M_L is 0.0008 (Table 9.3), and the average value of M_L for the sampled firms is around 20% (Table 9.2). Therefore, it can be said that on the average the main-bank relationship of the sampled firm has reduced the restrictiveness of the internal funds by 0.016, which is just 3% of the constraint (0.4955) when the firm does not have the main-bank relationship. Thus, our test suggests that the magnitude of effectiveness of the main-bank relationship is very small. The reason for this result may be that the sample of our test contains only leading firms listed in the first section of the Tokyo Stock Exchange. These firms may have accumulated so much "financial power" that they have been able to avoid the serious agency costs of external fund-raising without substantial support from their main banks.

In order to confirm the general validity of our empirical result, we should extend our sample by including small-scale firms that supposedly world require substantial support from the main bank. We should also extend the sample period from 1972–88 to the 1960s during which time the bank played much more important roles than the period after the mid-1970s.

---

[25] Even if the equity position does not particularly increase informational efficiency, there remains an incentive for the main bank to take equity positions in firms. As has been suggested in the previous section, it may be a main objective of mutual shareholding to give wide latitude to incumbent managers by reducing the possibility of hostile takeovers from outsiders. If this is true, we cannot regard shareholding by the banking sector as an efficient method of reducing agency costs in corporate finance.

Concluding remarks

In the second section of this paper we explained various roles of the banking sector in reducing the agency costs associated with external financing by focusing on the working of the Japanese financial system. Then we tested the hypothesis that the main-bank relationship reduces the agency costs of external funds, thereby mitigating the restrictiveness of the internal funds for investment expenditure decided by individual firms. The basic formulation of our test is similar to that adopted by Hoshi, Kashyap, and Scharfstein (1991). But we are careful of quantifying the strength of the main-bank relationship.

Our empirical test in the third section brought forth the following results:

1. The availability of internal funds exerts a substantial influence on individual firms' investment behavior. This suggests the existence of the agency costs with external fund-raising.

2. The main-bank relationship, the strength of which is measured in terms of the relative share of the main-bank loan in the total borrowing, contributes to mitigating the restrictive influence of the internal funds, although the magnitude of the contribution is very small.

3. Shareholding by the main bank does not contribute to reduction of the agency cost.

Chart 1 presents changes in composition of fund raising by major Japanese companies (around 600 top companies belonging to various industries) since 1960. According to this chart, a drastic change occurred in Japanese corporate finance during the 1980s. The major companies reduced their reliance on borrowed funds and instead increased the relative share of internal funds starting in the early 1980s. This phenomenon can be interpreted as follows: Those companies did not need to borrow heavily during this period because the growth rate of capital accumulation of the companies significantly declined. They tended to decrease the relative importance of external fund-raising associated with agency costs (i.e., borrowing).

It is noteworthy, however, that the amount of funds raised by issuing both stock and equity-related bonds (i.e., convertible and warrant bonds) substantially increased from mid-1980s. Japanese companies appeared to exchange their capital structure aggressively from debt to equity. In spite of this remarkable structural change, our investigation affirms the role of main banks in reducing the agency cost of debt. This result is worthy of emphasis, though it remains to be investigated whether the structural change has exerted any influence on corporate governance in Japan.

We must also acknowledge the tentative nature of our research. First, we should extend the scope of our sampled firms. Particularly, it is interesting and important to include small-scale firms in our sample, because they suffer from incomplete information more seriously than do leading firms. Therefore, the main-bank relationship would be more important for small-scale firms than for leading firms.

Second, we need to investigate the validity of our basic assumption that the main-bank relationship is an exogenous factor in explaining the investment behavior of firms. We must explain why some firms have relatively close relationships with their main banks while others do not. In other words, if the main-bank relationship is effective in reducing agency costs, why do not some firms depend on the main bank-relationship? In order to answer this question, we need a theoretical framework to explain the choice of the main-bank relationship both on the part of borrowing firms and on the part of banks. This is a problem still to be solved.

Appendix: an explanation of data

Sampled firms, the sample period, and data sources: The sampled firms in this paper are 38 firms in the electric equipment industry the financial data of which are available from Mitsubishi Research Institution's *Analyses of Corporate Management* dated continuously from 1971 to 1988 (fiscal year). The financial data (i.e., the capital investments, the tangible fixed assets, and the internal funds) are based on *Analyses of Corporate Management* and Nikkei NEEDS/COMPANY. The data source of the main-bank variables $(M_L, M_s,$ and $M_0)$ are Toyokeizai-shimposha's *Kigyo Keiretsu Soran* and Nihonkeizai-shinbunsha's *Kaisha Nenkan* (Yearbook on Corporations).

Definitions of variables: The main bank: In principle, we define the main bank of a firm as the bank that supplies the largest amount of loans to the firm. If there are more than two banks that supply the largest loan, we define the main bank as the bank that holds the largest share of the firm's stock. If still there remain two or more banks as the main bank, we take personnel connections into account to define the main bank for individual firms.

Capital investment (I_t): The increment of tangible fixed assets during the current fiscal year t.

Stock of capital (K_t): The tangible fixed assets outstanding at the end of the previous fiscal year $t - 1$.

Stock of debt (B_t): The total of debt outstanding at the end of the previous fiscal year $t - 1$.

The internal funds (F_t): The "net income after tax" plus "business depreciation" minus "dividend payout" during the previous fiscal year $t - 1$.

The cost of capital (u_t): The weighted average of the call rate and the discount bill rate during the previous fiscal year $t - 1$. Although long-term interest rates are more desirable than short-term interest rates, we find no reliable long-term interest that can be traced back to 1972 in Japan.

The marginal efficiency of capital (e_t): the growth rate of operating income from period $t - 2$ to period $t - 1$.

The ratio of the main-bank loan (M_L): The percentage of the main-bank loan of the total amount of borrowing of the firm.

The ratio of the main-bank officials (M_0): The percentage of executive officials coming from the main bank of the total number on the executive board. The concurrent case is included.

References

Asako, K., M. Kuninori, T. Inoue, and H. Murase (1991), "Capital Investment and Corporate Finance: Estimation by Simultaneous Equations" (in Japanese), Research Institute of Capital Formation, The Japan Development Bank, Feb.

Barnea, A., R. A. Hangen, and L. W. Serbet (1985), *Agency Problems and Financial Contracting*, Prentice-Hall, Inc.

Campbell, T. S., and W. A. Kracaw (1980), "Information Production, Market Signalling, and the Theory of Financial Intermediation," *Journal of Finance*, 35, 863–82.

Chirinko, R. S. (1987), "Tobin's Q and Financial Policy," *Journal of Monetary Economics*, 19, 69–87.

Easterbrock, F. H. (1984), "The Agency-Cost Explanations of Dividends," *American Economic Review*, 74, 650–59.

Fama, P. F. (1980), "Agency Problems and the Theory of the Firm," *Journal of Political Economy*, 88, 288–307.

Fazzari, S., R. G. Hubbard, and B. Petersen (1988), "Investment and Finance Reconsidered," *Brookings Papers on Economic Activities*, 141–95.

Franks, J., and C. Mayer (1990), "Capital Markets and Corporate Control: A Study of France, Germany and the UK," *Economic Policy: A European Forum*, 10, 189–231.

Gerter, M., and R. Glenn Hubbard (1988), "Financial Factors in Business Fluctuations," NBER Working Paper 2758.

Greenbaum, S. I., G. Kanatas, and I. Venezia (1989), "Equilibrium Loan Pricing under the Bank-Client Relationship," *Journal of Banking and Finance*, 13, 221–35.

Grossman, S., and O. Hart (1980), "Takeover Bids, The Free Rider Problem, and the Theory of the Corporation," *Bell Journal of Economics*, 11, 42–63.

Hayashi, F., and T. Inoue (1990), "The Relation between Firm Growth and Q with Multiple Capital Goods: Theory and Evidence from Panel Data on Japanese Firms," NBER Working Paper 3326.

Horiuchi, A., F. Packer, and S. Fukuda (1988) "What Role Has the Main Bank Played in Japan?," *Journal of the Japanese and International Economies*, 2, 159–80.

Hoshi, T., A. Kashyap, and D. Scharfstein (1990), "The Role of Banks in Reducing the Costs of Financial Distress in Japan," *Journal of Financial Economics*, 27, 67–88.

——— (1991), "Corporate Structure, Liquidity, and Investment: Evidence from Japanese Industrial Groups," *Quarterly Journal of Economics*, 106, 33–60.

Hsiao, C. (1986) *Analysis of Panel Data*, Econometric Society Monographs, New York: Cambridge University Press.

Hubbard, R. G., and A. Kashyap (1990) "Internal Net Worth and the Investment Process: An Application to U.S. Agriculture," NBER Working Paper 3339.

Isaacs, J., and T. Ejiri (1990), *Japanese Securities Market*, Euromoney Publications PLC.

Jensen, M. C., and H. W. Meckling (1976), "Theory of the Firm: Managerial Behavior, Agency Costs and Ownership Structure," *Journal of Financial Economics*, 3, 305–60.

——— (1986), "Agency Costs of Free Cash Flow, Corporate Finance, and Takeovers," *American Economic Review*, 76, 323–329.

——— (1989), "Eclipse of the Public Corporation, "*Harvard Business Review*, 61–74.

Leland, H. E., and D. H. Pyle (1977), "Informational Asymmetries, Financial Structure, and Financial Intermediation," *Journal of Finance*, 32, 371–87.

Meyer, J., and E. Kuh (1951), *The Investment Decision*, Cambridge, MA: Harvard University Press.

Myers, S. C. (1977), "Determinants of Corporate Borrowing," *Journal of Financial Economics*, 5, 147–75.

Prowse, S. D. (1990), "Institutional Investment Patterns and Corporate Financial Behavior in the United States and Japan," *Journal of Financial Economics*, 27, 43–66.

Sharpe, S. A. (1990), "Asymmetric Information, Banking Lending, and Implicit Contracts: A Stylized Model of Customer Relationships," *Journal of Finance*, 45, 1069–87.

Sheard, P. (1986), "Main Banks and Internal Capital Markets in Japan," *Shoken Keizai*, 158, 255–89.

——— (1991), "Delegated Monitoring among Delegated Monitors: Principal-Agent Aspects of the Japanese Main Bank System," Center for Economic Policy Research Publication 274, Palo Alto, CA, Stanford University.

Shleifer, A., and L. H. Summers (1988), "Breach of Trust in Hostile Takeovers," *in* A. J. Auerbach (ed.), *Corporate Takeovers: Causes and Consequences,* Chicago: University of Chicago Press, 33–67.

Ubukata, S. (1989), *M & A: Management Strategy in Corporate Takeovers,* Kodansha (in Japanese).

Uzawa, H. (1969), "Time Preference and the Penrose Effect in a Two-Class Model of Economic Growth," *Journal of Political Economy,* 77, 628–52.

PART IV

Strategic and policy issues for international banking

CHAPTER 10

Risk-adjusted deposit insurance for Japanese banks

RYUZO SATO
RAMA RAMACHANDRAN
BOHYONG KANG

Introduction

The necessity for public institutions to bolster the liquidity and the solvency of the commercial banks, even in economies committed to unregulated markets, is recognized by all but a small minority of scholars committed to free banking. The justification offered is that there is a beneficial externality to the vitality of the banking sector that must be preserved from contagious runs created by public suspicion of its solvency.

A recurrent theme in this literature is the consequences of the support and supervisory responsibilities for the central bank (as the controller of currency and the lender of the last resort) overlapping that of the deposit insurance corporation. The American model of deposit insurance has been widely adopted elsewhere [McCarthy (1980)], but the system cannot be judged independently of the nexus of banking relationships. Though the objective of this paper is the use of the Ronn and Verma (1986) model to rank the city banks and 22 regional banks of Japan by risk-adjusted insurance premiums, we shall begin a selective review of the literature on deposit insurance and the characteristics of the Japanese banking system.

In this context, it is common to differentiate between the macrofunctions (pursuit of monetary policy) and the microfunctions (supervision and control of individual banks) of the central bank. Even though the insolvency of an individual bank would reduce the money supply by making its deposits illiquid, it is in itself no justification for interfering with the market. Bentson (1983, p. 5) points out that the losses to depositors from bank failures were not excessive before the Great Depression. Losses were only 0.10% of total deposits per year from 1900 to 1920, and 0.42% per annum between 1921 to 1929. Such losses to liquidity can be rectified easily by a central bank through its open market operations. Another argument is that insolvencies will disrupt the payment system and increase the cost of transaction for the rest of the economy. An individual's use of the means of payment has a positive effect on the system, as this will facilitate other people's use of the same means. The individual will consider only his private benefit and ignore the greater social return. Bentson (1983) is skeptical of the argument that the banks should be given a Pigovian subsidy for the optimal exploitation of this positive externality. He notes that the use of checks spread considerably before the introduction of deposit insurance and that the check anyway carries with it the danger of inadequate funds. Goodhart (1988, p. 102) goes further in arguing: "Monetary payment services not only could be provided, and are increasingly being provided, by other collective-investment funds but could also be thus provided more safely than by banks."

Another argument that had a wide circulation in historical literature and has received support in recent theoretical analyses is that there is an informational asymmetry that prevents depositors from enforcing the normal market discipline on banks. Assuming risk aversion, depositors will require that riskier banks provide a higher return; but they are numerous, small, and possibly poorly educated and do not have the necessary information, which is very expensive to acquire. Even brushing aside Henry Thornton's comment about bank credit being used by persons of lower class, called snobbishness in his time, an early advocate of deposit insurance in the New York legislature put the matter rather eloquently [quoted in Karekan (1983, p. 2)]:

The loss by insolvency of banks generally falls upon the farmer, the mechanic, and the laborer, who are least acquainted with the condition of banks and who, of all others, are most illy able to either guard against or sustain a loss by their failure.

Informational asymmetry is common to the provision of many other professional activities, including medical and legal services. But the special relevance of the problem for banking was analyzed by Diamond and Dybvig (1983, 1986) and Hirsch (1987). Commercial banks as financial intermediaries do more than arbitrage between lenders and borrowers. In the process, they create a mismatch between the maturities of their assets and their liabilities. The banks issue liabilities redeemable on demand, but their assets consist of loans to "idiosyncratic borrowers" [Federal Deposit Insurance Corporation (1989, p. 44)]. The loans have not only longer maturity but are also illiquid in the sense that they cannot be sold except at severe capital loss, as any hands-off purchaser would discount it for the limited information he has about the borrower (as compared to the bank's more complete information).

The creation of the liquidity by the commercial bank makes it very hard for an individual depositor to evaluate the soundness of the bank's assets. It is extremely hard to determine whether the higher returns offered reflect the greater efficiencies attained by the bank or a trade off for the higher risk it is taking [Goodhart (1988, p. 64)].

If the individual suspects the solvency of an uninsured bank, he has every reason to seek an expeditious withdrawal of his deposits. This would enable him to receive the full value of the deposits as against the prorated amount. If this opinion is shared by many, then the resulting withdrawal is adequate to create a liquidity crisis for the bank. Also the public would at times of suspected crisis show a preference for lower risk, higher quality, and more liquid assets like legal tender or gold, creating a further need for "fire sales" of assets by commercial banks. Bank runs are not the act of frenzied mobs, but the actions of rational individuals (in the economist's sense) with incomplete information [Karekan (1983, p. 4)].

Technically liquidity crisis must be separated from the solvency problems. An individual commercial bank with assets whose equilibrium value (value under normal conditions of sales) is well in excess of its immediate liquidity needs can rediscount some of its assets either with other commercial banks or the central bank. The central bank as the lender of the last resort is responsible for providing liquidity in times of crisis. One common problem faced by all central banks is that they have difficulty in separating the run on an individual bank from the run on the system. The Federal Reserve has been criticized for its failure to act decisively and effectively during the crises of the 1920s and 1930s. Recent criticisms tend to accuse the central banks of being too solicitous about the solvency of individual banks. A deposit insurance, by reducing the probability of a run on the individual bank, reduces the pressures on the lender of the last resort in making these awkward choices.

Deposit insurance is not a costless or distortion-free system. All insurance schemes must address the twin problems of adverse selection and moral hazard, and various voluntary insurance programs have devised schemes to classify risks. But schemes to do so depend on actuarial estimations of normally occurring events whose temporal trends are fairly predictable. But bank failures depend on nonrecurring economic trends. Another difference is that the emphasis in deposit insurance is more on avoiding losses due to insolvency of banks than on compensating the insured for the losses. The Federal Deposit Insurance System adopted a flat rate of 1/12 of 1%, with rebates for revenues in excess of costs so that the actual cost comes to 0.03 to 0.04% of total deposits. The individual deposit covered was increased from $5000 in the 1930s to $40,000 in 1974, and to $100,000 in 1980. Another characteristic is that the insurance fund of less than 1.2% of insured deposits maintained by FDIC is far below what would be considered prudent for a private insurer; it is their public character and tax-payer backing that make the system credible [Kane (1986, p. 176)].

The flat-rate scheme is shown to encourage banks to take excessive risk taking as it biases the firm's risk-reward trade-off. Depositors not concerned with the riskiness of their deposits do not demand a higher return from the banks that undertake riskier investments. But such firms receive a higher return associated with the higher risk. Relieved from market discipline, so the argument goes, the banks as profit maximizers will seek a higher-risk portfolio of assets than they would otherwise do. This in turn increases the risk of insolvency in the future and adds to the expected cost of FDIC. To minimize this distortion, the banks are subject to a number of regulations that can be classified under four categories: asset limitations, capital adequacy, bank holding company permissible activities, and interest rate ceilings [see Flannery (1982) for a simplified exposition].

Karekan and Wallace (1978) argued that if bank deposits are insured under the FDIC-type scheme, then bank regulations were in a sense necessary. Subsequent discussion led to identification of further distortions created by the "implicit" insurance given by FDIC through their failure-resolution techniques. If the failing bank is purchased by another bank with the assistance of FDIC and FRS, then all the deposits are protected to the full amount and not to the legal limits. Also the banks could believe, as with LDC loans, that such protection will be more easily available when the central bank thinks that the risk is widespread and will affect the entire banking system. Hence they will have a tendency to convert as much of their idiosyncratic risks to systemic risks [Penati and Protopapdakis (1988), Spiegel (1989)].

The deposit insurance is but one component of a network of supports offered to commercial banks, and the interrelationships within the network must be taken into account in evaluating the system. Hence we shall review those features of the Japanese system that is of interest to the study of the deposit insurance. But what is striking, even to a casual observer, is that the Japanese banks are, in contrast to their American counterparts, unwilling to publicize the existence of a deposit insurance scheme.

Banking system and deposit insurance in Japan

The modern financial system of Japan is generally considered to be the creation of the Meiji restoration of 1868, which sought to transform the economy from a feudal to a modern capitalist society. The American national banks system was the preferred mode, and a large number of national banks with issuing rights were established [Federation of Bankers

Associations of Japan (1984, p. 1)]. This system collapsed by 1882 when the Bank of Japan became the bank of issue.

The commercial banks followed the European rather than the British pattern and played an important role in providing long-term industrial funds. The number of banks increased to a peak of 1867 banks in 1901 and then declined rapidly. The minimum bank capital requirement of the Bank Law of 1927 disqualified half the 1400 banks then existing; most of them preferred amalgamation with other small and medium-sized banks. This brought about the dual structure in Japanese banking, with the city banks concentrating on serving national corporations and international commerce and regional banks serving the rest of the country.

On the basis of historical origin, the city banks can be divided into four distinct groups [Bronte (1982)]. In the first group are four major *zaibatsu* banks that had a dominant role in the Japanese economy until the end of the Second World War; they are Sumitomo, Mitsui, Mitsubishi, and Fuji. Six city banks – Sanwa, Tokai, Toiyo Kobe, Kyowa, Daiwa, and Saitama – were formed by amalgamation of regional banks. Dai-ichi Kangyo and Hokkaido Takushoku were the products of privatization of state banks during the U.S. occupation. Finally the Bank of Tokyo began as Yokohama Specie Bank, half owned by the Emperor, and changed its name after the end of the war.

Legally there is no distinction between city banks and regional banks. They perform all the functions permitted under the Banking Law, but they have developed over time certain special functions. City banks act as "main banks" for large corporations with which they maintain close relations. The loans to the corporations are technically short term, but they are regularly renewed and so are in effect long term. In addition they are among the largest holders of securities of different maturities. They also assist corporations in times of difficulties.

The regional banks are based on a prefecture, though they frequently extend their activities to neighboring prefectures. The increasing economic integration of the country since the Second World War has provided an inducement to the regional banks to expand their activities to big cities like Tokyo and Osaka. The regional banks provide services to local enterprises and to local governments. They are important suppliers of funds to the money markets.

The Japanese banking system is said to have four distinctive characteristics [Susuki (1980)]. *Overloan* is the funding of loans and investments for sources other than deposits and equity capital. Part of this is financed by borrowing from the central bank. While overloans existed from the Meji restoration, more recently it has been a city bank phenomenon. The bank rate in Japan in post-war years was below the short-term money market rate, and the banks had no incentive to reduce or repay the central bank credit. In England and Germany, the penalty rate charged on such loans provided a price mechanism to restrict their demand; here it was achieved through credit rationing by the Bank of Japan [Suzuki 1980, pp. 12, 57–58)].

Another characteristic is *overborrowing* resulting from low internal financing and limited issue of securities by the commercial corporations. Related to this is the propensity of these corporations to resort to *indirect financing*, defined as resources provided by financial institutions through the purchase of securities or other means. In recent years, major corporations have resorted to a greater use of internal funds than in the immediate post-war years, and their dependence on main banks has been reduced to that extent. Finally the *imbalance of bank liquidity* refers to city banks being short of reserve assets while regional banks have an excess; as noted earlier, regional banks are significant lenders in the money market.

The Ministry of Finance and the Bank of Japan both have supervisory powers over the banks. The Ministry of Finance acts as the Japanese equivalent of the U.S. Treasury, the Securities and Exchange Commission, and state banking commissions. Insofar as it has oversight over the deposit insurance system, it also has some of the supervisory powers of the Federal Deposit Insurance Corporation. The bulk of the Ministry's authority comes from the Banking Law, which permits it to license and supervise all banks. It has powers to approve or deny mergers, acquisitions, and other changes in the operation of banks, including the opening of new branches.

The Ministry can enforce its policies in two ways. It can issue an "administrative guidance" either orally or written. Given the extensive powers of the Ministry of Finance, the administrative guidance is universally obeyed even though it is not legally binding. Most of the supervisory powers rest with the Banking Bureau, but the international operations of a bank are under the oversight of the International Finance Bureau.

The Bank of Japan was established by an act in 1882; some scholars contend that it was modeled on the National Bank of Belgium, though Goodhart (1988, p. 150) questions it. It undertakes all the standard micro- and macrofunctions of the central bank. Its discount rate is the reference point for most interest rates in Japan. In 1981, the Bank introduced the new lending facility similar to the Bundesbank's Lombard rate.

The overloan position of the city banks was mentioned earlier. Hence the loan policies of the Bank of Japan have a tremendous impact on these banks and the economy. It also permits the Bank to use the "window guidance," which sets the bank-by-bank quotas on customers in periods of monetary restraints. Window guidance also has no legal basis and again depends on the close relationship between the city banks and the central bank. Recent financial deregulation, the reduction in the dependence of corporations on bank loans, and the rise of postal savings are all considered to have diluted this interdependence.

The Deposit Insurance Corporation was established in 1971 and was originally capitalized at 450 million yen, of which the government, the Bank of Japan, the private financial institutions each contributed one third. Regular deposits, installment savings, and money in trust with principle guaranteed, are covered by the insurance, originally to an amount of 3 million yen. Interbank deposits and deposits of Japanese branches of foreign banks are not covered. Until 1988, the Corporation charged a premium of 0.008% of insured deposits during the previous year. It can also borrow up to 50 million yen from the Bank of Japan with the permission of the Ministry of Finance.

On the recommendation of the Committee for Financial System Research that the deposit insurance system should be strengthened to maintain orderly credit conditions in the face of financial deregulation, the following revisions were made in May 1986: (1) The protection per depositor was raised to 10 million yen; (2) the premium was increased to 0.012% of deposits; and (3) the limit on borrowing from The Bank of Japan was increased to 500 million yen, and the Corporation was allowed to borrow from other financial institutions to repay the loans to the Bank.

The system was tested when the Heiwa Sogo Bank ran into problems in 1986 and had the potential of being the first bank failure in 50 years. Sumitomo Bank agreed to absorb all the uncollectible loans estimated to a limit of 170 billion yen. Thus, in contrast to the rescue efforts in the United States in recent years, neither the Bank of Japan nor the Deposit Insurance System suffered any loss. However, the difference may be due to the "shadow price" that Sumitomo Bank attached to the branches of the Heiwa Sogo Bank.

Hirsch (1977, p. 243) argues that, due to limitations and asymmetries of information, the dependence of well-functioning markets on certain individual behavioral characteristic can be regarded as a collective inter-mediate good that will not be produced in socially optimal quantity by maximization of individual welfare. Without implicit or explicit cooperation, the insurance element in central banking is an example of this type of market.

The moral hazard issues can be in theory resolved by one of two methods. The central bank can take the "English" route of inculcating a club arrangement among the commercial banks, by which they receive extramarket facilities in return for submitting to a paternalistic and moral leadership. The alternative strategy is to enforce market discipline by treating equity and large deposits as deductibles from the insured risk. The cost of this approach is that the public may believe this rule will not be applied uniformly to banks of different sizes. The public will consider larger banks safer, as the central bank will consider its failure disruptive of the entire financial system and will therefore intervene in its capacity as the lender of the last resort. Hence the market would move the system to an oligopoly. Hirsch (1977, p. 252) argues that the predominance of large banks in Germany is the result of this policy.

A question naturally arises: Which of these systems prevails in Japan, and what is its impact on the deposit insurance system? This short survey of Japanese banking has shown the prevalence of a small number of city banks that work closely with the Bank of Japan, subjecting themselves to administrative guidance from the Ministry of Finance to an extent unheard of in western countries. Further, the smaller regional banks have a cash surplus that makes them net lenders in the money markets. Accepting the argument of Karekan and Wallace (1978) that flat-rate deposit insurance will work only in conjunction with administrative oversight of the banks, it is reasonable to conclude that the inefficiencies of not having a risk-adjusted insurance system may be less in Japan than in a country like the United States. But one should bear in mind the structural changes taking place in the Japanese financial system and also the fact that, in spite of the controls, the Heiwa Sago bank had to be rescued.

Deposit insurance pricing

While there is unanimity about the suboptimality of flat-rate premium, there is less consensus about an alternative. In general, the various proposals could be divided into those that use market information and those that continue to rely on implicit administrative pricing. Among the market pricing models a distinction must be made between those that seek to generate *ex ante* and *ex post* risk measures. The literature was reviewed in a recent FDIC study (1989). The purpose of this paper being the use of the Ronn and Verma (1986) model to evaluate the Japanese deposit insurance system, we shall confine ourselves to a review of the option pricing model of deposit insurance. Merton (1977) argued that the pricing of deposit insurance can be based on the one-to-one relation between deposit insurance and put option, which permitted the application of Black and Scholes (1973).

If the value of banks assets, V, is greater than the value of the liabilities to depositors, B, then the depositors will receive B, and equity of the bank is worth $V - B$. However, if the asset value is less than that of the liabilities, then the equity holders will receive nothing, and the insurer will have a net payout of $B - V$. In other words, if the value of assets falls below that of liabilities, then the bank has purchased a put option to sell the assets to the insurer at the value of its liabilities. If $G(T)$ is the value to the firm of the guarantee T years from now when solvency of the firm is evaluated, then

$$G(0) = \text{Max}[0, B - V] \tag{10.1}$$

The following assumptions are made [Smith (1979)]: (1) homogeneous expectations (about the dynamics of the value of the insured assets) prevail, with the distribution of the end value of any finite-time integral being lognormal with constant variance; (2) the constant instantaneous riskless rate for borrowers and lenders is r; (3) capital market is perfect; (4) trading takes place continuously; and (5) the insured asset generates no pecuniary or nonpecuniary flows. Then the value of the guarantee can be written as

$$G(T) = Be^{-rT}\phi(x_2) - V\phi(x_1) \tag{10.2}$$

where

$$x_1 = \left(\log\left(\frac{B}{V}\right) - \left(r + \frac{\sigma^2}{2}\right)T\right)(\sigma\sqrt{T})^{-1}$$

and

$$x_2 = x_1 + \sigma\sqrt{T}$$

Here ϕ is the cumulative normal density function, V the current value of the assets of the firm, σ^2 the variance rate per unit time for the logarithmic changes in the value of the assets, and B the face value of the liabilities at time T. Since most bank deposits are encashable on demand, a model with term-debt issue is not strictly valid. Merton, however, argues that the time of maturity should be equated to the length of time until the next audit.

The advantage of the formulation is that the pricing of deposit insurance is based on five observable variables: (1) the value of bank assets, (2) the variability of the value of banks assets, (3) the exercise price as measured by the total amount of insured deposits, (4) the constant riskfree interest rate, and (5) the time of maturity or lifetime of the option. Like all models, this one is also dependent on the realism of the assumptions.

An empirical assessment of risk-adjusted deposit insurance premium was made by Ronn and Verma (1986). Unlike some earlier studies, they concentrate on the interbank differences in estimated rates. The equity of the firm is represented as a call option on the value of the assets of the firm with the same maturity as that of the debt of the firm and a striking price equal to the maturity of the debt. But FDIC does not liquidate a bank when the net worth becomes negative; rather by an infusion of funds or purchase and assumptions options, FDIC tries to sustain the bank in the interest of avoiding the disruption created by a bank failure. It is assumed that there is a limit to this tolerance of the resource drain that FDIC exposes itself to, and the limit is expressed as a percentage of the total debt of the bank. Thus when the value of the bank falls between B and ρB, the insuring agency infuses up to $(1 - \rho)B$. On the other hand, if the value falls below ρB, then it takes steps to dissolve the bank.

Given the closure condition, the value of the firm is related to the equity by the equation

$$E = V\phi(x) - \rho B\phi(x - \sigma_v\sqrt{T}) \tag{10.3}$$

where

$$x = \frac{\ln(V/B) + \sigma_v^2\sqrt{T/2}}{\sigma_v\sqrt{T}}$$

$$\sigma_v = \frac{\sigma_E E}{V\phi(x)}$$

$$\sigma_E = \begin{array}{l} \text{the instantaneous standard deviation} \\ \text{of the return on } E \end{array}$$

Under the assumption that all preinsurance debt is of equal seniority, holders of the debt are entitled to either the future value of their deposits or the prorated fraction of the value, whichever is less. Thus they will receive

$$\min\left\{FV(B_1), \frac{V_T B_1}{B_1 + B_2}\right\} \tag{10.4}$$

where $FV(\cdot)$ denotes the future value operator, V_T is the terminal value of the bank at time T, and B_1 and B_2 are the face values of insured and all other debts, respectively. The presumption of equal seniority can be justified on the ground that the bail-out practices of the FDIC are equivalent to a *de facto* insurance of all debt.

The value of an insurance is equivalent to the value of a put, written with striking price equal to total debt, and then scaled down by the proportions of demand deposits to total debt B_1/B, where $B = B_1 + B_2$. Hence d, the per-dollar deposit insurance premium, is

$$d = \phi(y + \sigma_v\sqrt{T}) - (1 - \delta)^n \frac{V}{B}\phi(y) \tag{10.5}$$

where

$$\delta = \frac{\text{dividend per dollar of the value of}}{\text{the assets, paid } n \text{ times per period}}$$

$$y = \frac{\ln[B/V(1-\delta)^n] - \sigma_v^2 T/2}{\sigma_v\sqrt{T}}$$

It will be noticed that the per-dollar insurance premium does not depend on the risk-free interest rate. It is only the *present value* of the striking price that is relevant for the Black-Scholes option pricing; here the present value of the debt is B, and so there is no need to enter the rate explicitly. Second, the insurer is concerned with the future stochastic behavior of assets, and the model does not compare the preinsurance and postinsurance values of assets. Finally, the per dollar premium depends on the total debt and not on the insured deposits; this, as pointed out earlier, is to reflect the policies of the Federal Reserve in protecting all the creditors of the bank. These assumptions differentiate the Ronn and Verma (1966) model from some of the other papers on risk-adjusted insurance models. Deposit insurance based on the option pricing models suffers from the sensitivity to measurement errors in the value and riskiness of assets and the misspecification due to effect of forbearance (supervisory restraint on institutions that fail soundness criteria).

Estimation of deposit premium for the Japanese banks

The Ronn and Verma model is applied to determine the premiums of all 13 city banks and a selective list of 22 regional banks. No specific scientific criteria were used in choosing the regional banks, though many of them are among the largest in this group. Stock market data were gathered from the Nikkei Telecom Japanese News and Retrieval online database for the period January to March 1988. The daily rates of return were calculated from the stock prices for these months; then the standard deviation of the rate was calculated. Under the assumption that the daily returns were independently and identically distributed with normal distribution, the annualized standard deviation was taken to be $\sqrt{275}$ times the daily standard deviation. Other financial and accounting data, such as the face value of the total liabilities, the number of shares outstanding, and dividend information were found from the quarterly Japan Company Handbook (winter 1988) published by the Tokyo Keizai Shinposa.

We calculated the deposit premium using Eq. (10.5) for two values of ρ in Eq. (10.3). The value of $\rho = 0.97$ was chosen to compare the results

Table 10.1. *Relative premiums of city banks*

Bank	Insurance rate when $\rho = 0.97$	Insurance rate when $\rho = 0.94$
Dai-ichi Kangyo	3.00	0.0803
Hokkaido Takushoku	1348.33	13.9427
Bank of Tokyo	211.33	2.4510
Mitsui	1.33	0.0367
Mitsubishi	79.50	0.8033
Fuji	0.17	0.0060
Sumitomo	18.00	0.2288
Daiwa	1302.50	6.4312
Sanwa	34.33	0.4384
Tokai	5.17	0.2190
Kyowa	87.17	1.8420
Taiyo Kobe	264.50	3.2038
Saitama	1.00	1.0000

Table 10.2. *Relative premiums of select regional banks*

Bank	Insurance rate when $\rho = 0.97$	Insurance rate when $\rho = 0.94$
Chiba	1044.9	38.729
Bank of Yokohama	217.1	10.194
Joyo	3276.3	77.339
Gunma	522.3	20.253
Ashikaga	3072.7	74.980
Musashino	4442.4	131.834
Chiba Kogyo	46.0	15.847
Kanto	2274.7	152.411
Tokyo Tomin	672.0	31.137
77 Bank	139.0	14.165
Aomori	845.0	113.744
Yamagata	961.4	38.692
Bank of Iwate	144.4	52.794
Toho	1403.3	51.028
Hokkaido	1560.0	81.011
Shizuoka	701.1	23.819
Juroku	0.1	0.783
Hokuriku	390.0	28.863
Sugura	2346.3	69.270
Hachjuni	0.6	0.234
Yamanashi	1053.9	31.033
Ogaki Kyoritsu	1.0	1.000

Table 10.3. *Relative premiums of select American banks*

Banks	Normalized annual premiums
Continental Illinois Corp.	43.20
Wells Fargo & Co.	40.84
Marine Midland Banks, Inc.	31.22
Manufacturers Hanover Corp.	28.20
First Interstate Bancorp.	19.02
Citicorp	9.78
Chemical NY Corp.	6.00
Security Pacific Corp.	3.60
Bank of New York, Inc.	1.00
Morgan J.P. and Co., Inc.	0.02

Source: Ronn and Verma (1986), pp. 892–93.

Table 10.A1. *Estimation of deposit premium of city banks when ρ is 0.97*

Bank	σ_E	σ_V	V	B	d
Dai-ichi Kangyo	0.24986	0.04061	52701820	45555712	0.0000018
Hokkaido Takushoku	0.41267	0.03523	9877987	9325576	0.0008090
Bank of Tokyo	0.33695	0.04219	22648814	20469390	0.0001268
Mitsui	0.23865	0.04056	23895550	20469390	0.0000008
Mitsubishi	0.31647	0.05153	47905920	41531892	0.0000477
Fuji	0.20785	0.03538	49325348	42284180	0.0000001
Sumitomo	0.28500	0.05084	50751376	43148564	0.0000108
Daiwa	0.44859	0.06895	14500066	12697296	0.0007815
Sanwa	0.29639	0.04801	45531512	39428728	0.0000206
Tokai	0.24540	0.03201	30341354	27211686	0.0000031
Kyowa	0.29883	0.03318	14466365	13267993	0.0000523
Taiyo Kobe	0.33828	0.03979	23419866	21372480	0.0001587
Saitama	0.27213	0.03081	12696297	11300773	0.0000006

with those in the Ronn and Verma (1986) paper. It will be recollected that ρ is a policy parameter and reflects the willingness of the Deposit Insurance Corporation to save banks at a loss to itself. To test the implications of the conjecture that the Japanese Deposit Insurance System may tolerate a higher risk, and to check the sensitivity of the results to the value of the parameter, the rates were recalculated for $\rho = 0.94$. The results are given in the appendix, Tables 10.A1 to 10.A4.

Table 10.A2. *Estimation of deposit premium of city banks when* ρ *is 0.94*

Bank	σ_E	σ_V	V	B	d
Dai-ichi Kangyo	0.24986	0.04169	51335148	45555712	0.0000280
Hokkaido Takushoku	0.41267	0.03626	9587194	9325576	0.0048632
Bank of Tokyo	0.33695	0.04336	22034734	20469390	0.0008549
Mitsui	0.23865	0.04163	23281466	20469390	0.0000128
Mitsubishi	0.31647	0.05290	46660004	41531892	0.0002902
Fuji	0.20785	0.03631	48056796	42284180	0.0000021
Sumitomo	0.28500	0.05217	49456924	43148564	0.0000798
Daiwa	0.44859	0.07080	14119196	12697296	0.0022432
Sanwa	0.29639	0.04928	44348124	39428728	0.0001529
Tokai	0.24540	0.03289	29524992	27211686	0.0000764
Kyowa	0.29883	0.03412	14068324	13267993	0.0006425
Taiyo Kobe	0.33828	0.04090	22778578	21372480	0.0011175
Saitama	0.27213	0.03168	12014247	11300773	0.0003488

Table 10.A3. *Estimation of deposit premium of regional banks when* ρ *is 0.97*

Bank	σ_E	σ_V	V	B	d
Chiba	0.42088	0.04593	6723701	6194408	0.0007314
Bank of Yokohama	0.35592	0.04792	11028505	9840827	0.0001520
Joyo	0.53471	0.06014	5938844	5455316	0.0022934
Gunma	0.39435	0.04946	3753603	3386084	0.0003656
Ahikaga	0.51108	0.05834	5223826	4785281	0.0021509
Musashino	0.55016	0.04250	1576923	1505252	0.0031097
Chiba Kogyo	0.25568	0.02088	1315220	1245137	0.0000322
Kanto	0.37858	0.02193	699121	679145	0.0015923
Tokyo Tomin	0.39519	0.04093	1722498	1592691	0.0004704
77 Bank	0.31340	0.03128	3097915	2875056	0.0000973
Aomori	0.39221	0.03362	1238271	1167613	0.0005915
Yamagata	0.41889	0.04328	1168257	1080776	0.0006730
Bank of Iwate	0.27223	0.01911	1284158	1230952	0.0001011
Toho	0.44522	0.04421	1642354	1526766	0.0009823
Hokkaido	0.42428	0.03127	2890448	2762080	0.0010920
Shizuoka	0.41387	0.05330	5681097	5106311	0.0004908
Juroku	0.15817	0.01381	2757307	2594373	0.0000001
Hokuriku	0.27208	0.03117	6394374	6004897	0.0002730
Suruga	0.49313	0.04914	2361717	2197072	0.0016424
Hachijuni	0.21833	0.02949	4417765	3939244	0.0000004
Yamanashi	0.44126	0.05737	1419803	1275146	0.0007377
Ogaki Kyoritsu	0.20900	0.02212	1964045	1810449	0.0000007

Table 10.A4. *Estimation of deposit premium of regional banks when ρ is 0.97*

Bank	σ_E	σ_V	V	B	d
Chiba	0.42088	0.04723	6537897	6194408	0.0031409
Bank of Yokohama	0.35592	0.04924	10733274	9840827	0.0008267
Joyo	0.53471	0.06183	5775213	5455316	0.0062722
Gunma	0.39435	0.05083	3652025	3386084	0.0016425
Ahikaga	0.51108	0.05998	5080297	4785281	0.0060809
Musashino	0.55016	0.04290	1529318	1505252	0.0106917
Chiba Kogyo	0.25568	0.02150	1277864	1245137	0.0012852
Tokyo Tomin	0.39519	0.04206	1674750	1592691	0.0025252
Kanto	0.37859	0.02259	678747	679145	0.0123605
77 Bank	0.31340	0.03218	3011657	2875056	0.0011488
Aomori	0.39221	0.05076	1202451	1167613	0.0092246
Yamagata	0.41889	0.04451	1135853	1080776	0.0031379
Bank of Iwate	0.27223	0.02291	1247225	1230952	0.0042816
Toho	0.44522	0.04548	1596533	1526766	0.0041384
Hokkaido	0.42428	0.03219	2807588	2762080	0.0065700
Shizuoka	0.41387	0.05479	5527893	5106311	0.0019317
Juroku	0.15817	0.01421	2679487	2594373	0.0000635
Hokuriku	0.27208	0.03205	6219265	6004897	0.0023407
Suruga	0.49313	0.05054	2295823	2197072	0.0056178
Hachijuni	0.21833	0.03029	4299621	3939244	0.0000190
Yamanashi	0.44126	0.05893	1381545	1275146	0.0025168
Ogaki Kyoritsu	0.20900	0.02275	1909731	1810449	0.0000811

To evaluate the results, we normalized the premium by taking among city banks that of the Saitama Bank and, among regional banks, that of the Ogaki Kyoritsu to be unity. Notice that the absolute values of the premiums of the Saitama Bank and the Ogaki Kyoritsu are very close to each other when $\rho = 0.97$, but the premium of the latter is about 4 times that of the former when $\rho = 0.94$. The values of the relative premiums are given in textual Tables 10.1 and 10.2. For comparison, 12 U.S. banks from Ronn and Verma (1986) were chosen, and a similar table prepared for them (see Table 10.3).

The tables show that, among city banks, Hokkaido Takushoku and Daiwa Banks have the highest risk-related premium. At the other extreme, Fuji and Mitsui have the lowest. These groupings are not affected by the change in the value of ρ from 0.97 to 0.94. The other banks fall in the middle, and their rankings change with the value of the parameter ρ.

There is even greater instability in the ranking of the regional banks. The two banks Shizuoka and Suruga have the lowest premiums though their relative ranking changes with ρ. There is no invariant ranking of banks with high premiums.

Both in the United States and in Japan, the interbank variation in the risk-adjusted deposit rate seems to be quite large. It is reasonable to say that this range is beyond the realm of what is politically feasible in a democratic society. Also, as pointed out in earlier studies, the actual numbers seem to be sensitive to the parameter value assumed and any misspecification of risk.

If the risk-adjusted measures are correct indicators of the riskiness of the banks, then it is clear that the use of a flat rate could create serious distortions. Yet it is not clear why the banks with low risk-adjusted premiums did not choose a riskier portfolio for higher returns. On the other hand, if a risk-adjusted deposit premium is introduced, it is probable that the banks with the higher premiums would abandon some of the intermediation they are now doing. Would institutional innovations arise in the market to offer these services outside the banking system, or would the economy be adversely affected by the absence of such services even at higher cost? More fundamentally, if the service offered by the banks is the bearing of idiosyncratic risks that cannot be evaluated by an outsider, can the stock market correctly measure the aggregate risk born by an individual bank? The option pricing model offers a number of challenges to the study of the safety nets offered by the banks.

References

Bentson, G. J. (1983), "Deposit Insurance and Bank Failures," *Federal Reserve Bank of Atlanta Economic Review*, 69, 5–14.

Black, F., and M. Scholes (1973), "The Pricing of Options and Corporate Liabilities," *J. Political Economy*, 81, 637–59.

Bronte, S. (1982), *Japanese Finance Markets and Institutions*, London: Euromony Publications.

Diamond, D. W., and P. H. Dybvig (1983), "Bank Runs, Deposit Insurance and Liquidity," *J. Political Economy*, 91, 401–19.

Diamond, D. W., and P. H. Dybvig (1983), "Banking Theory, Deposit Insurance, and Bank Regulation," *J. Business*, 59, 55–68.

Federal Deposit Insurance Corporation (1989), "Deposit Insurance for the Nineties," Washington, D.C.: FDIC.

Federation of Bankers Association of Japan (1984), *Banking System in Japan*, Tokyo: FBAJ.

Flannery, M. J. (1982), "Deposit Insurance Creates a Need for Bank Regulation," *Federal Bank of Philadelphia Business Review*, 17–27.

Goodhart, C. (1988), *The Evolution of Central Banks*, Cambridge, MA: MIT Press.

Hirsch, F. (1977), "The Bagehot Problem," *Manchester School of Economics and Social Studies*, 45, 241–57.

Kane, E. J. (1986), "Appearance and Reality of Deposit Insurance," *J. Banking and Finance*, 10, 175–88.

Karekan, J. H. (1983), "Deposit Insurance Reform Is the Cart Not the Horse," *Federal Reserve Bank of Minneapolis Quarterly Review*, 3, 1–9.

Karekan, J. H., and N. Wallace (1978), "Deposit Insurance and Bank Regulation: A Partial Equilibrium Approach," *J. Business*, 51, 413–38.

McCarthy, I. S. (1980), "Deposit Insurance: Theory and Practice," *IMF Staff Papers*, 27, 578–600.

Merton, R. C. (1980), "An Analytical Derivation of the Cost of Deposit Insurance and Loan Guarantees," *J. Banking and Money*, 1, 3–11.

Penati, A., and A. Protopapadakis (1988), "The Effect of Implicit Deposit Insurance on the Bank's Portfolio Choices, with an Application to International Over-exposure," *J. Monetary Economics*, 21, 107–26.

Ronn, E. I., and A. K. Verma (1986), "Pricing Risk Adjusted Deposit Insurance: An Option Based Model," *J. Finance*, 41, 871–90.

Smith, C. (1979), "Application of Option Pricing Model," *in* J. L. Bicksler (ed.), *Handbook of Financial Economics*, Amsterdam: North-Holland.

Spiegal, M. (1989), "Risk Aversion, Deposit Insurance and Collective Action Problems Among Banks," C. V. Starr Center of Applied Economic Research Report, New York University. 1989.

Suzuki, Y. (1980), *Money and Banking in Contemporary Japan*, New Haven: Yale University Press.

CHAPTER 11

Competition in retail banking markets: a comparison of Britain and Japan

SHELAGH HEFFERNAN

Introduction

The purpose of this paper is to investigate the competitive structure of retail banking markets in Japan and the United Kingdom. It is part of a broader exercise aimed at investigating the impact of regulatory reform on competitive behavior in financial markets. A comparison of the Japanese and British retail markets is useful, because while banks in the U.K. have been subject to a number of reforms that encourage greater competition among retail banks, in Japan there has been little reform of this sort. The question then arises: Have the reforms in Britain meant that there is greater competition among banks in Britain than in Japan?

Definition of retail banking

The retail banking sector is defined as that part of a retail financial market that offers three products to the personal consumer: deposits, loans, and money transmission facilities in the form of a payments system.

The retail banking structure in Britain

By the late 1980s, two groups – banks and building societies – had emerged as the key participants in the British retail banking market. Traditionally, the banking sector was dominated by banks: four major clearing banks and a number of smaller (approximately eight) banks. Among the smaller banks (in terms of asset size) is the National Girobank, a subsidiary of the Post Office. In 1989, it was announced that a bid by one of the building societies to purchase the National Girobank had been accepted. Also included among the smaller banks is the Trustee Savings Bank (TSB), created by a merger of regional TSBs in 1986. The regional TSBs have been able to offer a full range of retail banking services since 1976. Prior to this date, they were largely deposit banks, and all funds were invested in public sector debt.

240

Historically, building societies were mutual organizations, formed to provide housing finance to members of the societies. Members would own shares (in the form of deposits) in the society and have voting rights (one vote per shareholder) in the organization. Shareholding allowed the member to take out a mortgage to finance a house purchase. However, since 1986, societies have been permitted to offer a full range of retail banking services and may convert from mutual to public limited company (PLC) status. Many of the very small societies have continued to offer the traditional products; it is the large societies that have expanded into retail banking.

In 1988, there were over 100 building societies in the U.K., but the largest three building societies had over 50% of building society shareholders (depositors) and just under 50% of society mortgage borrowers. Figures for the 10 largest building societies were, respectively, 85% and 78%. In 1989, the largest society (the Abbey National) converted to PLC bank status through a share issue. In this paper, figures for building societies go up to 1988 and thus include the Abbey National as a building society. Data reported in this paper are for the top six or seven building societies.

As can be seen from Table 11.1, banks and building societies dominate the retail market. In 1988, banks had a 33% share of savings, 81% share of consumer loans, and 20% share in housing loans. There are no figures on the market share held by building societies for consumer credit, though they have been allowed to offer personal loans since 1986. However, 1988 shows a 70% share of the housing loan market and a 53% share of total savings for building societies. Thus, taken together, these groups have just over 85% of the share of savings and over 90% of the housing loan market.

The British retail banking market has been subject to a number of regulatory reforms since 1971. An earlier paper (Heffernan, 1989) provides details of these reforms. They were diverse, ranging from Competition and Credit Control, 1971, to an introduction of composite rate tax on bank deposits in 1985. The effect on the retail banking competitive structure was a byproduct of some of the reforms. The main goals of the reforms were not directly related to retail banking. Others had a direct impact, such as the creation of the Association of Payments Services in 1985 and the Building Societies Act 1986. Finally, some of the reforms were not a product of government legislation but resulted from market pressures. A good example is the termination of the building society interest rate cartel in 1983.

Heffernan (1989) identifies eight reforms (1971 to 1986) that should affect the competitive structure of retail banking in the U.K. The primary conclusion of this paper was that in 1970, the structure of the market was

Table 11.1. *Market share of personal lending & savings: UK.*

% Share of consumer credit & housing loan markets (outstanding loans)			
	BKCC	BKHL	BSHL
1980	58.9		
1981	63.1		
1982	77.9	14.1	75.0
1983	79.8	16.4	74.7
1984	77.9	15.6	76.2
1985	77.8	16.5	76.3
1986	78.9	16.8	75.8
1987	79.3	19.5	71.9
1988	80.8	20.2	70.2

% Share of savings market			
	BK	BS	Other
1960	32.8	24.2	43.0
1970	32.1	34.6	33.3
1975	36.6	42.5	20.9
1980	33.5	46.2	20.3
1985	31.0	52.3	16.7
1986	31.5	52.4	16.1
1987	31.7	52.9	15.4
1988	33.0	52.5	14.3

Abbreviations: BK, banks; BS, building societies; Other, Institutions offering savings products include National Savings, Girobank, and, until 1986, the Trustee Savings banks; BKCC, banks offering personal credit (excluding housing); BKHL, banks offering housing loans; BSHL; building societies offering housing loans.
Source: Central Statistical Office, *Financial Statistics*, 1989, Tables 9.4, 9.5.

of two segmented cartels, each of which operated a uniform pricing system. In 1989, price-discriminating oligopoly was the most appropriate description of the retail banking market. It appears that banks and building societies engage in product innovation in order to segment markets and discriminate in prices.

The retail banking structure in Japan

In Japan, the question of what banks should be included in our definition of the retail banking system is more complicated than in the U.K. Apart from the city and regional banks, most other institutions tend to concentrate on offering one banking product. In many respects, it has some similarities with the British system before the Trustee Savings Bank Act (1976) and the Building Societies Act (1986). Both statutes brought about a change in managerial objectives. Profit maximization became the principal objective of these firms. This in turn increased the number of participants in retail banking. By contrast, in Japan, there continue to be participants in the retail market, where profit is not the main criterion for success. Examples include government institutions such as the Post Office and the Housing Loan Corporation.

By our definition, the following Japanese firms offer retail banking services:

The city banks: These banks are headquartered in a key city and each have an extensive branch network. In 1988, there were 13 city banks.

The regional banks: Regional Banks have their head offices in large or medium-sized cities; there were 64 in 1988.

The post office: The Post Office is an important player because it takes in a significant proportion of retail deposits, as may be observed from Table 11.2. Some of the deposits are lent out directly, but the largest shares are redeposited in the Trust Fund Bureau, part of the Ministry of Finance. Fixed amount deposits make up 90% of the postal savings market. The minimum deposit term is 6 months; the maximum term is 10 years. Tax is not paid on interest earned from postal deposits, but the maximum deposit for any one individual is limited to 3 million yen.

The Post Office offers funds settlement systems (e.g., an online system, automatic salary deposit schemes, automatic payment of public utilities charges, receipt services for interest, and dividends on securities) that are similar to those offered by private financial institutions. However, its participation in the personal lending market is of little significance.

The Sogo banks: Based on the Sogo Bank Law of 1951, these banks specialize in financing for small and medium-sized firms. Unlike the city and regional banks, Sogo banks are restricted in the type of credit they can offer but do offer installment financing (a slightly different product from installment savings offered by city and regional banks) to customers, though this part of the business is now relatively minor. Since 1981, the limitations on the business of Sogo banks was expanded to a level identical to that of the ordinary banks. In 1988, there were 68 Sogo banks, which now offer services similar to that of the city and regional banks, though with a special niche in small business finance.

244   Competition in retail banking markets

Table 11.2. *Market share of personal lending & savings: Japan*

	BK1	BK2	MLSBKS	HL	HLC	Other
% Share of outstanding housing loan						
1970	70.6	16.5	12.9			0.0
1975	41.0	8.5	9.4	4.6	23.4	13.2
1980	30.8	6.0	6.9	7.9	27.1	21.3
1984	26.0	4.5	5.8	9.0	35.1	19.6
1985	26.1	4.2	5.8	8.6	36.2	19.0
1986	27.6	3.8	5.6	8.8	36.8	17.4
1987	30.0	3.4	5.4	9.3	36.0	15.9

	BK1	BK2	MLSBKS	CA		
% Share of outstanding consumer credit*						
1970	89.0	1.8	9.2			
1975	77.7	1.4	21.4			
1980	55.5	1.6	16.0	26.9		
1984	45.0	1.2	26.4	27.3		
1985	42.1	1.1	30.2	26.7		
1986	40.3	0.9	33.6	25.2		
1987	46.8	0.8	31.6	20.8		

	BKS	PO	Other			
% Share of personal savings						
1978	33.9	26.4	39.7			
1979	33.5	27.3	39.2			
1980	33.1	28.0	38.9			
1981	32.1	29.8	38.1			
1982	32.1	30.1	37.8			
1983	31.7	30.9	37.4			
1984	31.4	31.7	36.9			
1985	31.7	32.0	36.3			
1986	31.7	32.4	35.9			
1987	32.2	32.5	35.3			
1988	32.9	32.1	35.0			

* Consumer Goods & Services (excludes installment credit).
Abbreviations: BK1, banking accounts of all banks; BK2, trust accounts of all banks; MLBKS, mutual loan & savings banks; CA, credit associations; HL, housing loan companies; HLC, housing loan corporation; Other (HL); credit coops, National Federation of Credit Coops, labour credit associations, mutual insurance federations of agricultural coops, life insurance companies, nonlife insurance companies; non-life insurance companies; BKS, city, regional, trust, long-term credit; PO, post office.
Sources: Loans, PMO (Stats Office), *Japan Statistical Yearbook*; savings, Bank of Japan, *Economics Statistics Annual*, various issues.

The Shinkin banks: Regional financial institutions, the Shinkin banks emerged from credit cooperatives after the Shinkin Bank Law of 1951. Those (largely urban) cooperatives that offered services like that of the ordinary banks became Shinkin banks. They take deposits, make loans, and offer settlement services, but unlike the city and regional banks, they are organized on a membership basis, so that in principle, only members have access to Shinkin credit facilities. They do accept deposits from nonmembers. In 1988, there were 455 Shinkin banks, somewhat reduced in number from 520 in 1968.

The credit cooperatives: Organized under a 1949 law, there were 422 such cooperatives in 1988. They are membership-based organizations, in which most members are from small businesses. They offer retail banking products but only to members of the cooperative. Nonmember activity is limited to a maximum of 20% of total deposits or loans. They also accept deposits and make loans to national and local governments.

The trust banks: Since 1954, regulations governing trust banks have drawn a sharp distinction between the trust and banking activities conducted by these banks. The seven trust banks concentrate on trust business (in particular, loan trusts), while one city bank and two local banks offer trust facilities but concentrate on banking services.

The trust banks are an important source for deposits, but these are in the form of trust accounts for investment. For example, securities investment trusts use deposits to invest in certain types of security. The trust bank is one party in this type of trust. They are not important players in the retail banking system.

Finally, one should include the Housing Loan companies and the Housing Loan Corporation as participants in the housing loan market, though these organizations are not active in the deposit markets.

Table 11.2 summarizes the market share of Japanese firms in personal lending and savings. In 1988, banks (city, regional, trust, long-term credit) and the Post Office took a 64% share of the savings, and "other" institutions (e.g., Sogo and Shinkin banks and agricultural and credit cooperatives) had 35% of the share in savings. The banks' share of personal savings has remained fairly steady through the 1980s, while the Post Office has gained at the expense of other institutions.

In housing loans, the largest market share in 1988 was held by the banks and the Housing Loan Corporation. Smaller participants were the Mutual Loan & Savings banks, the Housing Loan companies, and "other," which includes credit and agricultural cooperatives and insurance companies. The Housing Loan companies were established by the banks in 1971 – there are currently eight companies – in recognition of the specialized nature of personal housing loans. These companies are funded by the bank, which established them, though their lending has grown slowly in recent years, as Table 11.2 illustrates.

The personal credit market is made up of ales credit to finance the purchase of specific consumer items and personal loans; the consumer is the direct recipient of the loan. Installment credit is excluded from Table 11.2. The latter is offered by specialized consumer loan companies and Shinpan firms, neither of which offer other retail banking services. In 1970, the banks held close to 90% of the share of the consumer credit market; this had declined to 47% by 1987. The Mutual Loan and Savings Banks and the Credit Associations have seen a large growth in market share over this period.

Measures of competitive behavior

In order to study the competitive structure of the two retail banking systems, it is necessary to employ some objective measures of competitive behavior. In a typical market, one looks at the behavior of prices in order to assess the competitive behavior of firms. However, in retail banking markets, nonprice competition may be of equal importance. In a number of papers, it has been argued that in the presence of regulations that imposed ceilings on interest rates, nonprice competition would be important. See among others Feige (1964), Klein (1974), Mitchell (1979), Santomero (1979), and Startz (1979, 1983). This hypothesis can be tested if one compares Japan, subject to a high degree of retail interest rate regulation, and Britain, which has been free of formal interest controls since the early 1970s.

Interest rates in Japan and Britain

If one relied on this quotation from Suzuki (1987, p. 142)

The previous section has demonstrated that there was a gradual progression towards liberalization of interest rates in Japan after 1975

one would expect to observe competition in the setting of interest rates on retail banking products. Closer scrutiny reveals this to be anything but the case. Interest rates on deposit and loan products are subject to a high degree of regulation, to an extent at least compatible with the view that the Japanese retail banking system functions as a collusive cartel.

Loan rates are subject to the Temporary Interest Rates Adjustment Law (1947), or TIRAL. Under TIRAL, the lending rate is set at a maximum of 15% per annum for loans in excess of 1 million yen and loans that are short term. An agreement by members of the Federation of Bankers Associations in Japan means the maximum short-term interest rate has moved in line with the official discount rate since 1958. In addition, a standard-rate (similar to prime rate) system has been operated by the associations since 1959. The standard rate is pegged to the discount rate. It is currently 0.5% above the discount rate. This differential has been unchanged since 1977.

In principle, therefore, it is possible for individual banks to compete on short-term loan rates within the band between the short-term prime rate and the maximum lending rate. The rate charged to the borrower, within this band, is a function of credit worthiness and the relationship of the customer with the bank. It has been reported that there is a variation in interest rates offered by banks for personal loans, depending on the extent to which banks wish to enter this market. Unfortunately, it has not been possible to obtain information on whether banks do in fact compete for loans, whether or not they are subject to TIRAL. Japan does not compile a separate interest rate series for personal loans. But for housing loans, there is a uniform deviation from the prime rate. Normally, a few banks lead in the setting of the rate (in line with the discount rate), and other banks follow them.

Long-term rates are not subject to TIRAL, but rates are set through implicit agreement among the banks and official authorities. The long-term prime rate is a fixed spread above the fund-raising costs for 5-year money of long-term credit banks and trust banks.

Interest rates on deposits and savings at financial institutions are highly regulated, to the extent that banks in a given financial category are required to set the same rate. Hence there is no real deposit rate competition. The rates are regulated under TIRAL. A change in rates is recommended by the Minister of Finance, and the Policy Board of the Bank of Japan sets the maximum rate after consultation with the Interest Adjustment Council. These rates apply to all private financial institutions, except for postal savings rates, which are set by a different formula, discussed later.

Since April 1970, the Bank of Japan has set guidelines for deposit rates according to maturity, subject to the constraint of the TIRAL regulations. Deposit rates are set by firms at the maximum level set by the guidelines. Shinkin banks and agricultural cooperatives are permitted to set deposit rates 0.1 to 0.25% higher than other institutions. Since 1970, the maximum TIRAL rates and the guideline rates have moved simultaneously.

Over the last decade, new products have been introduced to which TIRAL regulations do not apply. But these are very much at the large-deposit end in the spectrum of retail financial products. The growth of these products was initiated with the issue of certificates of deposit (CDs) with free interest rates in 1979. Regulations governing the minimum size and maturities of the CDs were liberalized in 1984, 1985, and 1986. As of autumn 1989, time deposits in excess of 10 million yen (14-month term as of October 1987), CDs (minimum of ¥50 million for a term of 2 weeks to 2 years), foreign-currency denominated deposits, and nonresident yen-denominated deposits are exempt from regulation. "Small" money market certificates (minimum ¥3 million, falling to ¥1 million in 1990) have also been offered since 1989, but they are subject to a form of quasi-regulation: The maximum rate is the CD rate less 1.75% (3 months) to 0.5% (2 years). Three-year SMMCs (¥3 million) are paid the face rate on 10-year government bonds, less 0.7%.

Postal savings rates are set under a different system. The Cabinet sets the rates, based on the report by the Minister of Posts and Telecommunications in consultation with the Postal Services Council. With these rates being set separately from those of private financial institutions, there is always a potential conflict between postal savings rates and the conduct of monetary policy. In recognition of this problem, a tripartite agreement was reached in 1981 between the Minister of Posts and Telecommunications, the Minister of Finance, and the Director of the Cabinet Secretariat. Essentially it involved mutual understanding of the determination of postal savings rates if deposit interest rates are changed. But the agreement has proved problematic; there have been clashes between the Ministry of Posts and Communications and the Bank of Japan. Since 1984, the Ministry has called for a liberalization of small-deposit rates, possibly with interest rates linked to market rates. It is interesting that the pressure for reform is coming from the nonprofit postal savings system.

In the United Kingdom, there is no direct control over retail deposit and lending rates. The minimum lending rate (MLR), which had replaced the bank rate, operated until 1982. The MLR was the rate at which banks could borrow short-term funds from the Bank of England. Since this rate was abolished, the Chancellor of the Exchequer announced an interest rate change, and banks may or may not respond to the change, although they normally change their rates within hours of the announcement. Building societies also react to the change in interest rates, albeit far more slowly than the banks. However, there is no control over deposit and lending rates offered or charged to the public. Nor has there been any control of this sort since the bank interest rate cartel was abolished in 1971 and the building society cartel was abandoned in 1983.

These differences in the two structures of the retail banking systems permit some insights into competitive behavior. Indicators of competitive behavior that will be used here are product innovation, bank charges, and price dispersion.

Spreads on deposit and loan products:
a measure of price dispersion

One means of drawing inferences about competitive behavior is to look for evidence of price dispersion among firms. A good measure of price dispersion for banks is the spread earned by the bank: the difference between the rate offered/levied on a bank product and the market rate of interest.

For deposits, spreads were computed as the difference between an open-market rate and the rate offered on the product. In the U.K., the market rate used was 3-month £ LIBOR (London Interbank Offer Rate), and in Japan the call money rate (a rough equivalent for the interbank rate). An average of 2- and 5-year bank debenture rates was also used in the computation of spreads for Japanese time deposits of 1 year or more. Loan spreads were computed as the loan rate less the open market rate, which was LIBOR for the U.K. and the call money rate for Japan.

Tables 11.3 and 11.4 report on Japanese loan and deposit spreads. Table 11.5 provides the figures for Britain. Looking at loan products, the spread on housing loans in Japan (HL) is slightly higher than in the U.K. (RMORT or EMORT). In addition, the spread is falling in Britain, while it has shown a considerable rise in Japan, from 0.91 in 1981 to 1.92 in 1988. The spread computed from a Japanese average loan rate (AVLR) appears to be very low, averaging 0.71 for the period 1981–1988. However,

Table 11.3. *Spreads on Japanese retail loan products*

	AVLR	HL	LTP
1981	0.12	0.91	1.17
1982	0.29	1.53	1.67
1983	0.50	1.71	1.81
1984	0.55	1.64	1.50
1985	0.09	1.22	1.04
1986	1.44	2.84	2.02
1987	1.24	2.56	1.44
1988	1.43	2.91	1.96
Avg.	0.71	1.92	1.58

Abbreviations AVLR, average loan rate – call money rate; HL, housing loan rate (year end) – call money rate; LTP, long-term prime rate – call money rate.
Source: PMO (Stats Bureau), *Monthly Statistics* of *Japan*, Nov. 1989.

Table 11.4. *Spreads on Japanese retail deposits*

Ordinary deposits, etc.						
	OD	OPS	IS	PSIS	DN	DT	DS
1977	5.68	5.68			3.10	2.60	3.35
1978	3.35	1.83	1.64	1.21	4.56	4.96	4.81
1979	4.81	3.42	2.92	2.42	7.77	7.27	8.02
1980	8.02	6.77	5.67	5.46	4.79	4.29	5.04
1981	5.04	3.69	3.13	2.78	4.91	4.41	5.16
1982	5.16	3.80	3.34	2.96	4.39	3.89	4.64
1983	4.64	3.27	2.79	2.43	4.35	3.85	4.60
1984	4.60	3.22	2.70	2.38	4.71	4.21	4.96
1985	4.96	3.58	3.06	2.74	3.33	2.83	3.58
1986	3.58	2.17	1.66	1.31	3.30	2.80	3.55
1987	3.55	2.13	1.53	1.17	3.35	2.60	3.35
*1988	3.35	1.93	1.33	0.97	3.35	2.60	3.35
Avg.	4.73	3.46	2.71	2.30	4.33	3.80	4.50

* Preliminary figure.
Abbreviations: Bank, ordinary deposits (OD), instalment savings (IS), deposits with notice (DN), tax deposits (DT), special deposits (DS), ordinary postal savings (OPS), installment savings (PSIS); Spreads, call money rate – deposit rate. Rates are computed as a weighted average of interest rates reported for a given year.
Source: PMO (Stats Bureau), *Japan Statistical Yearbook.*

Certificates of deposit		
	CD1	CD2
1981	0.65	0.66
1982	−0.14	0.93
1983	−0.17	0.28
1984	−0.32	0.00
1985	−1.27	−1.56
1986	−0.37	0.11
1987	−0.42	−0.15
1988	−0.76	−0.20
Avg.	−0.35	0.096

Abbreviations: CD, certificate of deposit, term: 2 weeks to 2 years; CD1, call money rate – average annual CD rate; CD2, average of 1- and 5-year bank debenture rates – average annual CD rate.
Source: Bank of Japan, *Economic Statistics Annual.*

| Time deposits | | | | | | | |
BK3	BK6	BK12	BK24	PS1	PS1+	PS2+	PS3+
1978 2.56	3.79						
1979 3.27	4.52						
1980 5.42	6.67						
1981 4.46	5.71	0.98	0.73	0.98	1.98	0.98	0.73
1982 3.78	5.03	2.23	1.98	2.23	3.23	2.23	1.98
1983 3.75	5.00	1.09	0.84	1.09	2.09	1.09	0.84
1984 3.5	4.75	0.92	0.67	0.92	1.92	0.92	0.67
1985 3.5	4.75	0.68	0.43	0.68	1.68	0.68	0.43
1986 2.42	3.67	0.24	−0.01	0.24	1.24	0.16	−0.01
1987 1.76	2.72	0.32	0.37	0.62	1.62	0.52	0.37
*1988 1.76	2.64	0.77	0.52	0.77	1.77	0.67	0.52
Avg. 2.9	4.30	0.90	0.70	0.66	1.94	0.91	0.71

* Preliminary figures.
Abbreviations: BK3, 3-month bank time deposit; BK6, 6-month bank time deposit; BK12, 1-year bank time deposit; BK24, 2-year bank time deposit; PS1, 1-year time postal savings; PS1+, postal savings certificate for 1+ years; PS2+, postal savings certificate for 2+ years; PS3+, postal savings certificate for 3+ years.
Note: There are also PS certificates for 1.5+ and 2.5+ years. Spreads for BK12, BK24, PS1–3+: Average of 1- and 5-year bank debenture rate – rate for each product. Spreads for BK3, BK6, call money rate – rate for each product.
Source: PMO (Stats Bureau), *Japan Statistical Yearbook.*

it has been rising over the past 3 years. The AVLR figures should be interpreted with caution because they include commercial lending. There is no separate series on Japanese personal lending rates. By contrast, British spreads on nonhousing loan products are much higher. For personal loans and packaged overdrafts, the average spread for 1986–88 was, respectively, 8.67 and 9.72.

Turning to deposit products, average spreads for British products range from 3.36 to 6.6. The range for Japanese products is 2.3 to 4.73. If one looks at the period 1984–1988, when new deposit products were introduced in the U.K., Japanese spreads range from 1.71 to 4.1. It is notable that the highest spreads are for bank ordinary deposits (OD), deposits with notice (DN), and tax and special deposits (DT, DS). Spreads for postal savings deposits are lower, though it should be remembered that profit is not the driving force behind postal savings. Also, postal saving interest is exempt from tax.

A puzzling observation relates to Japanese certificates of deposits (CDs). Introduced relatively recently, the spread is close to zero and, in some years, negative. That is, in some years, banks are paying more on

Table 11.5. *Average spreads on U.K. deposit and loan products deposit products*

	7DAY	ATM1	ATM2	HID4	HID6	HIC4	HIC6
1976	4.83						
1977	3.52						
1978	3.32						
1979	2.50						
1980	2.23						
1981	3.72						
1982	3.43						
1983	3.68						
1984	3.31					6.01	5.28
1985	3.19			3.84	3.35	5.65	3.93
1986	3.38	6.68	6.07	3.83	3.31	5.68	3.64
1987	2.79	6.62	6.07	2.99	3.78	4.48	3.16
1988	5.54	6.56	6.05	4.38	3.78	4.99	3.61
Avg.	3.65	6.60	6.0	3.77	3.36	5.25	3.76

Loan products

	RMORT	EMORT	EQL	HIL	PL	PO
1986	1.76	1.58		10.05	9.07	
1987	2.19	2.24	4.56	7.68	8.60	9.87
1988	1.33	1.14	4.01	7.94	8.33	9.57
Avg.	1.76	1.65	4.30	8.56	8.67	9.72

Abbreviation and Notes: 7 Day, 7-day account; ATM, ATM access account, ATM 1: £150.00, ATM2: £765.00; HID, higher interest deposit account: HID4: £765, HID6: £4590; HIC higher-interest checking account: HIC4: £765, HIC6: £4590; RMORT, repayment mortgages; EMORT, endowment mortgages; EQL, equity loans; HIL, home improvement loans; PL, personal loans; PO, packaged overdrafts.
Deposit spread, LIBOR-net interest rate, except for 7DAY: LIBOR-gross rate.

CDs than they can earn in the call money or bank debenture market. This is in contrast to Britain, where spreads tend to be highest for the most recently introduced products. The puzzle is partly resolved by noting that the term structure of interest rates in Japan, in marked contrast to the U.K., has been sharply upward sloping for most of the period. Therefore, ideally, one should compare the CD rate with an interbank or treasury bill rate of the appropriate maturity for the period. However, choice of the call money rate, an average of 2- and 5-year bank debenture rates, or a 2-year debenture rate did not significantly alter the findings of a spread that is close to zero.

The spreads for Japanese 3- and 6-month time deposits are similar to those obtained on OD, DN, DT, and DS. However, they are much lower

Table 11.6. *British banks with bargain/ripoff spreads**

	Max spread	Min spread
Product		
ATM1	206	203
ATM2	206	203
HIC4	0	210
HIC6	401	0
HID4	203	403
HID6	203	0
7Day	0	0
EQL	203	206
HIL	204	203
PL	403/406	202
PO	204	201/203
RMORT	209	0
EMORT	208	0

* Firms that occupy a maximum or minimum spread position for at least 50% of the period studied.
20-, a bank; 40-, a building society; 0, no firm.

for 1- and 2-year bank time deposits and for postal savings of 1 year or more. In the U.K., time deposits are offered by banks and building societies but in recent years have tended to be superseded by the no-notice deposit accounts. Interest rates are slightly higher, but there has been no concerted attempt to reward those who commit their funds to deposit for a period of 3 months or more.

Trends in spreads are worth noting. In Britain, they are rising or have remained unchanged for the 7DAY and ATM accounts, while they have declined for most of the higher-interest checking and deposit accounts (HIC and HID). The 7DAY account is inferior in characteristics to the higher-interest deposit account, yet the spreads are roughly the same until 1988, when the spread on the 7DAY account rises. Finally, it is noteworthy that by 1988, the spreads on HID and HIC accounts were roughly equal, even though the latter offers a checkbook facility. Spreads on loan products are declining, although, in absolute terms (with the exception of mortgages), the spreads are still very high.

In Japan, there is a general downward trend in spreads. Spreads are declining for ordinary deposits instalment savings, CDs, and 3- to 6-month time deposits, and spreads have remained largely unchanged for notice, tax, and special deposits and for time deposits of 1 or 2 years.

It is also worth investigating whether any one British bank offers consistently good bargains to the consumer. Table 11.6 reports on firms that occupy a maximum or minimum spread position for a given product for at least 50% of the observation period. There are only 8 out of 26 zeroes in this table, suggesting that if a firm offers a best or worst spread at one point in time, it is likely to continue in the position for a considerable time. The firm occupying the Max or Min position varies considerably across products, and the large clearing banks (201 to 204) do not occupy any consistent spread position, suggesting the absence of any price leader. It is rare for building societies to appear in either column, and notable that they do not occupy the Min/Max spread positions for mortgages. It is not possible to conduct a similar exercise for Japan, since regulation virtually prohibits any price competition.

Product innovation

Product innovation is another indicator of competitive behavior, especially in a market where nonprice features may be an important source of competition. Heffernan (Table 2, 1989) reported on product innovation in Britain. In the period 1976–88, the number of retail banking products increased threefold. The number of products withdrawn from the market, or products that underwent a change in their nonprice features, was very small, firms preferring to introduce new products with different characteristics. Product innovation did not commence until 1980, 9 years after the bank cartel was abolished. Seven of the 10 new deposit products that pay interest were introduced after the demise of a tax levied on increases in banks' interest-bearing liabilities (the Corset, abandoned in 1980), but all but two were introduced a full 4 years after its removal. Three new loan products were introduced 5 years after the end of hire purchase controls.

Approximately 1.1 new products per year were introduced in the period 1980–88. While there does not appear to be a close link between regulatory reform and innovation, early work does suggest that new products tend to be introduced after a protracted fall in nominal interest rates.

The picture would be incomplete without noting the change in real bank charges over the period. In the United Kingdom, real bank charges apply to overdraft current account customers. Since 1986 the minimum balance requirement for exemption from charges has been zero. Prior to this, it ranged from £50.00 to £100.00. In the period 1981–1988, average real bank charges almost trebled. In Japan, bank charges are to trade secret. Fees are set by the Federation of Bankers' Associations of Japan, so there is no variation in bank charges across banks. Personal customers with ordinary deposits do not have a checking facility and bills are paid through credit transfers. A report that appeared in *The Economist* (vol. 17, Feb. 1990, p. 114) shows that the fee levied depends on the size of the transfer but varies between £3.38 for bills in excess of £123, and £2.52 for smaller transfers. The average charge is £2.95 per item, using 1989 figures. If one assumes that there are about 69 transfers required per year, this works out to a cost of just under £72.00. In Britain, the comparable average figure for 1988 was just over £28.00. U.K. banks do not have uniform rates, and the amount charged in 1990 varied from a minimum of £25.00 to a maximum of £40.00. Whereas the Japanese charges apply to all customers, in Britain only overdraft customers are subject to bank charges.

In Japan, there appears to be virtually no loan or deposit product innovation. The series on deposit (ordinary and time offered by banks and the Post Office) runs back to at least the early 1970s. Exceptions to this general rule are the variations of a Sogo account, which provides for automatic lending using a time deposit as collateral, introduced in 1972, and the "Swing Service" (1983), which may be added to the Sogo account and allows automatic transfer from the ordinary deposit to the time deposit. Other innovations are certificates of deposit (first offered in 1979) and the small money market certificates (SMMC) introduced in 1989. In 1990, the limit for purchase of a SMMC will be reduced from ¥3 million to ¥1 million.

In both countries, settlement methods have undergone a dramatic change, with the introduction of credit cards, cash-dispensing and ATM machines, and direct debit cards. However, these innovations can be explained largely by new technology, which have enabled financial firms in both countries to cut substantially their money transmission and settlement costs.

Further analysis

The United Kingdom is a country where the retail banking sector has been "deregulated" for a considerable period. Among other reforms that improved the competitive environment, explicit cartel behavior was abolished for banks in 1971 and for building societies in 1983. Observations on spreads, product innovation, and real bank charges suggest that firms in the retail banking sector are innovating to discriminate [see Heffernan (1989) for more detail]. Attempts to limit rapid increases in various monetary aggregates have been applied inconsistently and erratically, and with only mixed success, despite the stated objectives of the Conservative government since it was elected in 1979.

The picture is quite different in Japan. Compared to Britain, the Bank of Japan has traditionally exercised strict monetary control. In addition, there are ceilings on deposit and loan rates, and explicit collusion in the setting of rates on retail products. Thus, if one were to compare U.K. spreads (the result of price-discriminating oligopoly) with those of Japan (an apparently collusive cartel subject to tight monetary control), one would expect Japanese spreads to be higher. But with the exception of housing loans, this is not the case, and spreads in Japan appear to be falling. This suggests that while Japanese banks enjoy cartel conditions in the retail markets, it could be monetary control that inhibits the size of the spread they earn on deposit and loan products.

Given the contrast in competitive structure and monetary control, it is useful to test for the influence of these factors on retail interest rates. We have chosen to use the British 7DAY rate and the Japanese Ordinary Deposit rate because of the similar characteristics these products share. The idea is to test for the influence of competition, monetary control, and financial innovation on the movement of these rates. The presence of positive serial correlation in an OLS regression gave rise to the use of an autoregressive process (AR) using the Gauss-Newton iterative method on the following equation:

$$DR = a_0 + a_1 MR + a_2 MR1 + a_3 MS + a_4 FINN + a_5 SD$$
$$+ a_6 JUK + a_7 TTJ + a_8 TTUK$$

where:

DR: the average deposit rate offered on U.K. 7DAY and Japanese ordinary deposits
MR: the money market rate for U.K./Japan
MR1: the money market rate lagged by 1 year
MS1: the rate of growth of broad money ("money plus quasi-money") in U.K./Japan
FINN: the number of new products introduced in a given year
SD: the average annual standard deviation of the spread for 7DAY and OD accounts
JUK: a Japan/U.K. dummy
TTJ: time trend for Japan
TTUK: time trend for U.K.

The objective is to see the extent to which monetary regulation (proxied by broad money growth rates), competition (proxied by standard deviation of spreads earned by banks), or financial innovation (the number of new products introduced each year) explain movements in interest rates on the standard deposit account. Data covered the period 1978–88. The results are summarized below:

Regressor	Coefficient	T ratio
MR	.1890	1.41
$MR1$	−.1257	−2.93
MS	.0158	.3451
$FINN$	.1672	1.01
SD	13.24	4.23
JUK	−7.947	−12.52
TTJ	−.1922	−2.26
$TTUK$	−.8374	−7.73
CON	10.26	5.23
$R^2 = .999$		
$DW = 2.1$		
Number of observations $= 22$		

The results show that the monetary regulation coefficient, MS, is not statistically significant. The competitive measure, SD is positive and significant, as one would expect; a lower SD (zero for Japan) implies tighter collusion and is associated with a lower interest rate paid on deposits. Use of the standard deviation on the 7DAY account as a proxy for competition has its limitations, because it is not this product where one observes a high degree of competition among U.K. bank. On the other hand, choice of the SD from one of the more competitive products would prevent close comparison with the Japanese ordinary deposit account. Another potential problem is the fact that SD will be zero under either perfect competition or perfect collusion. But this is not really a problem when one uses Japanese and British banking data, because the retail markets are not even close to being perfectly competitive.

The coefficient on MR is positive and nearly significant; the lagged money market rate ($MR1$) is statistically significant with a negative sign. This suggests that the deposit interest rate rises with the level and the rate of change of MR. Note that in both cases, the coefficient is well below unity. Under perfect competition with constant deposit-related costs, the coefficient on MR would be close to unity. Under collusive oligopoly, it would be one-half with a linear deposit supply and less than unity for isoelastic deposit supply.

The JUK dummy is statistically significant: Interest rates are lower for Japan (1) than for the U.K. (0). The financial innovation term ($FINN$) is correctly signed though not significant. The results suggest that as financial innovation increases, interest rates rise. This tends to confirm a hypothesis of oligopolistic price discrimination in the U.K. Alternatively, an increase in MR (and hence the deposit rate) could trigger a burst of financial innovation in an attempt to compete for funds. The time trends fitted for the U.K. ($TTUK$) and Japan (TTJ) are negative and statistically significant: Deposit rates fall over time.

Conclusions

The objective of this paper was to investigate the competitive behavior of banks in Japan and Britain. A key question that was explored was: Does liberalization of markets induce increased competition? One can draw two main conclusions. First, it is naive to anticipate an increase in competition from certain forms of deregulation, especially those that dismantle cartels. The analysis of spread behavior showed that British banks are earning higher spreads on retail products than their Japanese counterparts. On the other hand, bank charges in Japan are about 2.5 times higher than in the U.K., where charges are applied only to overdraft customers.

Second, it is not obvious that control over retail rates (e.g., in Japan) induces more nonprice competition, though the Ministry of Finance regulates nonprice features of bank products. In the United Kingdom, termination of cartels encouraged more nonprice competition (rapid product innovation) than was present under the cartels.

Clearly, the determinants of spreads on retail products are highly complex. The simple regression carried out in this paper points the way forward on how spread determination might be analyzed employing data from more than one country. The task ahead is to collect the required data from several countries, and to refine some of the measures of the explanatory variables.

References

Feige, E. L. (1964), *The Demand for Liquid Assets: A Temporal Cross Section Analysis*, Englewood Cliffs, NJ: Prentice Hall.

Heffernan, S. A. (1989), "Regulatory Reform and Competitive Behavior in British Retail Banking," City University Business School, Discussion Paper #82

Klein, M. A. (1971), "A Theory of the Banking Firm," *Journal of Money, Credit and Banking*, 3, 205–18.

Mitchell, D. W. (19979), "Explicit and Implicit Demand Deposit Interest," *Journal of Monetary Economics*, 11, 182–91.

Sanotmero, A. M. (1979), "The Role of Transactions Costs and Rates of Return on the Demand Deposit Decision," *Journal of Monetary Economics*, 5, 343–64.

Startz, R. (1979), "Implicit Interest on Demand Deposits," *Journal of Monetary Economics*, 5, 515–34

———(1983), "Competition and Interest Rate Ceilings in Commercial Banking," *Quarterly Journal of Economics*, 98, 255–65.

Suzuki, Y. (1987), *The Japanese Financial System*, Oxford: Oxford University Press.

Index

259